Spike Mays was born in 1907. In 1969 he won
Post Best First Work Award for this, his first book. It was
followed by three further memoirs recounting his time with
the Royal Dragoons in Egypt and India, his repatriation to
England in 1934, going to university at the age of forty-four
and readjusting to life in 'Civvy Street'. He was married to
Vera with whom he had two sons. Spike Mays died in 2003 at
the age of ninety-five.

Spike and Vera Mays

The Only Way Was Essex

SPIKE MAYS

ABACUS

ABACUS

First published as *Reuben's Way* in Great Britain in 1969
by Eyre & Spottiswoode Publishers Ltd.
Published in 1973 by Pan Books Ltd.

This paperback edition published in 2013 by Abacus

A CIP catalogue record for this book
is available from the British Library.

ISBN 978-0-349-13879-4

Typeset in Baskerville by M Rules
Printed and bound in Great Britain by
Clays Ltd, St Ives plc

Papers used by Abacus are from well-managed forests
and other responsible sources.

MIX
Paper from
responsible sources
FSC® C104740

Abacus
An imprint of
Little, Brown Book Group
100 Victoria Embankment
London EC4Y 0DY

An Hachette UK Company
www.hachette.co.uk

www.littlebrown.co.uk

To Elizabeth Amy Mays

Contents

Map of Bartlow Hamlet drawn by Boris Weltman
from a sketch by the author

Acknowledgements

I deeply appreciate the help and encouragement of all those who have made this book possible; thanks are tendered especially to Mrs Leila Luddington, for whom I originally wrote the essay on Walton's Park, her old home where I was employed as a house boy; to Christopher Ketteridge, my oldest friend, who reminded me of many half-forgotten incidents of childhood and wrote down some anecdotes of the older characters in our village; to his sister Bess, my sister-in-law Mrs L. G. Mays; my cousin Ellen; and to my wife Vera; my sister Poppy, Mrs A. P. Flack, and my brother Fon, L. G. Mays. To these and to all who have contributed to my recollections I owe grateful thanks.

I regret any inadvertent omissions to this list; I have wherever possible obtained consent to mention living persons and I hope those I have failed to trace will accept the tribute intended. No offence is knowingly offered to anyone living or dead.

Thanks are also due to Mr Jack Singleton and the BBC Talks Department who broadcast my reading of 'The Horkey' on 18 September 1963; and to the editor of *East Anglian Magazine* for publishing 'Raise the Song of Harvest Home' in the issue of October 1958. To my editors at Eyre & Spottiswoode I owe thanks for valuable and helpful advice.

Throughout the period of this book I was 'Ced' to my family and contemporaries; but later in time, and in circumstances which belong to another story, I earned the nickname 'Spike' by which I am known today.

C. W. Mays

London 1969

Foreword

The author of this book was born in 1907, in a hamlet which he calls Reuben's Corner, near the little village of Ashdon, in the north-west of Essex bordering both on Cambridgeshire and Suffolk. That district is hilly, and most of it a plateau across which the north-east winds come in straight from the Ural mountains, across the flats of Europe. Spring is tardy there, and the soil heavy. But it is great country for wheat growing, and other cereals of lesser royalty. Root crops flourish there too. Great mounds of sugar-beet could be seen waiting by the roadside, to be carried away to the factories. The First World War encouraged that vegetable, for sugar ran short in our beleaguered island. During that time, Spike Mays was a child, in the village school, his father off at the war, his mother keeping the home together, with her brood around her. It is a picture told in millions over that period. But this lad registered it in his capacious memory, and it now forms the opening chapters of a remarkable story of rural East Anglia during the sad years that followed the war, before the Welfare State was created, and Lloyd George's 'land fit for heroes' was still no more than pie in the sky.

The author is a great man for detail, and I am able to vouch for its authenticity because I had a house, between the wars, in that same neighbourhood, up a cul-de-sac called Cole End, between Saffron Walden and Thaxted. I watched the decay of the agricultural world in Essex during those two decades; the villages emptying, the ancient cottages and churches seeming to sink into the neglected ground, the fences, gates and hedgerows neglected. All that is a political matter, no doubt, but to this boy it was the natural order of things, and he made the best of it.

His parents were thrifty, loyal and full of character. Father came home, one of few, from the mud of Flanders, to resume work on the farm. Thus the boy had a fulcrum on which to balance his universe. And his book shows what he has made of it. He is clear-sighted. The myopia of optimism does not smudge over the details of hardship, squalor, ruthless exploitation, the examples of human degradation which always form a substantial part of any community.

That clear sight is the genius of this book. It has prompted the author to miss nothing of the way of life as it went on at the very end of the old feudal world which had been our rural setting since Anglo-Saxon days. It is only just over forty years ago, but the younger generation today will read this book as a period piece, incredulous perhaps of the relationships, the ardours, the endurance of these folk on the farms and in the villages only some sixty miles from London. The setting of Thomas Hardy's novels is comparable to this; but they are a century earlier.

The young reader, however, will be forced to believe Spike Mays, for what he says is factual, down to the most minute detail, in all matters, human and connected with the goings-on of mother nature around him. His vitality is astonishing; his enthusiasm and curiosity percolate into every aspect of that rustic world, and his simple, unadorned prose records it all. We get to know every member of the village life, from the squire down to the local drunkard and the poacher. We learn the crafts of the woodmen and the farm labourers, and examine their tools, clothes, and personal idiosyncrasies. We taste the uncanny flavour of poverty. The boy's father had to go off to Canada for a while, to see what could be done there about making a living. The mother meanwhile waited for letters, and earned a bit picking stones off the fields, and 'making do'. At that time, the squire's house (the squire 'was a kindly, considerate man, ever tolerant of human frailties and shortcomings, and he was my first employer') was run by the full complement of domestic staff, from butler and housekeeper down to the boy who cleaned the knives, Spike Mays. So we are shown the benevolent interior of the squirearchy system, in full bloom, amid the countryside which was its compost. There is no sign of resentment or even criticism.

All is objectively presented, as are the author's observations of field and hedgerow, and his particularly close acquaintance with and passion for bird life. W. H. Hudson was not more intimate with them than is Spike Mays. And as for his attention to flowers and grasses, the habits and oddities of wild animals and farm stock, I think he has no rival, not even the Northamptonshire poet John Clare, or the west country Richard Jefferies. He is less poetic than the one, and less mystical than the other, but I believe that he approaches his quarry at closer range, and with greater benevolence. He has his moments of metaphysical speculation, as in his comment on a certain parson. 'He did not even call to "collect pennies for God", as had been his wont. I felt sorry for God. According to the parson God was deeper in the red than we were and that was deep indeed.'

That is an example of the myriad character studies which amplify the anecdotes in this book. What the late S. L. Bensusan did for East Essex of the estuarial marshes, in his many tales of its people, Spike Mays does for the uplands of the county. We meet them at work on the fields, in the byres, and in their homes; most especially in their clubs, the local pubs. Their conversation, arguments, superstitions, games and self-preservation tactics; all are here, presented in unhurried but richly dramatic realism. That sense of drama makes the dynamic of the book. It takes the reader by the heart, as in this simple statement about the wartime interruptions and final destruction of the ancient way of life which is here so fortunately preserved. 'I had heard that there would be many soldiers like my Uncle Bert who would never go down any long, long trails. Uncle Bert was killed soon after he was commissioned, and many others who crowded into the boats at Folkestone harbour were to be killed or wounded, but everybody sang as they went on. Nobody sang on the return journeys, there was hardly anybody about. For it was always at night when they came back.'

Inevitably, the author was to grow up, and to meet a girl with whom he fell in love. His account of this experience might have made him stumble as a writer; but no, there it is, unique and fresh, and lasting. When he too went off to be a soldier, like his father, he was able to return to the place of his upbringing and nurture, still as a member of that community of rustic folk, and to share their conversation. As he says, 'To hear them speaking of the fields they loved, mentioning them by name in what was almost a caress, was an inspiring experience – one which underlined what a great part these humble people played in the life of the nation without the recognition they well merited.'

The difference is, that Spike Mays has put it down in writing, which will, I suspect, get 'the recognition it well merits'.

Richard Church

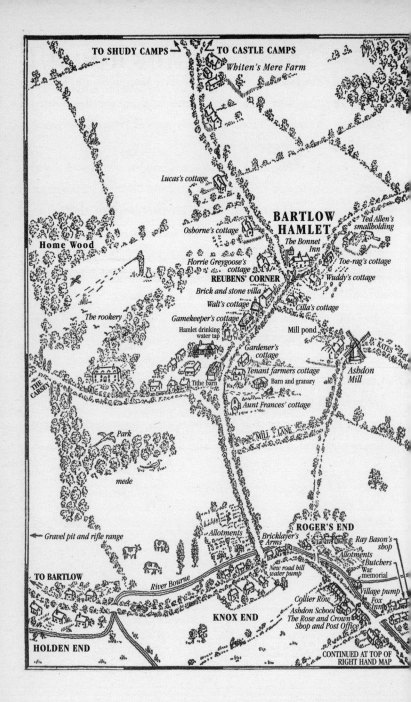

TO SHUDY CAMPS   TO CASTLE CAMPS

Whiten's Mere Farm

Lucas's cottage

BARTLOW HAMLET

Ted Allen's smallbolding

Osborne's cottage

Home Wood

The Bonnet Inn

Florrie Greygoose's cottage

Toe-rag's cottage

REUBENS' CORNER

Wuddy's cottage

Brick and stone villa

Walt's cottage

Cilla's cottage

The rookery

Gamekeeper's cottage

Hamlet drinking water tap

Mill pond

KATES

Gardener's cottage

THE CARSEY

Tenant farmers cottage

Ashdon Mill

Tithe barn

Barn and granary

Aunt Frances' cottage

Park

MILL LANE

mede

← Gravel pit and rifle range

Allotments

ROGER'S END

Bricklayer's Arms

Ray Bason's shop

Allotments

Butchers

War memorial

TO BARTLOW

River Bourne

New road bill water pump

Village pump

Fox Inn

Collier Row

KNOX END

Ashdon School

The Rose and Crown

Shop and Post Office

HOLDEN END

CONTINUED AT TOP OF RIGHT HAND MAP

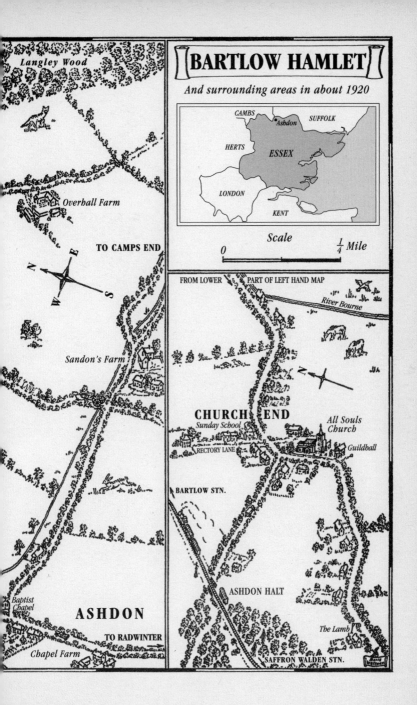

BARTLOW HAMLET

And surrounding areas in about 1920

CAMBS

SUFFOLK

•Ashdon

HERTS

ESSEX

LONDON

KENT

Scale

0   ¼ Mile

Langley Wood

Overhall Farm

TO CAMPS END

N
E
W
S

Sandon's Farm

LANE

FROM LOWER   PART OF LEFT HAND MAP

River Bourne

N

CHURCH END

Sunday School

*All Souls
Church*

RECTORY LANE

Guildhall

BARTLOW STN.

*Baptist
Chapel*

ASHDON

TO RADWINTER

Chapel Farm

ASHDON HALT

The Lamb

SAFFRON WALDEN STN.

The Only Way
Was Essex

Prologue

Reuben's Corner

Constable's country. Many artists with oils and water-colours, pencils and crayons came to my village hamlet in that north-west Essex frontier bordering on Suffolk and Cambridgeshire to copy or capture one of nature's masterpieces. Some came to paint the fields of Ashdon Place Farm, but only in the good weather, from springtime to harvest.

Few came in autumn and winter, but I was working at the farm every day of every month for two years after I left school.

Place Farm was on the fringe of Bartlow Hamlet, where I lived in a small cottage near the road bend called Reuben's Corner which leads off the Ashdon road by the Bonnett Inn towards the Camps, Castle Camps and Shudy Camps. The corner was named after my maternal grandfather, Reuben Ford, and it echoes for me . . .

Footsteps coming down past the Bonnett; the great hob-nailed boots of the farmhands going off to work on Place Farm; voices calling my grandad at half past five to get out of bed and go to work at Overhall Farm. Those were the morning sounds that used to ring in my bedroom when I was seven years old.

'Yip there, Reuben. Sun's up, bor; so should you be. Owt on it. Tell Sue ter stop layin' on yer night-shut!'

A few more paces, then the cheerful voices raised at Walt's cottage, demanding that Walt Stalley should also leave his bed.

'Come on, Walt. Yew bin in there too long, bor. Ain't as if yew've got a mawther (woman) ter keep ye abed! Owt on it, then!'

Walt was a bachelor, at sixty.

At about this point there would be furious activity from next door, Granny Ford's. The poker would nearly come through the chimney piece into our living-room as Grandfather raked out the ashes from his grate. Then I would hear footsteps round the back of our cottage and the sound of his enamel basin going into the rain-water butt to obtain the necessary for his morning ablution. This would be followed by the creaking of his armchair as he sat to have his first breakfast, which was always the same – slops of dry bread dipped into hot unsweetened tea. He would take his proper breakfast to the fields.

Then I would listen for the sounds of the stirrings of Stalley and a conversation of this kind.

'Mornin', Rue. Nice 'n' bright. Reckon we're in fer a tidy day.'

'Ah, not bad, by the look on it. Rooks are high, but it were cowd fust thing.'

Their heavy feet would be heard on the road as they went off to Overhall Farm. Not a day did my grandfather miss in sixty years. Greenfinches and chaffinches would pipe them up Overhall Lane and the first green of the high hedges, the elder and dogwood, would tell them of spring.

Calls were also made for me after I had finished my job as houseboy at Walton's and went to real work; but I would be bound in the opposite direction, for Place Farm. Toe-Rag Smith would call me. Horse-keepers always started half an hour earlier than the farmhands, to feed the horses before they were taken to the fields. Sometimes I would walk the half-mile with old Wuddy Smith. Above the thuds of our clodhoppers we would hear others coming up from the village – Barney Bland, Walt Nunn, Tom Symonds, Cribby Smith. Barney's thumps were different from the rest. He was crippled.

Great wooden creakings would waft across the fields as the farm gates swung wide.

Then there would be the thunderings of feed tins, snorts and whinnies and neighs from happy horses, the plaintive mooings of heifers in season singing love calls to the isolated, frantic, sex-crazed bull. Over all this would be heard the voice of Bidwell, the tenant farmer.

'Rollin' an' harrowin' ter-day. Woodshot, Hungerton, Old Lay. Usual teams. Jack, you go with Tom.'

To me, 'Best go with Poddy. Git the hay fust, then the straw fer the yards.

'Barney, Bartlow Station. Fetch the cattle cake. Best take a wagon; there's a tidy load.'

When we had our instructions Bidwell would move off, chewing straw, to his milking.

Into the stables I would go to collar up. I would lift down a great horse collar, black with old leather, bright with brasses, scarlet with painted wooden hames, heavy with steel chains, and try to thrust the collar over the chestnut's fiery head. My arms were not long enough when his head was held high and my arms were not long enough if he poked his moist muzzle – smothered with oat chaff – into my face. This he always did.

'Stand on a feed tin, then, yew fool,' Poddy Coote would say. 'Yew'll larn, boy. Yew'll larn!'

Soon there would be the thudding of horses being led to the cart shed which was packed with great wagons, tumbrils, horse-rakes and steel rollers, their shafts to the ground like soldiers resting on arms reversed. This would be followed by the slithering of hooves as the great horses were backed between the shafts accompanied by the jingling of chains, creaking of leathers, snorts of horses and the voices of men.

'Barney, when you git to Bartler Station see if there's a parcel for me. Seed taters, comin' from Cambridge b'rail.'

'If it's there you'll hev it, bor.'

'Toe-Rag, better hev a look at owd Jockey. Snot's runnin' from him like candle-grease. Reckon he's caught a cowd!'

Then would be heard a sure voice of spring – the heavy,

steel-ribbed roller on the way to the spring rolling. Barney's wagon and our tumbril would roll – their iron-clad wheels rattling through the great yard ruts – ours to the stackyard for Poddy and me to get hay and straw; Barney's thundering off to little Bartlow Station via the 'Carsey', the private road of Walton's Park estate.

There would be music at our hayrick; great swishings of the hay-knife; great gruntings from Poddy as he incised the stack to hack from it its hay. Crows and rooks would be a-cawing in the nearby rookery, inviting us to sing. Then off we would go with a hymn or two, good practice for the choir.

> Fair waved the golden corn
> In Canaan's pleasant land
> When full of joy, some shining morn,
> Went forth the reaper-band.

We did not stick to seasonal hymns and were as likely to sing 'God rest ye merry, gentlemen' in August as a harvest hymn in November.

We always sang something. Occasionally it would be Poddy's favourite:

> There was a bull in Derbyshire
> Who had two horns of brass;
> One grew outer his head, Sir,
> The other grew outer his . . .
> Rye-dingle-Derby-dingle-Derby-dingle-dey . . .

He were the finest bull, Sir,
That ever did feed on hay.

There were several verses, each a bit bawdier than the previous one, but I liked the last verse best:

Now when this bull was dead, Sir,
He were buried in Saint Paul's;
It took two men an' a boy, Sir,
Ter carry one of his . . .
Rye-dingle-Derby-dingle-Derby-dingle-dey . . .
He were the finest bull, Sir,
That ever did feed on hay.

I loved the scent and sound of the hay . . . the gentle rustling of it past my ears as great masses were pitched to me by Poddy and the bouncy softness which sometimes reassured me in my dread of falling from the top of the load down the rutted track to the stockyards. I would listen for the creaking of the stockyard gates as Poddy opened them to let in our hay-load; the squelch of tumbril wheels on soiled and wetted straw which would soon be ripe enough to enrich the soil for another season's plantings; the moos of appreciation from the heifers as they nuzzled at our load; the squeals and grunts from impatient pigs who had yet to be fed with pollard, swill and root-crops; and the music from the tall trees and the roof of the harness room, where wheeled and squatted fan-tailed pigeons and turtle doves in a harmony of cooings and love murmurs.

'One more load, then breakfast,' Poddy would say.

Half an hour for breakfast. By half past eight we heard the stirrings of the rest of the hamlet and the laughter of children as they made their way to school. If we happened to sit on the grass verge outside the big barn we would hear the clip-clop of pony Joey down Walton's drive as Bill Leonard drove Major Luddington in his brougham to Ashdon Halt – a diminutive railway station consisting of one disembowelled passenger coach. Stripped of its former furnishings, and with a new wooden seat running throughout the length of the distant side and both ends, it was notorious as a meeting place for lovers on wet Sunday afternoons and every dark night.

Standing off a single line track connecting Audley End Junction to Haverhill – the Cambridge line to the Colne Valley – the Halt featured the furious whistlings and puffings of four trains a day as they approached and departed. From those whistlings we could tell the time and we did. We had no watches. The Halt and its sounds are no more. Instead there are now jet-shriekings from fighter aircraft at Duxford and other such places. George Sutton, the trim, bearded, thirsty railway guard, will never wave his red and green flags there again. His trains are gone, his track overgrown. I shall always remember when he blew his little whistle in vain after emerging from the pub at Audley End and rushing into the guards' van. The engine driver whistled his usual reply and the engine chugged its way to Saffron Walden . . . leaving George in his van wondering why he had failed to notice that the passenger carriages had not been coupled to that departing, whistling engine.

Wild strawberries still grow in rich profusion along the steep, wooded banks of that railway. But there are also wild flowers and weeds in profusion where George was once an important link in the life of the community.

Along the country lanes and bordering almost every field stood the great hedges that are no more. In them lived little mammals in complex and fascinating colonies. Around those hedges I used to learn the secrets of stoat, squirrel, weasel, hedgehog and rat; of shrews, bank voles and dormice ... and listen to all their voices. But they have gone elsewhere, perhaps to the woods.

Stealthy stoat, rapacious rat, wily weasel ... they dwelt in hedgebank, with heroic hedgehog – a neighbour shy but cunning as they, disguised in dead leaves and a ball of protective prickles at the hedge-bottom. Tuned ears could detect the scuttlings of all from cover to cover. Shy and timid until dusk, lacking valour to disclose themselves in daylight – unless in pursuit of prey – they lurked in honeycombs of bank-burrows, not always their own. Stealthy walkers and attentive listeners heard, too, the bank voles' nut-gnawings; the faint shrillings of shrews in endless bickerings and quarrellings; and sometimes the squeak of the lazy dormouse.

When corn canaried the fields at ripening time, the symphony of sounds was modulated as man-made notes dominated the scene – the scythe-swishings round the headlands as sweaty mowers cut avenues for horse-drawn reapers;

the steely chatterings as triangular daggers raped the corn-stalks close to the soils; the clonkings as the mechanical reaper's fork paid out great sheaves in tidy lines ready for 'shocking'; the guiding calls from the driver to his horses ... 'Gee, then, Boxer!' ... 'Walk-a-meller, Gipsy!'; the clinkings of pint pots; the gurglings from the neck of the wicker-encased earthenware jars as ale gushed forth from the two-gallon treas-ure for 'levenses; the shots from farmers' guns; yelps of delight from women, men and dogs, as hares and rabbits streaked in fear from the last few rods of uncut corn; the voices of the reapers themselves.

'Good owd yield. They sheaves are a-layin' tidy thick this year. Clean, too, nary a thistle, nary a dock.'

Later would be heard the rattling and rolling of wagons across the stubble seas to net the golden corn and the shouts of warning to the 'loader' from the boy horse-leader.

'Howd-ye-toight, howd-ye-toight! Whoa there, Boxer!'

Then, after celebration, the fruits would go to the miller.

There is a sadness in me that mill sails are now static, silenced; no more does the western wind whisper through rotating vanes; never again will be heard the great creaking of wooden cogs or the grinding of flat circular stones to powder the grain of wheat to nourishing flour; the voice of old Bragg, the miller, can no longer be heard:

'Thass roight, bor. Le's hev another score o' sacks. Keep the grain a-pourin', keep it a-pourin'!'

Whirring steel rollers at Cambridge and elsewhere grind instead, at greater speed, in a higher key, to produce inferior flour. By their processes of 'selectivity' the germ of the wheat – the life-giver – is extracted from the flour to produce fancy breakfast foods – and profit! Bread was once the staple diet because it contained the magic of the soil.

No more do we hear the dung-spreaders. Instead of ripe dung from the stockyards, spread good and thick by singing men with four-tined forks, there crash through the fields mechanical monsters – grey-powdered, clanking, ghostly automatons, their spinning trays broadcasting artificiality and their end product inferior crops.

Insecticiders infiltrate into the fields, armed with sprays ... their object to poison insects alleged to ruin the crops. Beetles and bugs, worms and centipedes, daddy-longlegs and cockchafers are killed; so, too, are the bees; the beautiful butterflies that make late spring and early summer gay, and the inoffensive moths that dance in moonbeams. Our birds are poisoned, those beneficial birds that kill destructive insects as nature intended, and more effectively. But our birdsong has diminished. Poisoners have silenced many of our singers of the fields. Although much of the song is ended, for me the melody lingers, for theirs was the music which accompanied me in my long walkings almost every day.

We always walked. Our nearest station, Ashdon Halt, was two miles and a bit away. Our school, over a mile and Sunday school and church two miles distant. Ashdon village was just over a mile from our hamlet. Unless we could beg a lift in a jam-packed tradesman's cart, or in tumbrils and wagons going off to the railway stations with loads of vegetables and sacks of corn, our traversing of the highways and byways was upon our clodhoppered feet. Nor was this the only walking. Each day we would walk miles across fields and paths to get to our points of work – unless horses were being used, and then we rode – for the great fields were widely scattered. In spring and summer it was joy. In late autumn and winter it was an ordeal of mud, water and cold.

During the open season when the gentlemen came to shoot game there would be the greatest walk – or so it was regarded – because old and young of both sexes would turn out in droves to beat game to the guns. Every acre of the vast estate, fields, meadows, spinneys, copses and the great woods of Home and Langley, would be marauded by the beaters, all armed with sticks, all yelling to scare the game to their destruction. This was regarded as pleasant walking, though tiring, because it was communal, with every walker enjoying every pace. But many more miles a day would be covered in sullen, dreary solitude; in the daily grind of following the plough, harrow, shim and roll. Our feet became leadened and hideous with mud-clogged boots, each new step was an effort of lifting, to make thigh and calf muscles protest with a sting of pain before developing into that long, dull, mind-devouring ache. After each such day in the fields there was to come the return walk to our homes, but there was little spring in our steps. Evidence of these walks was to be found in the gaits of the older men. Their legs were often distorted, their perambulations extraordinary, particularly on the hard highway. One could see the penalty they had paid for following the plough at too early an age, when the muscles of little boys had been asked to do too much, too early.

But from great distances one could identify the walkers, by the sound of their feet on the hard highway.

Reuben Ford at Walt's Cottage.

Chapter 1

Kuldysack

Hair, the hair of horses! Because I was three, perhaps less, when I first smelled it, I shall for ever remember the smell of horsehair. Sometimes noisome, rank and offensive, sometimes fragrant, redolent and balmy, that smell stole into and sometimes galloped into my three-year-old nostrils. All through the day, even on Sundays, and all through the night – on Sunday nights as well – that smell was my companion.

At the bottom of my father's garden, a longish garden which began at the back step of our bungalow home in Glemsford, Suffolk, there was a small factory. I used to sit there with the sun burning my head to sniff through the white-painted palings. Sniffing, I suppose, to get to the heart and soul of that smell. The palings separated me from the factory by about six feet; and when I put my head close to them and sniffed through them I could smell strong soap as well. I could also hear strange noises, busy noises; for in that factory were machines, big tubs of boiling water, soap, bubbles, clouds and clouds of white, wet steam, and little men who were so busy that they could not afford to take time off to speak to me; to tell me what they were doing in that steamy, noisy, smelly world . . .

But one day I did find out. My father told me. They were cleaning the dirty hair of old, dead, greasy-hocked horses – to make mattresses, cushions and pillows. After my father told me what it was all about I didn't sniff through the palings much, but the smell was always there.

My father and mother used to sleep on a mattress made from horsehair and I found that out all by myself, without being told by anyone. I wouldn't have known about it if one of those little leather bits which are used to stitch the ticking together had not come off to leave a little hole where it had been. Through that hole I could see bits of hair and I spent one lovely afternoon pulling out the hairs. Some were grey, others were dark or light brown, but the best ones were reddish gold, bits of the coats of chestnut horses. My mother did not appreciate my investigations and slapped my backside.

That slapping wasn't the best she could do, because I can still feel the sting of her best slapping after I went 'weeding', to help my father . . .

I did not see much of him, but I loved him very much. He was not like the fathers of other boys in Glemsford, for he was the village postman. He wore a uniform and a smart, stiff shako and his scarlet piping and shiny brass on navy serge always filled me with awe and pride. My father worked for the king. After walking many miles round the scattered community pushing bills and debt-summonses into letterboxes, he would arrive home, snatch off his coalscuttle hat and his beautiful jacket and gulp down a cup of strong tea and a hasty meal. He would smoke a pipe of tobacco, blowing out fragrant clouds to my delight. Then he would change into his old corduroy trousers, cloth cap and hobnailed boots, kiss us all round and go off like a greyhound to work on a broken-down farm. Father had to have two jobs to get the five of us enough to eat. I did not like it one bit. I did not think it fair of the king to make my father work all through the daylight.

Sunday was always the best day at Glemsford, because my father would take me to his allotment. I used to sit there in the sun, sometimes with my pretty frock and sash on, because we dressed up on Sundays, and watch his feverish hoeings, diggings and plantings, to grow us food. He was very good at gardening and used to grow parsnips so sturdy and long that they won prizes at the Flower Show. People used to say, 'Owd John carn't be beat at growin' parsnips, nor most vegetables, either.'

Even today I associate the word 'vegetables' with my father's rolled-up sleeves, his toil and sweat.

'We must watch out fer the weeds, young feller-me-lad, an' pull 'em up,' he used to say. 'Weeds don't never do nothing useful ... They choke the life outer the good things by stealin' their food ... They're just like a lot of wicked men in this wicked old world ... Growin' fat an' strong by stealin' from others ... If we don't keep a sharp lookout an' pull 'em up the minute we see 'em, we shall starve.'

Watching the big blade of his shut-knife slice through bread and raw onion, I sat on his knee and put my finger into one of his sweat beads, then into my mouth ... I remember the salty taste, the shock of his emphasis on the word *starve* ...

And that's why I got that good slapping. One Sunday, instead of going to his allotment my father went to sing his solo in the church choir for the Harvest Festival. Perhaps concerned that the wicked weeds might win if my father was not there to do them mischief, I went to his allotment alone, and without permission.

Hours later my mother, who had been driven to distraction by my absence, found me. I was weeding, wantonly. She arrived in time to see the last juicy young carrot uprooted from its tilthy bed; to see, too, that every bold and bulbous Spanish onion had suffered a similar fate.

Her hands flew to her face to hide her distress.

'You wicked, wicked child ... Your poor father's been a-slavin' to grow us food ... Now look what you've done ... Look at it! Jest you wait till I get you indoors ... Jest you wait!'

She dragged me by the hand to our bungalow, the last house on the right of a rutted lane leading to nowhere else, the 'Kuldysack', as she called it. I knew no words to tell her my fear of starvation; my fear that because my father was thanking God at the top of his voice for all things safely gathered in, instead of being at his plot fighting the weeds, starvation was imminent ...

'I were only weedin',' I said.

'You oughter know weeds don't grow in straight lines, only the vegetables,' she said, as she started slapping.

I didn't cry. And though my backside felt all sore and wasp-stingy, I would not cry because my little brother Leslie was watching. I thought he was her favourite, everybody's favourite, on account of his curls. Irresistible to friends and strangers alike, even to the tramps who came a-begging and the gipsies who came a-selling, Leslie's curls had to be touched, stroked, fondled, commented upon. Not a soul touched my lank string and I was jealous ... But they were lovely curls, all sun-burnished, rippling, cascading; and when he was in his pretty frock, all golden-topped in his best Sunday bib and tucker, he was the centre of attraction. I felt unshapely, unornamental, unloved.

But I was wrong. She loved me just as much, perhaps more; for I had been spared to her twice after nearly dying. Harvey and Harold, my two unknown brothers, had died, leaving myself, born 5 August 1907 and christened Cedric Wesley in the sub-district of Hartest, Sudbury, Suffolk; Leslie Gordon of the curls, born 9 July 1908; and my new baby sister Audrey Phyllis, born 24 February 1910, with her – at the Kuldysack.

I still disliked Leslie's curls. One day I sat him on our wooden three-legged stool. From my mother's wicker work-box I took a pair of scissors and in next to no time the curls were on the coconut matting. Leslie was very scared and wanted to get off the stool, but I would not let him. From all accounts, I had been to the toolshed and taken a nine-inch nail and a hammer. The nailend was on Leslie's shorn head and I was about to drive it home when my mother entered the room. From that moment I became the centre of attraction, but only to be watched as a potential murderer . . . But all was forgiven, if not forgotten, and the curls grew again.

We were in the heart of Constable country, about three miles from Long Melford and about seven from Clare, but well off the main road. There was great poverty, malnutrition and neglect. Corn areas had declined, good stubbles had reverted to grass. Cottages and farm buildings were decayed, fences neglected and lean cattle strayed in search of food. Roads and byways were in disrepair and many an East Anglian home-stead and smallholding had been abandoned. Worse, in that fertile region where grew such wonderful wheat, skilled farmhands had forsaken the land. In a once prosperous agrar-ian country the most inferior place was held by agriculture.

But there were still the fields. At the very doors of Kuldysack were worlds of interest, to be investigated, explored, understood; to be revealed to a hunter of three years of age. There were still the hedgerows, the woods, com-mons, ponds, waysides and wastes, the gardens and the farms; all brimming with life and vitality.

The life and vitality was of the birds, insects, bugs, beetles and small furry animals; of the plants, trees, grasses, fields and meadows: the vast living world of nature.

I was beginning to learn. I knew the difference between some weeds and some vegetables. Grass fascinated me. The thickness, greenness and softness was a comfort, and in its lushness there dwelt many creatures. Long, slimy worms that wriggled their way underneath to fill their bellies with dark, rich earth before surfacing to make their casts. I ate several worm casts, because they looked like chocolate, before I was told by the baker-boy never to do it again.

'Drat it, bor ... Don't you eat that, now ... It won't do you a mite o' good ... If you do, though, you'll go flat-footed an' deaf as a post.'

I got to know a bit about worms. How far they would stretch before they broke in half; that if you cut them in half instead of stretching them you could make two worms that lived. The stretchy ones died almost immediately.

There were trees and hedgerows round our bungalow and the trees seemed to touch the clouds some days, but were not tall enough to touch the blue sky on other days. I was puzzled by this and wondered why the sky was too high for the trees when it was blue, and too low when the skies were all fluffy and white and cloudy. But the trees were rostrums for birds and there were many kinds, all with different songs to sing and different plumage. My father taught me the songs and calls and the plumage. I liked the tits and chaffinches best, particularly the chaffinch whose call-note was very short and to the point ... 'pink-pink' and that was that, and he sang it nearly all day. The great tit had a song very like it, but he was not as pretty as the chaffinch with his rosy breast, bright blue head and black wings with corporal's stripes on them in white. His wife is not half so good-looking in a coat of dull green but the same wing markings. There were all kinds of tits near the Kuldysack, but the great tit was the biggest and fiercest and I could pick him out any old time, with his black head, white cheeks, yellow belly and black breast band. There were coal tits, marsh tits as well and another that I liked best for his nice blue head and the longest tail, and that was the long-tailed tit. The tits all had the same call, a very shrill 'see-see-see' and they usually sang it from the very tops of the highest trees.

We used to throw out food before my father started his questions and the minute they flocked down he would be at us . . .

'What's that one, then? Come on, you . . . whistle his call now!'

No sooner had the food hit the grass than we had other bird visitors: greedy yellow-beaked blackbirds who slur all their notes, and thrushes who cannot sing half so well – except one, that is the missel-thrush, who sings best on rainy days and is known in Suffolk as the storm cock. You can bet your life that if it is not raining when you hear his song it will rain in five minutes.

Sparrows flocked down, all notes, flutter, flurry and quarrel. The hedge sparrow should not have been there, but he was. He lives on insects, but is as greedy as the blackbird and will eat food put out for others. We did not mind the common sparrow, for he was far less quarrelsome.

'What's that one, then?' said my father, pointing to a hedge sparrow. But I soon told him it was an old 'hedgy'. I could tell by his bill, just like a pair of nail scissors.

We all had our favourites.

My mother liked the chaffinch best because of his song, which is far more musical than the 'pink-pink' call-note, and he sings it from the low branches – where I could watch him – full of pride, joy and pomp, puffing up his chest to make himself look twice as big; switching his head from side to side in quick jerks to attract attention – or to see if there is an audience worth singing to – and off he goes . . .

'What-what-what-what-do-you-r-r-r-r-really-think-of-ME-now?'

My father liked the yellowhammer. With his bright, canary-yellow head, which makes him look like a fireman in a brass helmet, he always sings from hedgerow tops, but looking a bit scared all the time . . .

'A-little-bit-of-bread-and-NO-cheese.'

But my favourite was the greenfinch. He sings best when he is courting. First he does a little dance. Then, leaving his perch, he starts to sing like billy-o, fluttering about in small circles and beating his wings so slowly that he can hardly fly. His is a simple song of only four notes . . . 'clip-clop-clump-and-sneeze', which he repeats many times in rapid succession.

Sometimes in the hedgerows we would find skulking a white-throat, but he is not an English bird and comes only in the summer. He is small and brown apart from his white throat and sings while dancing up and down from the hedgetop, jumping six to ten feet up, or more, straight into the air, then back to the hedge. I disliked him when my father said he was not English. But I got over that and did not dislike him any more when he said that all birds were God's birds, and equal.

I used to wonder why my father, who knew so much about birds, did not teach me to fly.

The lines in Father's brow deepened as the furrows appeared one spring in the wide Suffolk fields around us. Plainly life could not go on as it had been doing. We were existing but poorly from the fruits of the allotment and from the very occasional pig some neighbour killed which supplied our meat diet of a slice or two of pork or bacon once or twice a week.

Somehow my mother contrived, through it all, to look the prettiest woman of all just as my father was the handsomest man. She had been born in Bartlow Hamlet, Cambridgeshire, and christened Elizabeth Amy Ford. For some years before her marriage she temporarily left her beloved East Anglia to cook for various rich families in London. She excelled at household and culinary pursuits when she had a chance to follow them. But in her God-given gifts courage and sweet goodness were her greatest.

My father had been a soldier, at heart, by instinct and through training. Born in the parish of Barnadiston, he tired of working on the land and had enlisted as a young man in 2nd Battalion, the Suffolk Regiment, and in an engagement of seven and three-quarter years served nearly all that time overseas. He had been mostly on attachment to the East India Company as a telegraphist and ended his engagement at Karachi on 10 October 1903.

24

We had little or no social life at Glemsford. Occasionally my Uncle Wag, my father's eldest brother and companion-in-arms in the Suffolks – also a village postman, at Great Thurlow, Suffolk – would pay a fleeting visit, but my mother was ill-equipped for entertaining and far too busy looking after her flock to go out and about.

In the winter of 1910 I became ill again. At night in the dark I could see no birds through the window and I was frightened where in summer I had been bold. Family gossip has it that I was a most delicate child, so frail that I was medically barred from school until I was seven years and a bit. Fat and prosperous doctors prescribed for me full cream, Benger's Food and port wine ... but no mention was made of how to buy them.

I was still very ill when my father left us in 1911. Distressed by poverty, encouraged by advertisements, he left for Canada determined to find us a new home. The first indications of impending change came in unusual tensions between my parents and secret whisperings in the parlour, which I apprehensively tried to overhear through the keyhole. There were impressive-looking forms on the chest of drawers and a general air of unease. One day a man in a smart suit, with a funny voice, visited Father and explained to us all with false gaiety, so frightening to my barely comprehending ear, that Father was emigrating to Canada where work and money abounded. Soon we would follow.

Such were the promises made to seduce honest men from East Anglia in those hard times. Word was spread around that

Canada was a country of vast glistening wheatlands where people could afford three good meals every day and homes fit for the nobility were provided for labourers. I knew nothing of that. All I knew was that my father went from us and that my mother was well nigh inconsolable for weeks. After three or four months of missing him, his letters started to arrive once a week. Many came from Montreal; the largest batch in my writing desk bears the post mark of Ontario; others came from Saskatchewan, Alberta, and from British Columbia and the Yukon, where he toured in search of work. Some of those ancient envelopes had contained money, but not of fortune's size. All bore witness that anyone but a Limey could get work in the land of the maple leaf; Greeks and Italians, Scots engineers and Irish labourers, for ever.

Our poverty increased.

The neighbours had more than enough troubles of their own and there were few callers who could be told of our plight. One of these was Uncle Wag, who was a great strength to me in my illness. He had a stout heart and an understanding of my darkness, plus the capacity to speak words I could hold on to. He would gently squeeze my little hand and say, 'Don't yew get a-frettin', bor. They luvly owd birds'll be a-wingin' back, an' yewer owd father afore 'em. Yew jest sleep. They'll be back.'

When I survived, more from kindness than from recommended medication, Uncle Wag took me pony-tripping to Great Thurlow to meet my paternal grandparents who had a fair-sized smallholding and three towering trees lush with

William pears. Grandfather David Mays' temper was as short as his sturdy frame. He occasionally clouted my grandmother over the head with heavy iron saucepans, but one night he got his deserts. Full of beer he stopped off to recharge his home-made cartridges from the powder keg in his bakehouse. The sun had gone down. There was not much light, but that suited his purpose because he wished to shoot partridge – not on the wing, but as they squatted in the stubbles. He was as wicked as that. He struck a match the better to see the gunpowder. A spark flew. His bakehouse blew into splinters. He had not a hair of head, nor of lid, nor of brow left. His sight vanished as the keg flashed and he was totally blinded. Nevertheless, his saintly wife, my grandmother, tended him through his declining years with not one word of reproach.

Granny Mays was an angel, a furrowed and wrinkled little angel, whose eyes volcanoed love and sympathy for everyone, particularly her children. Except for fat Delphy, they were all God-fearing Christians with a capital C. Stewart, who I am supposed to resemble in looks, was a carpenter and cabinet-maker like the Christ he adored. Before he took his sharp chisels or planes to oak or elm he would spit on his hands, clasp them in prayer and thank God for the smell of the wood and the work he was about to perform.

Delphy became a bookmaker. He grew fat on food, whisky, cigars and the sight of horses at Newmarket. He was one of the first to introduce gambling to Great and Little Thurlow; and was one who could never differentiate between nieces and nephews in terms of titles in fifty years of trying.

Perce, my father's youngest brother, had the broadest Suffolk accent in the whole of East Anglia. At times he could hardly understand what he said himself. But when he went to his chapel to sing the Wesleyan hymns he loved he became almost embarrassingly articulate and understandable.

Reuben and Susanna Ford.

Chapter 2

Aunt Harriet's Funeral

I have no recollection of our leaving Kuldysack. But I cannot forget the privation we endured in our new village, Helions Bumpstead, about five miles south-west of Clare. In her loneliness and misery my mother struggled on. Fewer envelopes from my father had money in them; fewer meals were served upon our table, but there were distressing additions to the lines in my mother's brow. Our diet was stale bread (one farthing cheaper per quartern loaf than fresh bread), skimmed milk and potatoes. As a great treat for Sunday's dinner – and to last out the week as the meat dish for four – she sometimes bought a tough buck rabbit for sevenpence.

Sometimes my mother's eldest brother, old rheumaticky Uncle Charles, would hobble from Wethersfield – about nine miles – to give my mother a florin from his labourer's pittance.

And when the ever-increasing agony of his 'screws' put a halt to his perambulations he did his Christian best by inviting the attention of 'The Parish' to our plight. It was when the parish stepped in that I once again began to take notice, for my health had improved – after two years.

From that dread place there came a Good Samaritan to take an inventory of all we had. He didn't need a lot of paper. He needed less the next week. Through the 'special arrangements' he had made for us the week before, and to recover his benevolence, he arranged that one of his friends should buy my mother's wedding-gift pictures.

God, how I missed those pictures! They were in gilt frames, all ornamental and rich-looking. Lovely, well-nourished ladies as naked as nature were bathing in marble-encrusted pools; fanning themselves, or being fanned by black slaves, with fans of peacock feathers. The water was as blue as the Neapolitan sky above them. Other ladies, equally naked and beautiful, strolled in tree-canopied gardens where not a weed was to be seen. And when those pictures went there remained only the two nails, and two big squares of cleanish wall paper, and the lighter patches only showed how shabby and faded we were.

Mother was often on her knees. 'If You love me, You will help me,' she would say to God. And God must have loved her as much as we did for soon afterwards there was a temporary change for the better. Envelopes came from Toronto with money in them, but not for long.

The worst day was the one after my Aunt Harriet died.

Ashdon, where my maternal grandparents lived in their

small brick and stone cottage at a tied rental of two shillings a week, is nine miles from Helions Bumpstead. It was from there a letter came, all black-bordered and sinister-looking. My mother paled at the sight of it and her fear was communicated to me. Her eyes misted as she read. Her pale face twitched and strong sad noises came from her. 'Oh, no!' she said. 'Oh, no!' She cried a bit then with her head on her arms on the table. She stood up, searched in her thin purse and spoke to me. 'Granny Ford has written. We are going to see her, going to Ashdon. Your Auntie Harriet has died and Granny wants me for the funeral.'

Auntie Harriet's funeral, the first I ever attended, was a formidable operation for us. My little sister Audrey had not yet learned to walk very far. Brother Leslie should have been able to walk well at his age but his legs were curved by rickets. I could walk well, so could my mother, but nine miles is a long way to march on empty stomachs.

The food cupboard did its miserable best – left-over slices of yesterday's stale bread. My mother cut them into egg-dipping fingers. But there were no eggs, no margarine, no dripping. I bit into my piece. Tasteless and dry it clogged my mouth. I had to spit it out.

'It's awful, Mother. It doesn't taste. I can't eat it!'

She bit into her lip and a tear fell. She threw back her head to hurl that tell-tale wetness from my sight. She went once more to the cupboard, to mix vinegar into a cup of water. I watched her dip another bread-finger into the mixture, turning it so its hardness should yield. And then she smiled at me.

'There now, try it again. It's not dry any more and it'll taste of somethin'!'

She took a bite herself and tried to appear delighted. 'It's not so bad now, boy. You must eat somethin' for we've got a long way to go.'

How I tried to swallow it! But the sting of the vinegar assaulted my throat, my nostrils, and made me cough so hard that I vomited into the fireplace. She sobbed, 'My poor darling. If there's a God in heaven why does he let on so?'

That did it. I said very loudly, just for her: 'For what we are about to receive may the Lord make us truly thankful.' Then I forced myself to eat every scrap. God must have been listening, I thought, because that time I did not even feel sick.

Then came our next ordeal, the beginning of the long march to Ashdon. Still sleeping, looking frail and doll-like, Audrey was lifted into the old pram. Leslie stood on the axle nearest to the pushing end, his curls cascading over the handle and my mother's hands. She rocked the old pram about a bit, looked at its wheels and, seizing the push-bar with a grip which whitened her knuckles, she pushed off. Off to the house of her birth, the half-living going to see the dead.

If God had not been absent from Helions Bumpstead He certainly appeared to be absent when we reached Castle Camps, about three miles from Granny's house. As makeweight to our misery He threw in a nerve-shattering thunderstorm and a torrent of rain. As we sheltered under the eaves of a big barn on the Camps road, a big tree added to the drama when it shivered and split as it was done to death by lightning. But things improved a bit after that for soon the air was all rain-smelly fresh and out came a rainbow. We went on our way, with rain-drops falling from the distorted peak of my sodden cap, and I remember catching some of them with the tip of my tongue, drinking them into me with unnecessarily loud gulps, to make my mother laugh at something for a change.

Then, where Whiting's Mere Hill meets the Bartlow road, there was a fourteen-acre field, all rain-washed, fresh and green. We might not have noticed it from all the other fields had not the rainbow seemed to go straight down into its middle. But there it was, a heaven-sent field of swedes.

I crept through the hawthorn hedge and pulled a middling-sized swede. By rubbing it on the rainy grass I soon cleaned off most of the soil. With quick snips of my front teeth, I cut off the small roots, feeling the grit in my mouth. I then stuck out my bottom jaw and ran the swede along the sharpness of my teeth, spitting out the peel as it entered my mouth. In no time at all the preparations for our feast were ended. But we had no knife to divide a root intended for cattle into equal proportions for four human beings.

In turn, like old birds feeding their young, my mother and I bit off sweet chunks of swede to feed to Audrey and Leslie. It seemed so succulent after that stale, vinegary bread, that life brightened immediately. So much so that my mother started off with her 'inventions'.

'You jest wait till your father comes back from Canada,

33

m'lads. We shan't be a-trampin' abowt like gipsies, a-pushin' a silly owd pram.'

'What will we be a-doin' then, Mummy?' asked Leslie.

'Ah . . . ! Now you jest wait an' see.'

'See what?' asked Leslie the practical.

'Well now, we'll sartinly have a pony an' trap for weekdays. For Sundays we'll be different. A big shiny brougham with two horses. I think we'll have cream ones. They're the best! With red an' gold ribbons in their manes an' tails too. But that ain't all, we'll have a coachman; one with a shiny top hat an' a cockade, an' a long whip with white ribbons on it like they have for weddin's. You'll see! You'll see!'

When her inventions began to wear a bit thin through sheer exhaustion and her breathing became laboured with pushing up the steep incline of Whiting's Mere Hill, she took a bit of a blow and pointed. 'There it is. That's Granny Ford's. The one with the smoke comin' outer the chimney.'

It was all downhill from there and her breathing was easier. We were in Bartlow Hamlet, the smallest hamlet in Essex. When we turned Reuben's Corner by the old Bonnett Inn, there it was . . . a simple brick and stone cottage, almost two hundred years old. Granny Ford's! The house where my mother was born.

'Granny ain't home,' said Leslie. 'Look, she ain't pulled the blinds up. P'raps she's still a-bed.'

'Shush now! Keep you quiet now,' said my mother.

Without knocking she walked into her birthplace by the back door. I followed, after lifting Audrey from the pram.

34

We entered a small room shrouded in darkness. In two facing armchairs heavy with woollen antimacassars sat my maternal grandparents. Granny Ford held a mixing bowl in her lap, she looked squat and kind. Old Grandad Reuben Ford, with his long whiskers and purplish nose, looked like a broken-down King George V.

'So you've come then, Lizzie,' said Granny Ford, jumping up to kiss and embrace my mother and to leave the imprints of her floured hands on Mother's shoulders. 'Thank the good Lord you've come!'

Grandad did not say a word, he just nodded his head. He never wasted time on words.

Then, wiping her hands on a cheese-cloth, she addressed us.

'Now then, you young Bumpsteads, get they wet clothes off an' I'll get you a mite of vittels. Lizzie, Harriet's in the kitchen. Want to see her, now?'

My mother nodded and followed Granny Ford into the little kitchen. As the door closed behind them I caught a glimpse of big flower bunches and I smelled a smell but not of flowers. Through the gap where the kitchen door did not meet its frame I could hear them.

'Should've bin done two days ago,' said Granny Ford, 'but owd Starchy Williams got took bad, an' we had to wait fer the measurin'.'

They soon came out again pretending not to be crying. But I already knew about quiet crying with tight lips. I felt sorry for them and proud.

Granny busied herself around us but although I looked

hard round the little room I could not see much, because of the drawn blinds.

'Come you on, now,' she said. 'Come you on, you young Bumpsteads, le's see you git they owd vittels into you.'

'Oh, look!' said Leslie. 'What a big owd lump o' meat!'

And what a sight it was – wonderfully topped with crinkly rind; thick with pink-white layers of lean; and between the crinkle and lean enough white fat to render down to a mixing-basin of dripping.

'It's pork, boy, from the last of your Grandad's fat owd pigs.'

We ate the pork with pickled walnuts, cold boiled potatoes and crisp lettuce. When we had eaten every morsel – which did not take us long – Granny brought in a seven pound biscuit tin wedged solid with hungry-making caraway seed cake. She cut us thick slices, then gave us glasses brimming with her 'extraspeshul' home-made elderberry wine. I could feel it warming my belly at the first lovely sip.

Everything was wonderful until a funny man came in without knocking. He had a huge Adam's apple and untidy whiskers. His white apron had side pockets and from one he pulled out a big screwdriver. He spat on his hands, said 'Hello, Lizzie' to my mother, then looked at Granny Ford.

'All right fer me to go in now, Susan?'

Granny turned to my mother. 'Don't the boy want to see her, then?'

My mother hesitated, then spoke to me. 'Your Auntie Harriet is dead, in there. You'll not be seein' her again. Come, say goodbye to her an' see how pretty she is.'

She took my hand and led me in. I was more curious than scared at first, so I had a good look round. There were two carpenter's trestles. On them was a long box with shiny brass along the sides. The box lid stood on its end against the wall by the water pails and Mother read what was on it – the date she was born and the date she died. I could smell the lilies, roses and violets, but the funny smell was stronger in the kitchen, and spoiled the flower smells. All the cards had black borders; some had verses and kisses; but most exciting of all was my cousin Will's 'Daisy' air gun; and I wanted so much more to pick it up and stroke its shiny barrel than to look at a dead Aunt Harriet. But I had no choice.

My mother picked me up and leaned over the long box.

I looked down at her.

Her face was as white and waxy as the lily petals. She was smiling a sad sort of smile and looked beautiful. But the smile looked a long way off, almost as though it was not on her face at all. It made me think of being punished for weeding; exactly how I had felt after being spanked for doing good.

I had to touch her. To feel if she was real, but I was scared of her stillness because I had seen her before, full of fun and smiles and jokes.

'Don't be afraid,' said my mother. 'She's a-goin' on a long, long journey. Say goodbye!'

And then I did it. I pressed her cheek with my finger. She felt cold. It was like putting a finger on the ice in the water-butt, but on soft ice. There was another difference. Where I had pressed there was a little dint which did not fill up again. That scared me. I had spoiled the face of my pretty Aunt Harriet and I thought that because of my finger-puggling God might not let her into heaven.

My mother set me down and nodded to the screwdriver man, who winked and put out his tongue. Afterwards Granny said he was 'Starchy' Williams, the village undertaker, one who had derived his apt nickname through his professional dealings with 'the stiffs'.

Next day was funeral day. Our relations came from all over East Anglia; farmers, shepherds, farmhands, thatchers; all with wives and children; all gossiping like mad, eating Granny's 'vittels' and drinking her home-made wine. There were two young soldiers from the Essex Regiment who said they had 'wangled' leave; but the one I liked best of all was the one everybody else hated. Their dislike was based on the fact that he was 'chapel' and they were C. of E. like me. He had been a lay preacher but had turned to drink. He did not go to church with the others but stayed behind with the children. Soon he impressed us by laying into three kinds of wine – parsnip, dandelion and elderberry. When he had had what he called 'a fairish owd draught', he began to sing.

Whiter than the whitewash on the wall;
I'm whiter than the whitewash on the wall.
You washed me in the water that has washed your dirty
    daughter,
And now I am whiter than the whitewash on the wall.

I liked that, but the next one made me laugh fit to burst:

> Jesus loves me, this I know,
> 'Cos the Bible tells us so.
> He has washed away my sins,
> Very much obliged to Jesus.

He kept giving me wine until I had learned both ditties but I got a swift clout from my mother when I sang them to her later. 'Good gracious alive, boy. It must be that owd Stalley who taught you that – the owd Devil-dodger!'

When our relations returned, some gave money to my mother; I thought it a pity Aunt Harriet had to die for such help to be forthcoming. After we returned home to Helions Bumpstead our fortunes continued to improve for a time. Welcome parcels of food and clothing were sent to us by these scattered benefactors.

For months after the funeral I had frightening dreams about death and burials. All the people I was fond of died in my dreams to leave me all alone. They floated in the sky in boxes, rejected equally by heaven and hell because of the holes I had bored in their faces with my finger. I told my mother about it when she came one night to find me sweating and screaming. She cured me pretty swiftly with a gentle cuff and tea of senna pods, laced with castor oil.

When Easter came round the parcels had ceased altogether and we were more deeply embedded in poverty's rut. Easter and its East Anglian customs should have been a highlight of the year – with the hot-cross buns and the brown hens' eggs painted with funny faces and our pet names.

Leslie's nickname was Fon or Fonnie. There were two reasons. First, he had been born on 9 July, the same day as King Alfonso of Spain; and, irrespective of nationality, my mother always had a soft and reverent spot for all mon-archs. The other reason was that he was thin and crooked, and this conjured up 'Ffon' which is Welsh for 'walking stick', a word my mother learned from a Welsh maidservant in Kensington.

Although my sister had been christened Audrey Phyllis she was invariably called Pops or Poppy. This was because from the moment she could walk she would find her way to a nearby field of scarlet poppies.

I was christened Cedric Wesley – the result of my father's timely reading of *Ivanhoe* and his preference for Wesleyan hymns – but I suffered an abbreviation of my first Christian name to Ced, or in moments of affection, Ceddie. I detested both.

Anyway, Easter 1914, when I was six, was one I would like to forget. We had for breakfast the brown eggs with faces and pet names. We had been promised hot-cross buns the minute the baker arrived on his special run with them – piping hot buns, brown and glistening with flakes of un-sugary-like sugar – tasting of warmth, softness and cinnamon.

I was the first to hear the baker-boy shout 'Whoa, there' to his horse, so I ran round the front and did a dance of joyful anticipation on a vantage point – our high bank from where

I could look down into the baker's basket and be the first to see his beautiful buns.

Two bakers came our way that day, one to the front door of the next house, one to ours. Next door's baker screwed up his face, made a know-all wink and hissed in my hearing: 'Pssst! Don't fergit, now. No buns there, bor. Not unless she pays!' And then I thought we would have a bunless Easter as I followed our baker to our back door. My mother's apron was already lifted for the buns but I heard the conditions, all whispered. Also in whispers, so that I should not hear, she pleaded: 'Jest three, then. One a-piece for the children. Please!'

'I dussent, missus. More'n me job's worth. Not even fer the nippers!'

She could see I had overheard. I put my hand in hers and felt the squeezing. Quietly, humiliated and shamed we went together to the kitchen. Leslie, all agog with bun-fever, tugged at her skirt and demanded the biggest one with the most sugar. Her shame went in a flash. Then came her pride, her courage. 'They owd buns aren't up to much this year. We'll make our own, an' you must all help an' we'll start this very minute.' And by God we did! Made only of flour and water, lacking sugar, cinnamon and taste, they were at least hot and bore the insignia of Christ's cross. Although as flat as cow dung, they were the finest of buns, love-inspired buns, devoid of debt and poverty's indignities.

It was at Helions Bumpstead that I first went to school in the autumn of 1914 but I remember little of it.

Mother slaved daily to feed us in those difficult times. In

season she gleaned for us, picked stones for us and black-berries. I saw skin shredded cruelly from her fingers in her stone pickings from barren, lifeless fields. I saw the flesh of her fingers staining redly the jagged stubbles of scythe-hacked bean-stalks as she gleaned among them. She was never deterred. The reward for her stooping, scratching, mutilation and boundless courage meant survival. But what a reward! Nine English pennies for one bushel of beans, and if the gleaning was thin it could take two days to produce one bushel.

The outbreak of the Kaiser's War put a stop to that wretchedness. From Toronto came thick envelopes with money and photographs of my father in the uniform of 1st Canadian Pioneers. For us children there were badges of bronze – Canadian maple leaves behind crossed pick and shovel, on which perched a pathetic-looking beaver. At last the Canadians had found work for a Limey.

We were proud of our badges, and pinned them on our threadbare jerseys to show off to the Helions Bumpstead boys whose fathers were not Canadian Pioneers but ordinary clod-hopping farmhands. Soon we were put in our places, for the other boys began to wear brass and silver badges to show that their fathers were no longer clodhoppers but English soldiers of the Essex, Suffolk and Norfolk regiments.

The old men at this time used to gather in the village pubs, sing outside them, wave Union Jacks, urge young ones to enlist and flourish large pictures of Lord Kitchener exhorting all and sundry to join the army.

Come on and join; come on and join;
Come on and join Lord Kitchener's army.
Ten bob a week, plenty grub to eat,
Bloody great boots make blisters on your feet;
Come on and join.

That one seemed to be the top of the 1914 pops, but there were two others – one was the inevitable 'Jerusalem' and the other, which the old men never tired of singing with the fervency of profound personal conviction on England's green and pleasant land at Helions Bumpstead, was 'Britons never, NEVER, NEVER shall be slaves'. In all their feudal existence they had known nothing but slavery, exploitation and degradation.

The last Canadian letter came. Her face was a joy to behold. Her wrinkles seemed to vanish. She was young again and beautiful. She could hardly speak. Her news came to us in gasps and jerks ...

'An Expeditionary Force ... Canadian soldiers ... Coming to England ... Comin' to fight they owd Germans ... Your daddy is comin' home ... Comin' home!'

'When?' said Leslie the practical.

'He don't say,' and the tears blinded her. 'He don't say, but he's a sergeant-major an' he's a-comin' home.'

Chapter 3

Father's War

I was the first to meet him. Wishing to surprise us he had not written to say that he had arrived in England. I was on my way back to Helions Bumpstead School after dinner. There he was! Five hundred yards away and getting closer with every step. My father. The father who had taught me about birds and growing things and whom I had long feared I might never see again. I did not actually see him at first. Rather could I feel him coming to me. Then I did see him. He was not just 'coming home', he was 'marching home'.

Now I could see his shiny Sam Browne belt and sword-sling . . .

Now his shiny knee-boots and buttons . . .

Now his moustache – black and fierce with spikes like hedgehog quills.

Now he was close enough for me to see his eyes, damp with love, looking into mine.

He lifted me to the sky, hugged and kissed me without speaking. I was glad he spoke first because I did not know what to say. I had forgotten his voice after over three years. It was strange when it came.

'And where do you think you're a-goin', young feller-me-lad?'

'I'm goin' back to school, sir,' I said.

'SIR? SCHOOL?' His eyebrows jumped at the thought of it. 'You'll not be a-goin' to school today, young feller-me-lad. We'll soon see about that. Is this your school?'

He pointed with his big stick and I nodded. Mr Shaw, the headmaster, stood in the porch.

'I've just come home from Canada, sir. This is my son. I hope you won't be needin' him for a day or so!'

'Thank God that you have come,' said Mr Shaw, who knew about our struggles. 'Off you go, boy, off home with your father and God bless you all!'

I should have cheered, turned cartwheels, or even whistled like a blackbird. Instead I took my father's hand, led him to the house he had never seen, and cried all the way.

This reunion produced Arcadia for us all – a sudden trans-formation; an East Anglian paradise. My mother's cheeks bloomed. She was enraptured, transported and delighted. After three years of misery she was released from bitterness and heartache.

In some ways I resented my father's presence. Before he came home all attention had been given to us. He was getting most of it now. Also, when he spoke of things Canadian he sounded like a foreigner. His good old Suffolk dialect had become corrupted. I was jealous of his popularity. People who had ignored us in our hour of need came flocking to our house to listen to him.

In his big black trunk and three kit bags he had brought presents for us all. For my mother he had a brooch which spelled out 'ELIZABETH' in solid silver. She pinned it on her new black dress with the white ruffly collar and sleeves and looked more beautiful than ever. When she thought we were not looking she would stroke it and go all dreamy-eyed. We had sweets galore and packets of Spearmint or Chiclets which were nice and pepperminty to begin with but soon tasted of nothing and made our jaws ache – possibly because we had been out of chewing practice for a long time.

I loved to hear him tell old rheumaticky Uncle Charlie stories; and Uncle Charlie came very often to improve his health on big doses of Father's whisky. There was the night when he spent hours telling Uncle Charlie about the cold he had endured in distant Canada.

'Think yourself lucky that you've never encountered the Chinook, Charlie boy.'

'Chinook? Now what might that be, then?'

'It's a wind, so cold that when it blew it froze the boiling water in my shaving mug afore the steam had stopped coming out of the top.'

46

'Well, I never!' said Uncle Charlie, as he took another deep swig.

'You don't know what cold is in England, Charlie. When I was in Alaska the ground got froze so solid it couldn't be opened to dig graves. For months an' months the dead were stacked up in livin'-rooms like grandfather clocks, all a-waitin' for the thaw.'

'Gawd a-mighty!' said Uncle Charlie, repeating the dose.

'They got over it, though. An old Jew made hisself a fortune. He went round with a reindeer sleigh, collected all the dead and fer fifty bucks a foot took the stiffs to the sawmill and had their feet cut off at the ankles with a buzz saw.'

'Well, I never did! Funny owd lot out there, ain't they now?'

'Yes, they had to cut off the feet afore they could sharpen the legs, y'know.'

'Sharpen the legs?' said my mother ... 'Whose legs?'

'Why, the legs of the dead folks! The old Jew used to sharpen 'em up to a point with his axe and it were dead easy after that. He'd get a big buck nigger to hold the stiff up straight and another one to bash him over the head with a fourteen-pound hammer. And the stiff would go into the ground clean as a whistle.'

'Thunder an' lightnin' an' Gawd preserve us, tell us another!' said Uncle Charlie.

'Alaska was cold,' mused my father, 'but it were a sight colder in the Rockies. One day a young mountain goat was a-tryin' to jump from one hill to another an' froze solid in mid-air.'

'Now I know thassa lie, Jack bor. The law o' gravity wouldn't hev allowed it.'

'Now that's where you're wrong, Charlie. It was so bloody cold the law o' gravity got froze as well.'

'Jack, for heaven's sake! Such language in front of the children!' Then Mother went and hid in our now well-stocked pantry and I could hear her laughing fit to burst.

So our miraculous new life went on for three weeks. Then came a bolt from the blue. Old Sarah Unwin, who had lived next door to Granny Ford for sixty-odd years, died, believed to be one hundred and two. I had seen her in her cottage when we went to bury Aunt Harriet, filling her armchair with layers of clothing she had wrapped round her little wizened body.

I recalled that she had worn a tall poke bonnet – strapped under the chin with a dog-lead – plus a black candlewick shawl and scarlet mittens. Her gown had been of indeterminate material and colour and had hidden her feet.

She was a crinkly little nut in an over-large shell but her fierce eyes had gimleted their way into my conscience and scared the living daylights out of me. I was told she could still read the *Christian Herald* without spectacles. But she was anchored to her chair. When she wished to move she relied upon her broomstick. This she kept in constant readiness to thump the fireplace and so summon Granny Ford. This was her last resort if her high-pitched shriek of 'Susanna' failed to get a response.

But now her chair was empty. So, too, was her cottage and it was ours for the asking.

'Would you like to go to live next door to Granny Ford?' asked my mother, her eyes imploring us to say yes because she so much wanted to be where she had been born.

'Shall we have seed cake and wine there again?' asked Leslie.

'Of course! We shall be making our own.'

Within a few days we were settled in Ashdon at Bartlow Hamlet, or Stevington's End as it was sometimes called, which was a good mile from Ashdon village and overlapped bits of Essex and Cambridgeshire. It was Lilliputian, an agrarian microcosm. One farm, three smallholdings, a few houses, a pub and a dozen scattered cottages in a setting of rural loveliness. We had not a church, a chapel or a shop. But ours was that precious thing, a true hamlet. Ashdon's other extremities were merely Ends ... Church End, Knox End, Holden End and many more, for these Ends were endless.

Each was a community with its own code and a dialect quite distinguishable from the rest. Each tiny community considered the others suspect and inferior. But if some stranger from another End was sufficiently ill-advised to criticize our parent village Ashdon, there would be instant cooperation to denounce and confound the critic.

Father soon went off to France to fight the Germans.

In 1914 Bartlow Hamlet was not over-blessed with children, perhaps a dozen at most. Some were nearing school-leaving age. But like myself most were about to begin their education at Ashdon's elementary school. This was just over a mile from the Bonnett Inn, the geographical and social nucleus of our hamlet.

The day came when there were finger rappings at window panes, kicks on the front door, girlish gigglings and shrill 'coo-ees' . . . Dolly and Milly were calling to take me to school.

'Come on, Ced, bor, it's nigh on ten t'nine. We'll have to run all the way.'

Twenty to nine became a key time in my life from then on – the time when I went off to school each weekday with Dolly and Milly who were the only other two children of school age in our part of Bartlow Hamlet. Dear little Milly, her cheek all marmalady, her dark eyes and hair wild and unbridled as an unbacked colt, was especially my pal.

'We got sums ter-day, Ced. Hate owd sums! Wish it were silent readin'!'

'Sums'll do YOU better'n silent readin',' snorted Dolly. 'YOU never read the books they give you. On'y they dratted owd comics an' sich.'

Milly was an orphan, a skinny one whose natural grace was not concealed by her pitiful dress, an inartistic cut-down from her grandmother's faded smock. Despite her dress, and where and how she lived, she looked the little lady that nature had intended.

There had been three thatched cottages opposite our front door. Now, where Milly lived with old Cilia Cooper, there remained but half a cottage, a monument to neglect and decay. Jagged joist-ends protruded from slattern thatch like dark bones. Unshiny, sombre ivy festooned the crumbling plaster walls. Clematis clung desperately to the remnants of the porch, as if trying to hold its ruins in one piece. Where once were gardens there was a chaos of weeds; fractured, distorted palings; monster elder shrubs being strangled by bellbine. But the birds loved this riot of green confusion and came there in flocks every morning and evening to sing to little Milly.

Dolly was different. She lived with her parents and brothers, Chris and Ernie, at the Bonnett Inn. Her father and brothers worked on the land and also served beer in the pub. Dolly was in standard seven, and would be fourteen in September. She was far too old for us!

'Let's go across the fields,' said Dolly one morning, 'seein' as it's a nice day.'

Because she was so old and wise we did as we were told. Instead of walking down Ashdon Road as usual we crept through the opening of Sparks' Mede. Dolly was right. It was better going by fields when the sun was shining and the earth was dry and warm. That lovely day Sparks' lush grass was bejewelled with buttercups and daisies, clumps of dandelion, patches of sorrel and wide ringlets of darker grass under which lurked potent spawn, just sleeping there until late September when it would erupt overnight to thrust up giant mushrooms for our breakfasts.

Five-acre Shortlands was canaried with flowering mustard, after a year of lying fallow and resting to regather its strength. Mill Meadow's pond was betrayed by frog croakings and the 'chirra-chirra' of reed warblers. It would be far better, thought

I, to explore the pond for water voles, otters and shrews – perhaps to see a rainbow-plumed kingfisher – than to be shut up in school! Water hens were 'kur-r-rucking' at full throttle, perhaps frightened by a vole, or just because they had laid their eggs . . . And then the bell sounded.

'Bugger it!' said Dolly. 'Five minutes' warnin'. We're late ag'in!'

Hand in hand we ran like hares, the brown hair of Dolly, the black mane of Milly and three school satchels streaming behind.

Crossing the open fields we always saw the rabbits. We could not go far in Ashdon's fields without seeing them. In the evenings they would come out to feed. We could get quite close to them before one or two gave the alarm signal. Then there would be a great scurrying and flashing of white tails before they would disappear into their burrows. Our knowledge of nature expanded regularly. We learned that rabbits are mute, except for a kind of subdued grunt, and that they give the alarm signal by quickly and strongly striking the ground with their hind feet. We learned that hares have no burrows in which to hide but rely upon their great speed to keep them from danger; that if you want to catch a hare it is the easiest thing in the world provided that the wind is not behind you and blowing in the direction of the hare; that usually the hare squats in a bit of a nest which he makes with his body in the grass; that this is called a 'form'; that if he's got his back to you, and the wind is right, you can walk up to him and grab him by the ears; but that the minute he spots or smells the enemy, he is off like the wind. I regarded Mr Hare as a truly wonderful sight, with his big ears flat back, bounding over the ground in leaps of ten feet or more.

The owls' techniques were fascinating, too. We would watch them avidly – floating, gliding and skimming close to the ground on silent wings, up the field, down the field, following the plough furrows with great regularity.

Milly did not like owls, especially the barn owl which screeched and looked a bit like a ghost because it was white except for its light chestnut back. Sometimes it frightened me, too. But I admired the brown owls with their two songs – 'kee-wit, kee-wit', and 'to-whoo, to-whoo' – and soon realized that they were much appreciated by the farmers, living as they did on the larvae and pupae of insects – leatherjackets, wireworm, daddy-longlegs and cockchafers.

We would see flocks of all kinds of birds in autumn and winter – redwings, fieldfares and flocks of pigeons, goldfinches and partridges.

There was also much to learn when we went by road. Along the winding tracks, lanes and roads around our village flowers grew in rich profusion. I understood why my mother's favourites were, of all flowers, Ashdon violets – blue ones, pink ones, mauve ones and white ones – in clusters of heart-shaped leaves and bedded in soft green moss. They were not like the Parma variety that were sold in London at sixpence per bunch. Ashdon violets smelled like violets. Any time we wanted the smell of them in our nostrils we did not pick the flowers or dig up the roots; we just squeezed one little bloom between our finger-tips and rubbed our fingers inside our noses. The smell would remain there for a long time.

Daffodils, primroses, wild hyacinths, dog-daisies. They coloured and covered the road-banks and blazed carpets of glory for our spring and summer days. And in the fields behind the roadside hedges the poppies blazed like waving blood. Dog-roses, with briars as thick as a boy's arm, caressed the hedgerows, putting out their pink and white petals to blend with the scarlet of the hips and haws of the year before.

Between the delights of all these goings and returnings we were in school from nine to half past four, with an hour's break for a midday meal.

Because I was too old for the Infants and too ignorant for the Juniors – I had not learned overmuch at Helions Bumpstead – I had been tested and was allowed to sit with the Juniors – 'ter try an' ketch up'.

One day when our private nature study had made us rather late, we heard music as we tore sweaty and breathless up the steps. This meant that Mabel Eason, Bill Smith the blacksmith's daughter, wife of Reg Eason the shopkeeper, church organist, choir mistress and Sunday school teacher – as well as day school teacher – was playing the entry march on the tinny piano. She always played the same tune but there was no time this particular day to sing softly the words we had invented to fit that tune:

The donkey cocked his tail up, his tail up, his tail up;
The donkey cocked his tail up, and I shoved a nail up.
The donkey cocked his tail up, and showed his dirty bum.

We were in time for prayers . . .

OwerFatherwichartin'eaven, 'allowedbeThyname.
Thykingdomcome, Thywillbedone, onearthasitisin'eaven.

We had time during the mumble-jumble pleas to get back our
breath. Then Milly and I went one way and Dolly another.

From time to time in 1915–17 during this period of my
schooling we left the peace of our hamlet to be near my father.
He was wounded five times in France and five times he was
sent back to England. It was difficult at first to understand why
my mother appeared to be less distressed when he had been
wounded in the Kaiser's War than when he was uninjured but
unemployed in distant Canada. Sometimes she seemed to be
pleased, but I began to realize she thought he was out of the
danger of France when he was being tended in military hospitals in England, where she could take us to see him. I could
not believe that a man so big could be damaged by puny bullets, or that such a strong voice could be reduced to a croaky
old whispering by mustard gas.

Because of his wounds, we followed him like medieval
camp-followers to the new war-created garrison towns, to
Hounslow, Folkestone, Shoreham, Hastings and various parts

of London, as he was switched from one camp or hospital to another. Occasionally too we went home – when he was on leave or in France again.

Never settling in one place for more than a few weeks or months, I found this moving around most disrupting and sometimes distressing. No sooner had I settled in a new class in a new school and made friends than we would be off again. Sometimes I was a bit too bright for a new class whose standard was less advanced than the previous one. More often I was too dull, which made me feel miserable, incompetent, idiotic and ashamed. The London boys were particularly cruel to a country bumpkin who was less clever than they, and lost no opportunity to ridicule, bully and to criticize my country speech. I soon found that a good punch on a Cockney nose would get over most of the difficulties, but I had to take a good few in return because I was small for my years.

Our staunchest friends were Canadian soldiers and we got to know many of those from 1st Canadian Railway Troops and 1st Canadian Pioneers by their Christian and nicknames. They were forever putting on children's parties and field sports and gave fine prizes to every participant of each event. There would be air guns and dolls and candy galore; but the mothers received the most appreciated prizes: great slabs of salt butter and cheese, hunks of rich pink ham, tinned meats and fruit and strange-tasting buns and cakes called 'goodies' or 'cookies'.

We liked the Canadians. When they were not eating, drinking, singing or flirting they would look after all the children near their camp.

At Hounslow the officer in charge of finding billets – the Town Major – found us a lovely house on the London–Bath road. It was three-storeyed and stood next to St Paul's Church. From the topmost bedroom window, Leslie and Poppy and I used to look out at local bits of the war long after the time we should have been sleeping. Our greatest delight was to watch the searchlights sweeping the sky and painting the bottoms of clouds with long brushes of light. One of these lights we called *ours*. It was the dearest because it was the nearest and it was the only searchlight in the whole world to be mounted on a tram. The tram ran from the Hounslow Bell to Hounslow Heath, along the London–Staines road, parallel to the Bath road. Its light was brightest because of its nearness and we used to pray to God that *our searchlight* should find all the Zeppelins and Gotha aeroplanes which wicked old Kaiser Bill could send from rotten old Germany.

'How did Captain Robinson, VC, escape when he got shot down?'

That was one of the riddles the Hounslow boys used to ask us. The answer was rude.

'He greased his bum and slid down a searchlight.'

We had clips on the ear over that.

At Folkestone we enjoyed long walks along the Leas and South Downs and Mother took a well-earned rest and was happy. But she became good and worried once, and Leslie and I were to blame.

57

We decided to become German spies of exalted rank and quarrelled about who should be chief spy (Kaiser Bill). Because I was older I demanded my rights and Leslie had to settle for second chief spy (Little Willie). We 'borrowed' two smelly gas masks from the pegs in the hall and started our espionage in the underground trenches which ran along the coastline from Folkestone to Dover. Being first-class spies we kept this secret and did not even tell sister Poppy.

But we knew not the geography of that seven-mile labyrinthine burrow and were lost in the depths for two days and one night. Canadian soldiers from my father's platoon volunteered to conduct a search and they found us, dirty and tired but spying like mad on the problem of how to get out of the bowels of the Kentish earth. After a good ticking off from nine big soldiers and two hidings – one apiece from Father and Mother – we promised never to spy on anyone or anything again.

Along the Leas on Sundays bands played, flags were waved and men and women stood on the verges and steps, shouting, cheering and singing, as thousands of soldiers marched by.

'Come and join Lord Kitchener's army' was one of our favourites – because we could sing 'bloody' without getting a clip on the ear . . . 'Bloody great boots make blisters on your feet'. 'Pack up your troubles' was very jolly and good for marching, and we used to march along beside the soldiers, singing it fit to burst. 'It's a long way to Tipperary' came about third, and we sang it to the words adopted by the Canadians, 'It's the wrong way to tickle Mary' . . . The Canadians should have known the right way, because we would often see them practising in the shrubs and the shelters along the Leas.

But there was one song which made me sad and brought a lump to my throat, 'There's a long, long trail a-winding'. I liked the beginning because it said that nightingales were singing and the white moon beamed. The end bit upset me ... 'Until the day that I'll be going down that long, long trail with you'. I had heard that there would be many soldiers like my Uncle Bert who would never go down any long, long trails. Uncle Bert was killed soon after he was commissioned, and many others who crowded into the boats at Folkestone harbour were to be killed or wounded, but everybody sang as they went on.

Nobody sang on the return journeys, there was hardly anybody about. For it was always at night when they came back.

I should not have seen them myself, but we lived not far from the harbour and the boats' hooters used to waken me, and I would slip out to watch the big white ships with red crosses painted on their sides and funnels as they unloaded the wounded into ambulances. There were plenty of noises, but all different. Some like the shriek of a rabbit when it is stared out by a stoat or a weasel and knows it is going to have blood sucked from its neck until it is dead. Worst of all was the terrible coughing of men who had breathed in mustard gas. They would make me shiver and shake and wish I could cough for them and help to bring up the gas.

At Hounslow, and we were there twice when my father had wounds, it was different, for there were no Red Cross ships;

only soldiers of many lands going off on the outward journey after being trained on Hounslow Heath, where I saw my first cavalry horses.

We loved the church parades which converged each Sunday on St Paul's, next door to us. Soldiers marched from Hounslow Barracks, and Hounslow Heath. Some were as black as ink, others as brown as cob-nuts. There were different hats, Balmorals, Glengarries, Australian bush-whackers, New Zealand kiwis; and steel helmets were strung on their shoulders in case war should start in St Paul's while the collection was being taken. There were many different uniforms for the different kinds of bodies, and for the legs there were kilts, trews, riding breeches, leggings, knee-boots, shorts and puttees – but on every left shoulder there was a rifle.

There were many onlookers who cheered and waved Union Jacks before they followed the soldiers into St Paul's. And when the soldiers had 'piled arms' down the central aisle the onlookers piled into their pews, took up their hymn books and sang, 'Fight the good fight with all thy might', 'For those in peril on the sea', and other such hymns. Then they would drop on their knees to the hassocks and pray like the devil for soldiers and sailors and for King and Country. Everybody did it so enthusiastically every Sunday – except one man I shall never forget.

Jacko lived with us. His proper name was Sergeant Bill Jackson (1st Canadian Railway Troops). One of my father's closest friends, he had been a schoolmaster in Calgary. Unlike most of his Canadian comrades Jacko did more thinking than drinking and was mostly on the quiet side. He was good and noisy that day, after he had marched No. 10 Platoon to St Paul's.

I did not merely like Jacko, I loved him. I admired his great moustache which was even bigger and whiskerier than my father's, but I think I loved him because he taught me how to fight and had bought me boxing gloves from the Army and Navy Stores. He punched me in the belly and said, 'Keep your hands up to guard your chin and your elbows down to guard your solar plexus.' I did not know I had such a thing until Jacko told me where it was and that it was a nerve centre. I shall never forget that, or the last thing Jacko said to me in our house the week before they were so unkind to him in church.

'Always be able to look after yourself, Ced, boy, and learn to fight. I don't mean to fight in wars, wars are terrible things; but when nasty people try to do nasty things to nice people – nice people like you and me – we have to stand up for ourselves.'

We were sitting in our pew when it happened; my father and mother, sister Poppy, brother Fon, and old Jacko sitting next to me. Jacko went very red when the parson read out, 'Thou shalt do no murder.'

He jumped on to the pew and I felt the thump of his big brown boots before he hollered out, 'Yippee, yippee!'

All the people in front looked round, and then Jacko got busy on the parson.

'Do no murder, my arse! Look at those guns under your nose, you bloody hypocrite!'

All the world seemed to come to our pew. Soldiers pushed

me and trod on my feet as they pulled Jacko down. They put hands over his mouth and twisted his arms up his back and dragged him out of the church.

After the service I asked my father why they hurt Jacko, and all he said was, 'Don't ask questions, boy. Least said soonest mended.'

Jacko stopped living with us and did not come to see us for a long time. When he came he was not a sergeant any more. I could see the stitch marks where his big stripes had been. I saw that his nice red face had gone pale and that his hair was cut very short. He could not stay even for one night, and had to be back in Hounslow Heath's huts by ten o'clock.

After he had gone my father spoke to Mother about him.

'I feel sorry for Jacko. You can betcher sweet life he's missing us and the comforts of the sergeants' mess. He was quite right, when you come to think of it, but it don't always pay to speak the truth.'

I was surprised by this, and when my father came to my bedroom to say good night, I asked him a couple of questions.

'Why have you told me to always speak the truth?'

'It is because it's the right thing to do. To be honest.'

'Why did Jacko lose his stripes for telling the truth in God's house?'

He gave me a cunning old look and said, 'It's late. You should hev been asleep long before now. Don't worry about it, boy. Things are different in the army.'

This was the first time I had ever doubted my father. I knew that he had been joking when he told Uncle Charlie about burying frozen people by hitting them over the head with mallets and hammers, but this was a different kind of lying, and I was upset. Just when I had decided to forget it, or had forgotten it, he told another whopper. We were walking hand-in-hand to Hounslow Heath and he let go my hand and went into a house with a notice board on it marked 'CCAC'.

'What does CCAC mean?' I asked him when he came out.

'Oh that! It's short fer Charlie Chaplin's Army Corps. One o' them Yankee regiments who've just started to fight the Germans.' He put a finger to his mouth and said, 'Don't tell nobody I told you.'

I believed every word of it, and looked at the shoulder tabs of every soldier I met, hoping to be the first boy to find one of Charlie Chaplin's own; and though I had been sworn to secrecy I told two of my mates – just to show off. We knew about Charlie Chaplin being real because Father had taken us all to a cinema in Hounslow to see him. We did not see all the film because Poppy screamed the place down, she was afraid of the dark, and we had to leave. And I learned from Father the words of the song all the soldiers were singing:

> Let the moon shine bright on Charlie Chaplin;
> His boots are cracking
> For the want of blacking;
> And his little baggy trousers
> They want mending
> Before we send him
> To the Dardanelles.

Later, I learned the truth.

After my father had recovered from that wound he was returned to France, but within a month my mother received a letter which let the cat out of the bag. She was asked to call at the *Canadian Casualty Assembly Center*, because Father had been wounded again and was in Addenbrooke's Hospital, Cambridge. The Canadians paid our fares and off we went home to Ashdon, only twelve miles from Cambridge. We used to visit him twice a week in Dr Brown's pony trap.

When I told him he was a rotten old liar about inventing a regiment called Charlie Chaplin's Army Corps he laughed like mad and said it was only to keep us from worrying. But he had told me other names, places in France where a lot of our nice Canadians had been killed by shells as they were putting down railway tracks; the Somme, Zillebeke, Passchendaele, and Ypres, and I knew these names were right because I had seen them in the newspapers.

He was ill on our first visit, but was so pleased to show Mother a letter he had received in France, all the way from Canada. It was from the widow of his platoon officer. She thanked him for his kindness and his poem . . .

> Number Ten Platoon are sad this day,
> For our gallant young officer's passed away;
> His pleasant smile and cheerful face
> Were joys no one ever will replace.
> Always kind and courteous to his men,
> He will long be remembered by Number Ten.

In the danger zone, or on parade,
An example of how a soldier's made.
And now that he is laid to rest
We grieve, to lose one of the best.
To his lady so far across the sea
We extend our heartfelt sympathy.

On our last visit he looked fit and perky. Perky indeed. In his bed locker was a quart of rye whisky. His pals had been to see him. His eyes were diamond bright, until he showed Mother his *present*, and then they went quite dampish. It was a magnificent walking stick of ebony, to help him get about. Its knob was smooth, shiny and sturdy with the horn of a Canadian elk. But I think it was the engraving in the gold tip which made him weep a bit. They were simple words . . . 'Sergeant, you're a Dandy'. We took him home with us – *our* Dandy.

(Right) Elizabeth Amy Ford, Ced's mother.
(Left) Auntie Harriet Ford, Elizabeth's sister.

Chapter 4

Brick and Stone Villa

'Brick and stone villa' was the name my father gave to our cottage the moment we moved there in 1914. Unlike most villas, it was not overblessed with accommodation. Two up and two down, brick and flint on the outside, lath and plaster inside, the whole was less than twenty feet by twenty. There was no bathroom, no water, no wc – apart from the privy down the back yard and that was shared by the twin cottages. The downstairs rooms – living and kitchen – were divided by a four-inch wall of lath and plaster. Front, back, kitchen and pantry doors were of plain board nailed together, swinging on hand-forged iron hinges. All were opened by thumb latches. The main windows, up and down, were eighteen inches high and thirty-six inches wide. The windows of the kitchen and small bedroom were of the same height, but only thirty inches wide. Although out of square and of uneven surface, the walls had not the undulations of the red-brick floor. Much cunning and many wedges were required to keep the table level and steady.

A great oak beam ran through both cottages to support the low ceilings. Keyholes were so large that the wind whistled through them willy-nilly. The stair was a tragedy. Tortuous and steep it led to a diminutive landing and to a flimsy banister-rail rotted with worm holes. In the small bedroom – Leslie's and mine – great bits of wood extended from floor to ceiling, about a foot apart, and they would have challenged the ingenuity of the best paper-hangers in East Anglia. On them were iron hooks for overcoats which in winter were transferred to our bed.

The large bedroom, where my parents slept, had a great bulge where the chimney lurked on its way down to the big opening for the kitchen range. On each side of the chimney bulge was a recess, two feet deep and two feet wide. Curtained off, one functioned as the villa's wardrobe while the other held trunks and wicker baskets, the linen and clothing store for my mother. The upstairs doors were like those downstairs, but minus keyholes. All walls were papered and the ceilings white-washed. Downstairs, in the chimney recess, was our pantry. So small that one had to walk in sideways, but it was nevertheless large enough for our food and crockery. We could always find things, even in the dark.

'There's a place for everything and everything should be in

its place!' Having been a maid and cook for the gentry, Mother was most methodical.

Along the back of the two cottages ran a strip of concrete, on which we put benches for the chores of washing up, washing ourselves (always in cold rain-water caught by the butt at the front of the cottage), cleaning boots and shoes or vegetables and doing odd bits of carpentry. Later my father built a tool shed there, almost as big as a sentry box.

Shared by both cottages was the pride of the home, the bakehouse. In it was a twenty-four gallon copper over a fire grate. Our bakehouse was nothing if not versatile for it served as a laundry, wine-making emporium, cobbler's shop, barber's saloon, chitterling cleansing chamber, onion store, apple store, potato store and gossip-shop.

Most of our furniture was old but good. Mother's prize possession was a large mahogany table, a wedding present. It was her pride and joy, her workbench for food preparation and sewing and the place where she served our meals. Ordinary tables have four legs. Ours had one – a solid mahogany base, or pedestal, at whose corners, all four of them, were the claws of lions. One touch on a claw by a boy's foot and that boy's ear would receive a swift clout.

Mother's next most-highly prized possession hung on the east wall. It was a large bread board of some exotic wood, hand-carved by a Boer prisoner-of-war. My father had brought it back from Pretoria. Everyone commented upon its beauty, the painstaking result of a master-craftsman who – apart from the beauty of the carved centre-piece – had milled its circular edge as perfectly as the Royal Mint milled half-crowns.

Two framed pictures of troopships, the *Nubia* and the *Plassey*, hung below the bread board. The first had taken my father to India and the East Indian Telegraph Company; the second had brought him from Bombay to Southampton. The Soldiers' Home, Quetta, and the Officers' Mess, Darjeeling, were two more military pictures and there were framed photographs of Uncle Charlie and Uncle Will in naval and military uniform respectively, taken long before the Kaiser's War.

We had six Windsor chairs – sturdy, yellowish – plus two armchairs – hard-wooded, curvy and comfortable, one on each side of the fire grate. Under the window, taking up the whole length of the front wall, was one headed couch. Like the armchairs the couch was cushioned and it was God help the ears of the boy who failed to shake up and tidy a cushion after sitting on it!

The room also included one window ledge, bristling with potted geraniums, japonica and a maidenhair fern, and one tall chest of drawers, so polished that it reflected the daylight from the window opposite. In each of its drawers, three long ones below and two short ones above, tidiness prevailed. Everything was in its place, never out of its place in years. On the top of this chest were pictures of us children at various stages, one brass oil lamp with global glass screen, the family Bible, our prayer books and two biscuit barrels which seldom contained biscuits. The floor was covered with coconut matting – three heavy mats, one for each of the doors – and a black and red rug before the fire grate. The top and front of the fire grate were so polished – with more elbow-grease than grate-polish – that it seemed sinful to put fire-sooted saucepans and the stew-pot on top. Pokers and rakes shone ebony black against the hearth-stoned whiteness of the hearth. On the off side of the fire grate was an oven big enough to roast a brace of turkey. In this my mother baked the best batter puddings in Britain.

That was the living-room, the room around which our home life revolved.

The kitchen was not much to write abroad about. Under its window was a deal table so white with scrubbing it seemed a shame to put the red ochred flower pots on it. But there they were, always filled with flowering plants and green, feathery ferns. Shelves had been built round the walls by my father to house his black deed box, and after the war, the stationery of the Comrades of War; his razors – hollow-ground cut-throats from Krupps; his shaving mug and a looking glass. There were more racks on the floor, the shelves varying in size to take the different sizes of boots and God help the boy who did not clean his shoes before putting them on the rack! Nearby were two galvanized water pails, brimming with water clear from Sparks' meadow spring, and a blue enamelled jug to dip from the pails. Under the stairs was a cubby-hole. Only the deformed could get coal out of this with ease. Finally, on the inside of our kitchen door were roller towels.

That was the kitchen. Although tiny – perhaps too tiny at

times – it was always pleasant, tidy and clean. It was comfortable, too, a positive indication of the good qualities of my mother. She had made from it our home!

Sleeping space was the biggest problem. Leslie and I slept in the small bedroom in a three-quarter bed. It took up nearly all the room – and it was not possible to make the far side of the bed except by leaning over.

We had the tiniest of chests of drawers at the foot of our bed which we shared. When drawing the window curtain we had to keep a sharp look-out in case we knocked off its mirror.

Mother and Father slept in the larger room in a full-sized double bed and Poppy in a tiny bed crammed into the recess. It would not have been possible for her ever to fall from her bed. She was practically walled in. Mother and Father also shared a chest of drawers, complete with a mirror. This shut out some of the light from the window but there was nowhere else to put it. There was no water piped to any cottage in the hamlet; but four hundred yards down Ashdon Road a flimsy wooden bridge arched Sparks' stream and led to a communal tap. With galvanized pails hooked to shoulder yokes – far too big for schoolboys' shoulders – we would set forth to bring back, at four gallons per trip, the sweetest, purest water in East Anglia; fresh from the meadow spring behind our cottage.

Except for Walton's Park, Major Tansley Luddington's big house which had a dynamo, there was not one ampere of electricity in the village. We had brass oil lamps with smoky wicks, paraffin and tallow dips and candles. By their soft light we illuminated our lives through many years of autumn and winter nights and were content.

We had front and back gardens, the fertile soil of which nourished apple trees and a William pear tree. Along the bank of the garden stream grew other trees – black damson, white damson, greengage, Victoria plum, crab-apple and sloe. Years ago, the juice of the black damson was used as a dye to paint the cottages with colour-wash to make them Constable Pink. Alongside the far paths were fruit bushes – currant, gooseberry and loganberry, all much overgrown, a jungle of fruitfulness. Flowers abounded. Without human interference they had gone naturally to seed, sowing and re-sowing themselves year after year. There they were in their wild profusion, established, alive, thriving – begging, imploring that the skilled hands of my mother and father should disentangle their confusion and set them to rights in trim array.

Sparks' Mede was the best place for moles, field mice and hedgehogs. The hedgehogs, however, were always far fewer in number than the moles and mice and we saw them only occasionally, rolling themselves into a ball, head and tail well tucked in, spikes a-bristling in all directions.

I recall one early evening during the school holidays when Grandfather Ford cooked a hedgehog for us, in true gipsy style. He covered it with clay, without removing the prickles or skinning it, and cooked it in a fire he made in the back garden under some large stones. When it was ready he broke the baked clay. The prickles came away with it. He then opened the carcase and cut us off chunks to eat with hunks of newly baked home-made bread. No expensive barbecue equipment could possibly give the pleasure this simple country feast gave to us. The hedgehog meat resembled rich pork. That is by the way, but the important thing was that Grandad burst into speech and said, 'Should've took the guts out, but I forgot!'

When, in season, we delayed our homeward journeys from school until dusk, we would see the mice-hunters on the prowl – kestrels and owls of several kinds – and we would notice that unlike the owl the kestrel hovered to look for its prey. It was always a thrilling sight to see those big brown birds of the falcon tribe poised motionless in the sky, their keen eyes alert to the slightest movement of mice or beetles, even from a height of several hundred feet.

Grandfather Reuben Ford had spent the whole of his life regulating nature in the big fields around us. We could always hear the thumping of his feet next door through the cavity wall as he banged on his clodhoppers each morning at half past five. He was seventy then. For sixty years he had worked at Overhall Farm. He was the horse-keeper and a skilled farm labourer, and had served four generations of the Haggers' stock. He had never wished to do anything else or go anywhere else. But before I was born he used to drive a wagonette once a week from Ashdon to Covent Garden, filled with fresh fruit and vegetables. He had never seen the sea. But he was content and fulfilled.

Each day – and you could put your clock right by him – he

would be at the front door of the Bonnett Inn for his midday pint. In his labourer's frail – a straw-plaited basket bound with hemp – he had his bread and cheese with an onion, or a slice or two of cold meat. In the Bonnett he had his own pint pot and his own stool. They are there today: Ford's pot, Ford's stool.

Sawing logs and killing pigs were his pastimes. Not one millimetre longer one than another, the logs would be sawn with instinctive exactitude. Although they would squeal like banshees as they sensed their end at the flash of Grandfather's razor-sharp knife, the pigs would die painlessly.

Except for his wedding and the christening of his children, Reuben never attended church or chapel. He did not swear or curse, nor did he do mischief to a living soul. But each year he got blind drunk. This was on the night of the Horkey, a ceremony of thanksgiving for a successful harvest. On that night he would say, 'I reckon harvest home is the only thing in life worth celebratin'. Where should any on us be if it worn't for the land, the harvest?'

On that night, if he was not too tiddly, he would sing to the wrong words his favourite hymn . . .

We ploughs the fields an' scatters the good seed on the
    land;
An' it gits fed an' watered by God a'mighty's hand,
He sends the sun in summer, with warmth to swell the
    grain;
The breezes an' the sunshine, the soft refreshin' rain . . .

When we reminded him that he was wrong, that the third line should be 'He sends the *snow in winter*, the warmth to swell the grain', he would not take that at any price.

'Don't make sense, boy. I've sin a bit o' snow in me toime. Snow allus makes me cowd!'

Grandmother Susanna Ford was his junior by a year. They had been sweethearts from childhood and produced thirteen children. Four had now died, in addition to Harriet, leaving me with two uncles – old rheumaticky Uncle Charlie who had been the professional sailor, and Uncle Will, the ex-professional soldier turned village cobbler – and five aunts; Frances, Sally, Lillian, Polly and Nancy. All the girls had been in domestic service. They had become expert cooks, needlewomen, winemakers and laundrymaids.

Granny Ford had always kept them in their places. She was a strict disciplinarian, an expert cook and wine-maker. Her heart was so big and kind that there seemed no room for it in her squat East Anglian frame. To us children she was a fairy godmother, albeit with the waspiest of tongues.

'What you bin a-gettin' up to now, you boys?' she would ask. 'Look at your dutty owd faces. Git the face flannel an' come you here!'

With rain-water from the butt she would clean and ginger us up. The flannel was coarse, striped in red and blue – a bit of an old shirt of Reuben's. Holding us by the ear, one at a time, she would pummel and drub away at our necks and behind our ears until they were nearly raw – a kind of flannel flagellation designed more for correction than cleanliness.

'Now, ain't that better an' ain't you a-feelin' fresher? If you don't keep clean I'll do it all over ag'in. Remember now, cleanliness is next ter Godliness.'

She practised her precepts. 'Don't you come in, now, this is dustin' day.' Once a week she would dust everything within dusting reach. First the ornaments – big, hideous-looking china dogs; porcelain shepherds and shepherdesses; repellent urns and vases; china clogs and clocks; all kinds of boxes, coffers, caddies, caskets and tea chests; treasures brought by her children from fairs, fêtes and galas. 'You can come in now, I've done me ornaments,' she would say eventually and she would get out the big tin of Garibaldi biscuits plus a jug of rich elderberry wine.

In the cottage on the south side of Granny Ford's – one of wattle and plaster with sturdy oaken beams and a reed-thatched roof – lived Walt Stalley. With my grandfather he worked at Overhall Farm, but his was by comparison but a temporary job having lasted only forty years. Walt had not seen the sea either, but he had travelled as far afield as Cambridge – a good twelve miles – and had been to London and thoroughly enjoyed it. At least he thought he had. Actually he had got no further than Liverpool Street Station and had stayed there all day, wondering why London was covered over with glass.

Poor Walt was a martyr to rheumatics. Although over six feet, he was stooped in pain, the penalty for getting wet so often in the fields. We boys had great fun with Walt in winter when he would go to his bed at seven o'clock.

'Come on,' Leslie would say, 'let's go an' watch old Walt.'

Through the little mullioned window lit by the pale light of a tallow dip, we would watch his preparations for rest. Off with five pullovers and top waistcoat, out with watch from waistcoat pocket; wind watch, listen to its tick, place on bed-table; fetch candle and matches, place beside watch; off with bottom waistcoat; off boots, socks and down with trousers; scratch considerably under armpits and crutch; on with long woollen bedsocks, knee-high; on with blue flannel nightshirt, plus red woollen night-cap with pompom; scratch backside; turn down bedclothes halfway; ease legs gently into bed; take from under pillow one pair of mittens, one pair of bedsocks; pull bedclothes up to chest height; put on mittens; over mittens pull on bedsocks; bend forward, seize bedclothes between teeth and draw up to pillow level; sink back on pillow with grunt; goodnight!

Unaware that he ever had an audience – and his audiences were not always children but included inquisitive adults – Walt went on adopting this procedure nightly. Because there were few other entertainments in those days we took great delight in watching Walt go to bye-byes. Sometimes, just for the hell of it, we would wait until he had completed his ritual and then we would knock at the door before running away. He got up once or twice but soon gave it up.

Walt was a bachelor. 'I had a gel once, eyes like sloes, hair like raven's feathers. We got on tidy well together. Should hev married her. Found somebody else, from Thaxted. Never troubled lookin' much arter that!'

He loved children and flowers, but he had only flowers and fleas. He remembered all our birthdays and would be at our back door on those days. 'Happy buthday to 'ee!' and in the big horny hand half a crown and one of his Blenheim Orange apples.

John Mays and Elizabeth Amy Ford, after their wedding, 25 October 1905, near the Bonnett Inn, Bartlow Hamlet.

Chapter 5

Ketteridge and Kindness

Place Farm, one of three standing in Bartlow Hamlet, had fields so scattered that their extremities tentacled into three counties: Essex, Suffolk and Cambridgeshire. For much of each year only their rich brown earth was to be seen. Each springtime there could still be observed much of the earth between the first green flushes and fingers of wheat and early oats, whose long, straight drillings were springing to life from hedgerow to hedgerow.

The new life was beginning in mossy banks, trees and hedges; catkins, pussy-willows, violets, primroses, and the sticky buds of chestnut trees were swelling ready to erupt their great green hands. The music of the horse-drawn roller over the uneven country roads and lanes could be heard – a harbinger of good tidings.

In a few more months the ripe corn would be blazing those fields with gold, and in late August or early September, it would be harvest time.

As a schoolboy I used to work in those fields, leading the wagon-horses from shock to shock of grain, standing in serried ranks ready to be carted.

'Yeoman' and 'Little Josh', two of the finest wheats ever to be harvested from Ashdon's dark, fertile fields, used to be ground from sun-golden grain to fine white flour at Ashdon Mill. From the front window of Brick and Stone Villa we would watch the graceful turning of the four great sails. Only two fields away from us, the mill stood in Mill Meadow, a fine landmark and a great attraction, set on the highest point of the surrounding countryside. There were two millers' cottages adjoining. In one lived my bricklayer friend, Chris. Four years my senior, he taught me many things. Chris Ketteridge came from a family of bricklayers so adept in their craft that almost every year they would be selected to build houses, cottages and ornate dovecots in the exhibition halls of Earls Court and Olympia.

At that time 'Pelmanism' and Monsieur Coué's 'Auto Suggestion' were all the rage and Chris took correspondence courses in both. By candlelight on wintry nights he would initiate me into some of these mysteries in that old mill. In next to no time he was drumming into me 'word association techniques' to improve my memory. Without the slightest provocation he would subject me to 'thematic apperception drill' to ginger up my visual acuity. Before I could bleat a protest he would walk away from me, whispering softly the while and imploring me to listen intently until I could hear nary a whisper, just to improve my aural perception. The next night I would be subjected to tests, examination and trial to discover if my sensitivity and sensory perception had sharpened or blunted.

Because I was puny for my age – the penalties of illness and deprivation – Chris did far more than subject me to mental gymnastics. Tough and muscled by his concrete mixing, hod carrying and climbing high scaffolding, he took pride and delight in teaching me to climb. Scared stiff because I could not stand heights, I was ridiculed into climbing a long mill-rope, first to the floor where squatted that great pair of millstones and finally to the top where were housed the giant hub and cogwheels of the great sails. To begin with Chris climbed the lot, carrying me on his back.

Outside the mill, around its circular brickwork base, was a cemetery – a graveyard for cats. Bess, Chris's youngest sister – now my sister-in-law because she married brother Leslie – kept cats of all colours, sizes and classifications. They bred like rabbits and died in droves. To tune up my muscles I was appointed unpaid grave-digger; and there was a certain significance in the fact that the cats' resting places were out of all proportion to the cats' dimensions.

'Come on, Ced, I've got a job for you,' Bess would say.

'Sorry, I'm reading.'

'You can drop that book. Tiddles died last night, Torty got caught in a trap and we had to kill her. You've got two graves to dig. Chris says four feet deep, four feet long and two feet wide. They've got to have separated graves, so there! I'll get the cats and flowers.'

It was hard going, for the soil was heavy with clay and builders' rubble. After about an hour of my hard work, Bess would arrive with the dead cats stitched in white sheeting ready for some feline Valhalla. Sometimes coffins were made from bits of orange boxes; but there were always flowers in jam jars, little wreaths and a proper burial service. Only a bold man would refuse Bess. She honestly believed that cats had souls.

York Ketteridge was Chris's father. He was a tall hawk-faced man who strode through the fields with a gait like a marauding land-shark. I never heard him complete a couple of sentences without a curse word, for he was a most outspoken man with the courage of his personal convictions. He had several sons and daughters: all the men were bricklayers, carpenters or builders of some kind and each was an expert.

Young York, his son and heir, was a first-class natural comedian with the wryest of wits and one who could curse his father under the table. He was much older than Chris, his youngest brother. Crippled with arthritis and the 'screws' he was bent almost double and sidled around like a land-crab. For some years he and his wife thoroughly disenjoyed marital discord. To compensate himself for the lack of connubial bliss, Young York took to drink. As compensation for the same deficiency, his wife took to making mincemeat. Seven-pound jars of the stuff would stand in serried ranks in every nook and cranny of their thatched house at Church End. But, because of her marriage situation and the fact that she had won prizes for mincemeat manufacture at village fêtes, she could not stop making it. Until the day of the char-à-banc trip to Clacton.

Mrs Young York had gone off with the Women's Institute in the firm belief that she would be able to return in time to lay Young York's supper before pub-closing. But when Young York got home from the Lamb – halfway on the road to Saffron Walden – there was no supper laid. So he went to his toolshed. From it he brought into the kitchen his knocking-up board and a shovel. Upon the board he emptied the contents of every seven-pound jar he could lay his hand upon, knocked it up to the right viscosity with his shovel, and then set to work in earnest. When Mrs Young York arrived home from Clacton, late because the char-à-banc had suffered some mishap, she found that her kitchen had undergone a remarkable transformation. Young York was absent but mincemeat was present – spread evenly upon every wall. With his floats and trowels Young York had faced up the lot.

It worked. Soon there was another, but more important transformation. They settled their differences to become the happiest couple in Ashdon.

Kate, Chris's senior sister, was kind and warm-hearted but the harshness of her voice disguised or falsified her innate tenderness. Mrs Beeton could have learned much from her about cooking English dishes. Laundrymaids, young and old, would have been gainfully rewarded by inspecting the end-products of Kate's smoothing irons. And although unmarried and childless, Kate could have taught most mothers a trick or two on the care and understanding of children.

On one occasion towards the end of the war, she left her home in Mill Cottage to tend the children of her brother Ted who had suffered the supreme bereavement. To move more than a mile from an Essex hamlet is to become socially as well as geographically maladjusted, but Kate bore with characteristic fortitude what little ostracism there was when she moved to Collier Row, a collection of terraced cottages next to Ashdon School. Each day thereafter when the school emptied for the midday meal Kate would be at her new front door. Each day she would take in some half-starved child and feed him, nurse him, sing to him, comfort and love him.

One of her soothing lullabies was unorthodox to say the least. With a small boy or girl in her lap who had disdained the plate of cabbage and peas she had prepared, Kate would cheerfully sing, 'Peas make you fart, cabbages make you stink.' This was sung to the melody of the Wedding March. The challenge would be accepted, the platter cleared. Ketteridge and kindness were synonymous terms.

Chapter 6

Willingly to School

On schooldays I would sometimes be summoned by a bicycle bell. Ted Allen, who lived up Overhall Lane and helped to grow the finest strawberries in Essex, would wish to pace me to school as he cycled each morning to Saffron Walden's nurseries. I would run panting on the near-side of his bike the whole mile.

'That were nigh on half a minute quicker, boy. You'll make a good runner if you keep at it.'

Yes, I used to run to school.

Luckily, we lived only a mile away but the majority of the pupils had to trudge several miles down rutted lanes and flint-strewn roads every school day. In summer, and sometimes in late spring, many of them, like us, would short-cut across fields and meadows. But in winter the meadows were muddied and the paths water-logged. We had no Wellington boots, and if our boots and shoes let in water – and there were plenty of children without either – we would sit in class wet-footed and miserable, sniffing and snuffling with a new cold.

There were three classrooms, with three teachers and two playgrounds – one for boys, one for girls. Maps on the walls were prominent and characteristic features – maps of the world with big red blotches to indicate the British Empire which we were all taught to believe in. There were also the usual offices, one for each sex, of course, with rough wooden seats and buckets underneath.

William Tuck, the headmaster, lived in the red-brick house adjoining the red-brick school. Each morning he would emerge from his house, check to see that the big school clock on the outer front of the building was telling the truth and run the Union Jack up the white flagpole. Mr Tuck was a living symbol of those hard times, a kindly cultured gentleman whose mind was well-stocked with the classics, but one who restrained his own ambition and his belly, to send his two charming and gifted daughters to the ivory towers of learning at Cambridge.

Infant mortality was high in our village. Family limitation, if known, was seldom practised. Many a strong woman went prematurely to her grave through the worry and poverty brought about by annual child-bearing. Many children in the school were pot-bellied. Many had head lice. There was a high incidence of illness and school-absence born of malnutrition. And the efforts of some parents to conceal their children's lack of boots and clothing by the pretence of illness revealed pride as well as poverty. School inspectors would sometimes draw attention to those absences and alert the Essex County Council department responsible for education. Usually the inspectors were sent to investigate the families concerned, but once, in order to conduct a statistical survey on head lice, there was sent to our school a 'welfare woman'. She was ugly. She was unkind.

In the patch pocket of her white clinical overall she carried the tool of her trade – a little stick, about the size of a pencil. For the whole of the first day she lurked and skulked in the school porches, where hung the coats and hats, running her little stick along the seams of hats and threadbare garments. She was on shikar for lice and bugs.

Next day, presumably after examination of the resultant statistics, all children suspected of having head lice were called in front of the class in full and shameful view, before being sent to the huntress one at a time for confirmation of the crime. Whether or not her wand had the magical property of transferring or multiplying head lice will never be known; but if one had not head lice before encountering the lice-diviner's rod, one certainly had them afterwards. With quite unnecessary ferocity she dug her stick into little scalps – stirring with it, puggling with it, scratching with it until little heads were sore and bleeding.

When Mr Tuck returned from Saffron Walden and saw some of the results, he was infuriated. 'Get out, you monster,' he shouted at the welfare woman. 'Go away from here and never come back.' With a large cabbage stalk from the school garden he chased her from the school and out of our unhappy lives.

In his profound concern for his pupils' welfare, Mr Tuck went far beyond the requirements of his post. He would even wince and weep as he peeled brown paper strips from the torn and filthy feet of shoeless, stockingless children, or bathed sores and chilblains. Because his own boot soles were invariably wafer-thin, he knew, he understood. His tears would mingle with the warm water he poured from his cheap tin kettle as he knelt to bathe the little feet of his flock.

Our supremely sensitive headmaster had to cope with things other than the physical aspects of poverty. Country children knew about life. As far as we were concerned old Sigmund Freud was not far out when he postulated that experience relating to sex enters into a child's life from infancy. There was not a day when sex did not rear its head, in and out of school. Acute and sustained observation was maintained upon the sex behaviour of animals in the farmers' stockyards. Human refinements were gleaned – mostly on Sunday afternoons – through the absorbing pastime of playing gooseberry on courting couples. There being little incentive or scope for the more usual pastime of train spotting – there were but four trains per weekday upon the single-line track – careful records were mentally made of the sexual prowess of the 'engaged', the 'steadies' and the 'casuals'.

Many local girls had practical experience before puberty . . . sometimes with schoolboys, but more often with uncles and cousins. Nor were they in the least ashamed. Some even bragged about personal experiences, considering it their duty to inform the virginal minority who had preserved that intact and immaculate state thus far to the ripe old age of twelve years. In addition, those too shy for open discussion of the subject soon had their attention drawn to it, and their education was brought up to date, by drawings and sketches of alarming proportions. If the response was favourable there would follow a kind of correspondence course, culminating in written or verbal invitations to play mothers and fathers in Thruskells', a ten-acre field opposite the school where Little Josh wheat grew straight and tall, so tall that practical research into the mysteries of sex could proceed unseen – unless an audience was invited.

'What did she look like, then?'

'Nuthin' much. I were disappointed. Jest like two fingers put togither!'

Nor had the commercial aspect of sex been disregarded in our village.

At one farm there worked a lad of financial acumen, who earned a bit on the side by charging a penny a peep through a knot in a stockyard fence. By closing the disengaged eye and getting cheeks tar-stained one could determine the vigour of a shorthorn bull as he earned his cattle cake.

Despite their advanced knowledge, some of the bigger boys would ask questions specifically designed to embarrass our headmaster.

A hand would shoot up.

'Yes, Donald?'

'Sir, where do babies come from?'

Sturdy Donald could carry a sack of beans or linseed upon his back without faltering in his stride. His several brothers were equally strong. All kept and bred rabbits, ferrets, dogs, cats, white mice and pigeons. There would be many girlish gigglings but nary a blush.

'Now, Donald,' said Mr Tuck, putting on his angry voice. 'You know perfectly well where babies come from. Any more of this and I will have you out in front to lecture about it.'

Mabel Eason looked after standards one to three in the smallest classroom. She had never received any academic education but had all the qualities that count, including kindness, understanding and sympathy. Her smile was like springtime – winning, enchanting, captivating. Her laugh was like her music, articulate and melodious.

Our classes were always mixed for there was no room for anything else and no point in trying out sex discrimination in village schools. When the girls were engaged in needlework the boys would open their books for silent reading. When the boys had to do a bit of carpentry the girls would have their spell of silent reading. But for them this was a misnomer. They would chatter away, write love letters, ogle the carpentry squad, lift their skirts and do all manner of things to take the boys' minds off tenon saws and chisels. This certainly added to our education.

One day young Nellie, who sat farthest away from me, sent me a letter.

Dear Ced,

    If you see anything what hangs, pull it.

                    Love and kisses,

                    Nellie.

My fly was undone.

But life was going on in other parts of the classroom.

'Come out here, Fred Symonds ... at once. I won't have you eating in class.'

'I ain't eatin', Miss, honest I ain't. I were only chewin' me tongue.'

'Open your mouth!' Mabel looked inside, and sure enough she found nothing but a tongue. 'I don't believe you. You've been eating sweets. Your tongue is stained red. Turn out your pockets!'

Frederick obliged. There was instant confusion. Girls were up on forms, squealing, shrieking, skirts clutched tight to legs. In two seconds flat Mabel Eason joined them. 'Turning out' had produced the following:

One catapult, three snares, one pop-gun, one red hand-kerchief with white spots, a silver threepenny piece with a hole in it and the havoc maker – as white as snow, with the pinkest of eyes – one albino rat! It had fallen from the slippery desk and run around wildly. The girls remained aloft for some time.

Another day, one of rain and misery, Mabel tried to cheer things up.

'Who would like to come out and recite?'

Not a hand was raised. 'I don't mean a school poem, you can recite one Mother has taught you.'

Still not a hand.

Then Ethel, the freckled, did her mischief. 'Please, Miss, Ron knows one.'

'Come now, Ronnie. Out the front.'

Blushing, swallowing his spittle, as awkward as a carthorse in a pony-trap, Ronnie lurched out.

'Don't be shy now. Who taught it to you?'

'My Gran, but, er . . .'

'Be a sport. Let's hear it.'

'Roight, then.'

And off he went:

> 'Olly'ocks an' mistletoe;
> Set the baby on 'is po.
> When 'e's done, wipe 'is bum;
> Show owd Granny what 'e's done.

There were no more invitations to recite poetry that day.

We were glad of laughter in those hard, hard times. It was our chief weapon against life's indignities. Misfortune appealed to our sense of humour – as when we found my cousin George Ford sitting at a remote school desk eating his dinner, trying to prevent us seeing that he had only dry bread. Not a morsel of lard or butcher's hard dripping had he to help down three big doorsteps. The reason – which did nothing to qualify our mocking laughter – was that George's father, my

Uncle Will, had been badly war-wounded. He was in hospital and no money was coming through.

George took our cruelty well. He had already been conditioned against ridicule on account of his uniform. My Aunt Emma, his mother, had used her scissors with ingenuity and from a discarded khaki jacket and trousers no longer needed had cut enough cloth to make him a suit; a modified soldier's suit complete with the buttons of the Essex Regiment. He had also a cheese cutter cap complete with chinstrap, and puttees were wrapped round his little legs as though he was a horse with greasy hocks. George had attended school in his uniform for some time; he had nothing else to wear. But now we added to his discomfort by christening him 'Dry-bread Ford', a name he was to bear for years thereafter.

When Kaiser Bill's Gothas and Zeppelins raided London we came to have strangers in our school. Young Londoners arrived, mostly from Tottenham and East Ham. They were terrified of the country – no pavements, no street lamps, no shops, no dance halls or cinemas! They could not understand our language and we disliked theirs. Some had relatives in Ashdon with whom they stayed. Others had no relatives anywhere now, but were cared for by our war-widowed women who once had known love.

Mabel Eason altered the curriculum. Uncertain about the title of a new subject, but sure that it came not under 'botany' or 'horticulture', she settled for one better by far, 'Wild Flowers'. We were appointed mentors, practically to enlighten young Londoners about our countryside. Each week, Mabel would pick an afternoon to coincide with a sunny day and 'they owd Cockneys' would then be taken to see our woods, fields and hedgerows. Half of them found it difficult to walk across a field of soft, yielding grass. Their feet had been flattened by concrete slabs through thin soles. Even in the roads they would peer apprehensively over their shoulders as if anticipating a bus. There were no buses. In fact, there was but one motor in the village – an Austin 20 owned by Major Luddington, the squire, gentleman farmer. It was he who, as owner of Walton's Park and more than half the acreage of the village, gave instant permission for 'they owd Cockneys' to be taken into the delights of the woods of Home and Langley.

Later that springtide, a two-mile walk took us deep into Langley Wood. The London children were delighted and bemused to see bluebells carpeting the glades with blue and green. Interspersed with purple orchis, wild strawberry flowers, foxgloves, wild honeysuckle and cuckoo pint, the bluebells were looking their best with sunshine seeping through the tree-leaves to floodlight their beauty.

We were amazed at the ignorance of the Cockneys. They could not believe the cuckoo-spit was not a flower; that all that beardy froth was created by an insect, the frog-hopper, who had sucked out sap and churned it into foam by beating it with his hind-quarters. They did not believe that those flickering fairylights they saw at dusk were the mating calls, the beacons of female glow worms designed by God to attract their mates from afar. Until we took them to Ashdon Place Farm, where Mrs Bidwell filled our quart flap-cans and jugs with frothy, creamy milk, some believed that all the milk in their London world had been manufactured – and sweetened in advance – by Nestlés.

With accents strange and dialects misunderstood, there came to our school from time to time other strangers. Their short-cropped heads told us they were new orphan boys from Ashdon's Church of England Boys' Home, where Miss Whitehead taught and disciplined them with patience and love. Apart from not having parents, they were better off than most of us. Warm clothes, sturdy shoes and good food were primary considerations at the Home. These they had, together with every facility for learning games including a coach for cricket, a first-class sports ground and equipment of all kinds.

Standing opposite the Rectory, only a quarter of a mile from the village centre, their Home was a pleasant one, bright, clean and airy. Ashdon School education was for them but a fleeting thing, for each night they were taught better by far by Miss Whitehead. She spoke often of receiving letters from 'her boys', many of whom had written to thank her for her love and care and for the good posts they now held in the Church and the services. Although they had the characteristics of 'institutionalized' children – aloof, shy and unduly introspect-ive – they were fine boys with high principles, and they were always ready in winter to turn out in strength for a snowfight against the rest of the village boys.

In the winter months our return journey from school was often in total darkness. There were no street or road lights and the stars would not be out until much later. If there was snow or ice on the roads and fields we would be late home. Not because we were unable to negotiate the roads but because we would make slides, toboggan runs, snowmen, and would have long, fierce snowfights. In the snow-fighting there were often minor casualties. The big boys, the cunning ones who had seen a winter or two, used to cheat. They would press and press their snowballs until they were almost blocks of ice. Sometimes they would even slip a small stone into a soft snowball. There would be cut cheeks, blood on the snow and other fights – fiercer fights – without snow. Each End would challenge other Ends and Bartlow Hamlet to make the longest and most slippery slide in the road. Some were longer than cricket pitches but it was great fun to see the glowing cheeks, to hear the shrieks of joy and laughter as novices fell on their backsides. And when we had had enough or were getting hungry we would cover the long slides with snow so that no one could see them, hoping to see old men fall on them and curse like mad.

The toboggan runs were made on the steep slope of Hilly Meadow, behind Cobby Webb's farm, or Chapel Farm, to give it its right title. We made our own toboggans or sledges from boxes scrounged from old Vic Eason, the village shopkeeper – father of Reg, Mabel Eason's husband. If Bill Smith the blacksmith was not too busy making great iron shoes for the Suffolk Punches and Clydesdales, or was not bent in two with his crippling rupture, he would put iron runners on a sledge for sixpence. Then off we would go to Hilly Meadow, sometimes in total darkness, to whip down the steep slopes like lightning. A small stream ran along the bottom of Hilly Meadow. On its bank there was a great hawthorn hedge, quite ten feet high. If the sledges were overloaded, or we did not put out our feet quickly enough to do some useful braking, we would tear through the hawthorn hedge and land in the stream. Inevitably there would be casualties here, too, mostly gashed cheeks from the hawthorn spikes, ripped clothing or a total immersion in icy water.

In the evenings of spring and summer our return journeys were less energetic but no less absorbing. We would usually go home across the fields and visit ponds to collect frog-spawn, tiddlers and tadpoles in jam jars with handles of string. The ponds were alive. Flitting fairy-like over the surface there would be several species of dragon-flies – graceful flying slendernesses coloured bright blue and black, red and black, yellow and black. They would fly only in the sunshine and when clouds came over they would go off and cling to bits of herbage with their gauzy wings folded over their backs – hidden so cleverly that they could hardly be distinguished from bits of twig.

Our satchels would hold jam sandwiches, cheese sandwiches and sometimes hard-boiled eggs and salt. But there were no books or anything remotely connected with 'education'. Instead we carried mole-traps, snares, hanks of string, bits of wire for making snares, horseshoe nails, augers and shut-knives (the last two were the essential tools for making a couple of additions, whistles and pop-guns) ... and, in autumn, conkers as well. To make a whistle was but the work of minutes, following a plan that ran something like this:

Go to Mill Pond. Find willow tree. Cut from between two nodal joints a four-inch length. Must be straight. Chew all round, taking care that teeth do not split or puncture bark. Cut all round bark at central point. Hold half in left hand, half in right. Twist right hand until bark is freed from wood. Repeat with left hand. Slice off wood to make mouthpiece. Make two V-cuts in wood at ¾-inch distance. Cut out wood from between V-cuts. Make small V-cut in bark. Slide both bits of bark back on to willow wood. Put mouthpiece in mouth. Blow like hell. Slide bark up and down until whistle is heard. Trim ends to whistling point. Stow in satchel.

Result: one ear-piercing whistle. Time, five minutes.
Pop-guns took longer ...

Select from three-year elder growth one straight piece between nodal joints. Pith-hole should not exceed $^5/_{16}$-in. Cut to 9 ins. Heat Mother's fire poker to cherry red. Poke poker down pith-hole until most pith is burned away, taking care not to burn wooden barrel. Clean out pithy remnants until barrel is smooth and clean as a whistle. Select from hard wood (preferably oak) a straight 12-in. length. Cut round wood at 3 ins from one end. Whittle down remaining 9 ins until it exactly fits pith-hole in elder barrel. Chew stolen school blotting paper into wads. Insert two wads into barrel, one at each end. Insert hard-wood piston into one end of barrel (about 1 in.). Hold handle of hard-wood piston to belly by grasping firmly with right hand. Switch right hand to barrel. Hold left hand lightly over distant end to catch the bullet. Pull barrel back hard with hand, and quick.

Results: Loud 'pop'. Red mark on palm of left hand. Very sore indeed.

Great delight. Time, thirty minutes.

Having left or by-passed the Infants – with their beads, crayons and teddy bears – I was extremely happy with the Juniors under Mabel Eason. Following the ritual of school march and the babbling of the Lord's prayer, I was getting into my educational stride each day with the three Rs . . .

> Readin', writin', 'rithmetic;
> If we don't larn 'em
> We'll get Tuck's stick . . .

Upon the fly-leaves of my books I wrote the usual warnings . . .

> Steal not this book for fear of shame,
> For in it stands the owner's name.
> On Judgement Day our Lord will say:
> 'Where is that book you stole away?'

> And if you say, 'I cannot tell,'
> Our Lord will send you down to Hell.

Or, on a more personal note . . .

> Cedric Wesley is my name
> And England is my nation;
> Bartlow Hamlet's where I dwell,
> And Christ is my salvation.
> When I am gone, deep in my grave,
> And all my bones are rotten;
> Pick up this book, think you of me,
> And then I'm not forgotten.

I read what was there to read, *Treasure Island*, *Tales from Shakespeare*, *Robinson Crusoe*, *Gulliver's Travels*, *Grimm's Fairy Tales*, *Cuckoo Clocks and Carrots*; and in poetry, *The Arab's Farewell to his Steed*, *Skylark*, *Shipwreck*, *Lochiel's Warning*, plus a fair sample from *The Golden Treasury*.

Once a week the Reverend Hartley, ex-padre of the Royal Navy, would put us firmly in our inferior places with Bible readings, catechisms, collects and hymn snatches. The accent was always upon our servile state. We should be humble. The meek would inherit the earth. We should not envy, covet or desire. Before blessing and leaving us he would ask us to sing his favourite hymn, 'All Things Bright and Beautiful'. Young though I was, I detected significance in these lines:

> The rich man at his castle,
> The poor man at his gate,
> God made them, high or lowly,
> And ordered their estate.

In green-covered copying books, their pages resplendent with copperplate examples, we would write further enjoinders to thrift and humility:

> A penny saved is a penny gained.
> Waste not want not.
> A fool and his money are soon parted.

We had nothing to save or waste but we were fools all right.

Dictation and composition were the only other 'language' subjects. Long passages were read to us from Shakespeare, the Bible and *Pilgrim's Progress*. The reader's voice would be suitably raised to indicate commas; slightly lowered for semi-colons; and dropped for full-stops. I cannot recall what occurred for colons. To test our aptitude we were asked to write upon subjects of which we had no knowledge: 'What I did on my holiday' ... 'My trip down the River Nile'.

Having mastered the tables by chant and rote, we progressed to arithmetic until we learned how many gallons of water would remain in a fifty-gallon bath with three holes of specified dimensions and with both taps running full-hole. It mattered not that we had no baths.

I would have liked to go to a better school and envied the

superior well-dressed boys of Newport Grammar whom I saw sometimes in Saffron Walden. They carried books and always looked at me with disdain.

In June 1916 the national press devoted a lot of space to a meteor or comet by the name of Pons-Winnecke. It was the talk and fear of the hamlet, because folk still remembered an eclipse of the sun. We had been in school when that happened and had looked at the sun through bits of smoked glass, watching the moon's shadow eating it away until only a toe-nail clip was left. Then a strange darkness had fallen and the birds had stopped singing and it became eerily cold. Half the children were really scared ... most particularly my sister Poppy who damped her drawers in fright.

But Pons-Winnecke! Rumour had it that at incalculable speed it was tearing straight at Mother Earth – at us. It would be the end of the world! Never before had so many children got out of beds at night to inspect the heavens. The rumours intensified and worsened. The target was Bartlow Hamlet. The end would come any minute. Poor Poppy! Leslie and I plagued her. We would point out Mars to her, remarking how red and hot it was. 'Here it is, any minute now!' and the drawers would receive another damping. My father, who was at home on leave, ticked us off and told Poppy if she did it again he would rub her nose in it, like a puppy, to teach her manners.

She did it again. Her nose was rubbed in her knickers. She has never forgotten Pons-Winnecke.

Chapter 7

'T'Church a-Sundays'

I goes t'church a-Sundays,
T'hear owd parson shout;
I slips me farthin' in the bag,
An' sneaks a tanner out.

Sunday mornings in our cottage were lunatic, bedlamic. It was the only day in the week when the family would breakfast together. Throughout the hamlet it was the same wherever there were children.

'What's the time? The collect? The catechism? The text?'

'Where's my prayer-book, psalter, hymn-book, Bible?'

'Somebody's swiped two stamps out of my Sunday school attendance book. Now I won't be able to go to the Sunday school treat.'

Everybody would be trying to get a peep into the looking glass over my father's shoulders. Often there was blood on the towel because his arm had been jogged while shaving. He always had to shave and wash first on a Sunday because the vegetables had to be dug and washed in Walt's brook before he left to sing in the choir. It was his Sunday ritual – broken only by army camps or, after he had come home for good, when his wounds were bad.

Leslie, Poppy and I had to get to Sunday school and then to matins at All Saints, Ashdon parish church. Two miles there, two miles back, but there could be no excuses. Les and I were in the choir with our father.

Sunday dinner would be followed by afternoon Sunday school. Then we would go to Aunt Emma's for tea to save time, for we were due back to sing in the choir for evensong. What a rush it was!

Most children and all adults were members of one of three churches.

C. of E.s would have been christened and confirmed at Ashdon or Bartlow Church, both two miles away from our house. But because our Bartlow Hamlet was not like an ordinary End of Ashdon, we could go to either village church. But we had to steer clear of the village chapel, whose Baptists had been initiated or made members, sometimes at the ripe age of seventy years, by the wet and perishing public process of total immersion in 'that owd sheep-dip', wherein many gallons of holy water stagnated beneath the rostrum of the chapel. Thus we had three preparatory schools for Paradise, whose parsons did their best to lure sheep from other flocks by cottage visits, flattery and cajolery. And Lord have mercy on the soul of one who switched from church to chapel – or *vice versa*, for the villagers would never forgive a 'Devil-dodger'.

Granny Ford was not a Devil-dodger. Because she had been christened at Bartlow Church she would not attend another except for Harvest Festival. She had been christened, confirmed, married, and would be buried at Bartlow, as would several of her children. For fifty years she had walked over two miles back and forth to Bartlow Church each Friday to clean, dust, scrub and polish it. This took all day and was done solely for love. She had not missed one Friday in those fifty years.

Also, once a fortnight Grandfather Ford would walk there and back for equally selfless reasons – tools over bent shoulders – to tidy verges, rake grass and paths and put in trim untidy, neglected graves.

Every Sunday morning and evening the church bells delighted us in pealing their music across the wide fields and woodlands from other parishes. If the wind had 'gone back west a bit', we heard Saffron Walden, Thaxted and Newport. But if it kept to its prevailing direction we heard not a peal from them; instead we enjoyed the higher notes from Shudy Camps, Castle Camps, Steeple Bumpstead, Helions Bumpstead and sometimes Haverhill. We always heard Ashdon and Bartlow.

On Wednesdays we would listen to the bells intently. Wednesday was practice night for bell-ringers and choristers alike. At eight o'clock the bell-ringers' signals would go out to bell-ringers at other parishes and pubs; two quick ones on the tenor meant, 'We'll meet at the Rose and Crown for a swift one.' Three quick ones meant 'The Three Hills at Bartlow'. And although some of the pealings could not be classified as masterpieces, the tugs on the tenor were music to many ears.

Leslie and I were once disgraced and got hidings on account of Poddy Coote who sang with us in Ashdon's choir.

'Wanna bit of a larf?' asked Poddy. 'Tell yer what ter do. You an' Les swop choir stalls with the Fishers an' watch owd Starchy Williams sing the bass solo in the Trinity hymn nex' Sunday.'

Starchy Williams was the village undertaker who had screwed the coffin lid over my Aunt Harriet.

We swopped, watched and laughed till our bellies were sore. In front of a shocked congregation we were publicly rebuked by the Reverend Hartley.

He looked very angry.

Starchy had to sing all by himself 'Holy, holy, holy, Lord God Almighty', with not even Mabel Eason's organ to accompany him. He had the biggest Adam's apple in Anglican history. When he sang the first syllable of 'Holy' his Adam's apple bolted down his cassock like a rabbit into its burrow and when he sang the second syllable it shot up again and dithered about something dreadful. We were in hysterics in that choir stall.

Later, at choir practice night, there was a kind of clerical Court of Inquiry at which my father was asked to be present during our questioning. We did not want to blame old Poddy but we told the truth.

Then, when we went into the choir practice room with the others, the Reverend Hartley asked Starchy to sing his solo just for him, without telling him what it was all about. Starchy got as far as 'Holy, holy, holy', but it was my father who said the next bit, 'Lord God a'mighty!' Hartley laughed, my father laughed, and everybody else laughed, but on this occasion Les and I were most serious. We were scared of the consequences. It all turned out all right, apart from a hiding from Mother who was furious at what the neighbours had told her – that Hartley had ticked us off.

Nobody said a word to Poddy Coote!

Parsons old and parsons new would proceed often from their churches, vicarages and rectories to talk to my mother, who adored parsons. Les and I did not – especially one who always came at tea-time, had several cups of tea on the cheap and always stood with upped frock-coat tails in front of our fire.

He came one afternoon when we were about to have tea and we wanted to get the meal over quickly because we were going out rabbiting.

'Now, Leslie! Who remembahs last Sunday's text?'

Not Leslie! The parson turned to Mother. 'Well, Mrs Mays. What did you think of my sermon, eh? Do you think that I am now finding the hearts of my flock?' and so on.

'Come now, Leslie, do have a try!'

Leslie had a try, a poor one.

'No, no, no, Leslie! ... "To do MY duty in THAT state of life unto which it shall please God to call me." That is how it goes, Leslie! Not "THAT" duty in "MY" state of life. Oh, deah me NO!'

At this point there came an almighty bang; smoke swirled, fire flew and the parson ran yelping down our back garden as though the Devil had him by the coat tails.

Somewhat disobliged because our rabbiting was being held up, Leslie had slipped into the fire a 12-bore Ely cartridge loaded with No. 4 pigeon shot.

We stamped out minor conflagrations on rugs and coconut matting, dislodged bits of coal and cinder from wallpaper and doors, swept up soot and ash and were given another good hiding. Before the restoration and retribution were completed we had another visitor, old Steve, from his allotment.

'What's bin a-gooin' on here, then? I reckon things hev come to a tidy owd pass when a man's gotta stop pullin' parsnips ter pick pellets owter a parson's arse!'

We did not see that parson for years. He did not even call to 'collect pennies for God', as had been his wont. I felt sorry for God. According to the parson God was deeper in the red than we were and that was deep indeed.

Anthems, hymns, psalms and songs of praise! We rehearsed and remembered them. For Harvest Festival we practised with particular fervour, with Mabel Eason guiding and teaching us the beauty of words and music. Then, when we had finally mastered the anthem by singing it over and over again in our bed at nights, with my father joining in from his bedroom all bass-baritony and corrective, we were ready and willing for the big day.

At Harvest Festival our church looked more like God's garden than God's house. Flowers and fruit festooned the altar. On walls, pillars, pew-ends and window sills were spread the good things from the earth, from farms and cottage gardens. Small plaited corn-sheaves were interwoven into the brass chains supporting the oil lamps.

In the vestry, long before the due hour, men and boys would have already changed into black cassocks and newly laundered snow-white surplices; all would have their books and anthem sheets; all would be humming snatches of hymns, psalms and anthem, tuning themselves up, bursting to sing to God.

Above us the great bells would be pealing welcomes to farmers and farmhands, their downy, multi-coloured rope-ends dancing to the weight of the cast metal, soaring so joyfully and strongly that they would sometimes take the lighter bell-ringers aloft with them.

Whole families would be flocking into our church – children first, then the parents. There would be a brief pause at the centre aisle, an almost imperceptible bow to the altar and then rustlings and gropings for hassocks. Knees and heads bent in prayer, hands sometimes clasped, sometimes just shielding eyes, they would wait humbly for the bells to stop. There would then be a single tolling for two minutes, after which the vestry door would open to admit the parson. There would be a quick glance from him and a nod from the churchwarden or leading chorister. Young Sid Williams, six feet tall and ruddy of face, would take the long cross and move to the door, whereupon Mabel Eason would play the opening bars of the processional hymn, while the parson offered up a short prayer.

In double file behind Sid Williams we would then process, boys first with the small ones in front, then the men and last the parson. When the organ gave the appropriate note we would move slowly up the aisle – Sid Williams trying not to hit the low lamps with his tall cross – and would sing the Processional.

> Come, ye thankful people, come,
> Raise the song of Harvest home ...

This was always a great day in our village lives, when in our church we gave thanks for what little we had. The men's voices seemed more powerful that day, the women's eyes were moist. Flowers and corn were taken to hospital wards soon after the last service; fruit and vegetables to our village old and poor.

Once a month we would get up very early on Sunday to get to Holy Communion at eight o'clock. On those days we would make five attendances in all; two at Sunday school, three at church.

I felt very sorry for my sister Poppy when she was con-firmed in 1922. Because we were so poor, my father still being out of work because of his war wounds, we could not afford the white dress, stockings and shoes the other children had; but my mother did her best to keep it dark by getting Poppy confirmed at Hadstock Church, where none of us was known. Poor Poppy! She was made a full member of the Church in laced top-boots, grey skirt cut down from Granny Ford's old dress, and green jumper. My parents were much distressed by this, but my father used his Suffolk cunning to disguise the truth from Poppy, saying that it was God's wish, and a punishment into the bargain, because she had played hookey from Sunday school all that spring to go bird-nesting. This was partly true, for Poppy was not all that enthusiastic about Sunday school in springtime. My father softened the punishment by saying that she was the finest bird-nester in the whole of East Anglia; one who knew every nest in a twenty-mile radius. That cheered her up a bit. But she has always remembered those other girls in white.

Although it was pleasant to go to church in spring and summer, it was hard going in winter and sometimes in late autumn, when Church Hill would be thick with snow drifts. We would arrive at church so out of puff that we had no breath to sing without resting a bit.

At Christmas it was a different matter. Most of the choir, and sometimes Bartlow Hamlet only, would band together for carol singing. We would walk miles and miles through the deepest drifts, to all the Ends, singing louder and longer than we ever did at church.

For this we made our own lanterns – jam jars with candles, of which we each had one. Usually a dozen or more of us would set out, all jam-jarred and collector-boxed. Muffs, helmets, scarves, winter-warmers and leggings made from old sacks were the garments we wore to keep out the cold. People could see us for miles before they heard us for our lights were easily discerned in a largely lightless land. It must have looked a pretty straggling torchlight procession from the distant view but close up we no doubt looked much better and more Christmassy – all red of cheek, our frosty breath blowing into the air pinked and yellowed by the candlelight. Farmers were the best payers – Tilbrooks, Furzes, Haggers and Webbs. Usually they would invite us in, particularly if they had been at the bottle, to sing to them in the warm, and we would then get silver instead of copper plus mince pies and lovely yellow apples, the latter all mellow and brown-pippy through ripening on oat straw in lofts. Now and again they would give us wine and small beer. The wine was all right because it warmed us up but the small beer made our teeth chatter and our voices quiver.

Sometimes we used to cheat a bit by not singing the proper words.

Beer by the pailful, makes us gay, triumphant,
Bring some, ye citizens of Stevington's End.
Fetch out the mince pies, hot and sweet and tasty;
If you don't we'll bash your door in;
We'll bash your silly door in;
We'll bash your silly door in,
As sure as we're born.

We only sang such words to those who were too mean to open the door. If we sang one word wrong inside a house the news would go round the village and the parson would tick us off for not doing the job properly.

Old Johnny Purkis came with us one night. He couldn't sing a bit, nor could he do the church job he had as well as it should have been done. Johnny was the organ blower. Many a time he let Mabel Eason down by not pumping when wind was required. He would sit in a little recess at the back of the organ all by himself, screened from the congregation by green curtains. Mabel would know the moment he arrived, for he would swish the curtains closed with a great flourish, making the brass rings dance and jingle on their rail. From that moment she had to hope for the best. Sometimes he would drop off to sleep and the organ would groan and splutter to a stop in the middle of a hymn or psalm. Sometimes he would snore, or make the loudest of rude noises, and the church-warden would nip smartly round to tell him off and ginger him up.

We took him carol singing because he was the best man in Essex for walking straight in snow and could lead the way. This was curious because when roads were clear he would lurch from side to side – as though completely without control of his spindly legs. In this day and age old Johnny would not have lasted ten seconds.

Between Christmas and the New Year there was always a spate of choral and bell-ringing practice. On one occasion the Reverend Hartley had got a bit frosty over something or other

113

and had doubled practice nights to two per week. Rumour had it that Starchy Williams had complained and advised that we choirboys should be gingered up. With that end in view we were ordered to report to the parish church where the campanologists were ringing out wild bells to the wild sky, instead of to the Sunday school building. There was plenty of flying cloud and several degrees of frost on that wintry night – enough to crisp the top of a thick blanket of snow.

Poddy Coote, the leading choirboy, thereupon hatched a plot. When everybody else was wending their way to home and fireside, there was one who was not. Lo and behold, it was Starchy. By some unaccountable circumstance he found himself alone . . . locked in the belfry.

And when all the Christian folk of Ashdon had gone upstairs; were on their knees a-saying prayers – including the Reverend Hartley – a sound rang through the wintry night. One wild bell alone was ringing to the wild sky. It was not the customary steady toll, more of a feverish clanging.

When the Reverend Hartley arrived at the church, after plodding through half a mile of deep snow drifts, to let Starchy loose, he had to make the same trip all over again – twice. He had forgotten the key.

'Retribushun!' said the leading choirboy. 'That's what it were, retribushun!'

He may have been right. Anyway, the choir practices were halved forthwith.

In those days Ashdon Church was well filled, with far more men than women at morning service. Sunday's dinner, soon

114

after morning service, was not only a meal, it was the meal of the week, a challenge, and the women would be hard at it while the remainder of the family were worshipping. For the menfolk 'church going' had advantages. Some of the 'characters' could be seen taking furtive looks at their big turnip watches. If the sermon dragged a bit – and though it might well be doing them a power of spiritual good – twelve of the clock was opening time and by the fidgetry one could assess those whose concern was spirituous rather than spiritual; who wished not to lose one second of Sunday drinking time – the main occasion in the week for talking about their work with friends from other farms.

They would be the first off their knees after the blessing and the first in the church porch the minute the oak doors swung open. Although my father was handicapped by having first to enter the vestry to divest himself of surplice and cassock, his friends would not be far down Church Lane before he overtook them.

'Owd Hartley were a bit long-winded ter-day, John, bor'; and others would say, 'He were a-watchin' us; dragged it owt deliberate 'cos he knew we was dry . . . ' 'I'm proper parched, dry as a lime kiln; couldn't spit a tanner if ye paid me.'

And then my father would make his usual joke. 'Like you, gentlemen, I've developed a thirst – after Righteousness!'

There was social discrimination in the church seating. The squire had a pew at the front, right under the pulpit. Farmers, according to acres and means, would sit behind the squire; and the ex-soldiers of officer rank, Captains Reville, Lucas

115

and Collins, would be close behind, on the near-side facing the altar. Such professionals as postmaster, grocer, baker and other tradesmen would be on the offside, their social standing indicated clearly by the degree of proximity to the lectern from which were read the scriptural passages to provide the text.

Then came the family pews, all with personal books bearing various inscriptions on fly-leaves ... some of love, some exceedingly scriptural or scriptuous, and some in odd odes.

> Matthew, Mark, Luke and John,
> Bless the bed that I lie on.
> Four corners to my bed,
> Where four angels nightly spread.
> One to watch and one to pray,
> And two to carry my soul away ...

Or, if the boys had been at it:

> Matthew, Mark, Luke and John,
> Went to bed with trousers on.
> Mark got up in one big fright,
> 'Where's my nightshirt on this night?
> I can't settle, I'll not stay,
> For my nightshirt I shall pray.'

And:

Old Willy Tuck, that be his name,
He goes to church each Sunday.
And prays to God to give him strength
To cane we boys on Monday.

For no apparent reason Guy Fawkes crept into the psalter
with this:

Remember, remember the fifth of November,
Gunpowder, treason and plot.
I see no reason why old Mabel Eason
Should ever be forgot.
And best of luck to Old Bill Tuck!

Last, the children . . . 'Chillen should be seen an' not heard!'
That was the doctrine of some villagers. But in Ashdon's
church some children could be seen – and heard. Always
seated farthest from the pulpit, ill-clad, undernourished, but
attentive and silent during prayers and sermon, they were in
the last four rows of pews, nearest to the vestry – learning
about life from words. Sometimes they would stir hearts as
they sang their own hymns unaccompanied by church organ
or adults. Perhaps they gained some comfort from the words
in those hard times. I certainly did.

There's a Friend for little children,
Above the bright blue sky,
A Friend Who never changes,

Whose love will never die.
Our earthly friends may fail us,
And change with changing years,
This Friend is always worthy
Of that dear Name He bears.

The Brick and Stone Villa, Walt's Cottage and the Keeper's Cottage,
Bartlow Hamlet

Chapter 8

Walton's Park

The squire's house was spacious, tranquil and beautiful in its Ashdon setting. Great windows looked out on velvet lawns, gravelled drives and walled gardens; on the rookery and other leafy woodlands; on undulating meadows lush with clover and sorrel, as buttercupped and daisied as Sparks' Mede. Snowy clouds of fan-tailed pigeons whirled about the red tiles of stables and out-houses. They rested in rafters over the harness room and stables, dotting the hay-lined joists with bushels of pink-white eggs and filling the country mornings of springtime with their soft cooings and love murmurings. Other days we would hear the huntsman's horn and see the picture of hunting pink and velvet black, of glistening pawing horses and impatient baying hounds awaiting the end of the stirrup-cupping ceremony, framed by a backcloth of stately walls, sturdy oaks and lofty elms. And in the bright clear mornings of autumn the estate's employees, old and young, man and maid, would throng the environs, ready with hazel sticks to beat game to the guns of the friends of Major Tansley Luddington, gentleman farmer, owner of Walton's Park and Place Farm.

Although fresh in my memory, that was before the cruel flames burned down Walton's and the Luddingtons left our village. It could never be the same after that tragedy. My pigeons went too. Black, cawing rooks and hysterically-shrieking jays replaced my love birds. Drives were forlorn. Where once blossomed flowers there were weed tanglings and unsightly mounds of leaf mould, dank, decaying and depressing. I wonder if Major Luddington's portrait perished in those all-consuming flames. Long before my father shaved the last hairs from the death-waxed face of the squire, his painted portrait in that fine drawing-room where I used to clean the silver played tricks with my senses – looking at it I fancied I could smell the faint aroma of his cigarettes, specially blended to his taste by Freeman's of London. Perhaps the fact that Major Luddington had given me my first cigarette had something to do with it.

He was a kindly, considerate man, ever tolerant of human frailties and shortcomings, and he was my first employer. My father asked for me to be taken on when I was ten during the holidays, so even before I left school I was engaged to clean his boots, knives and forks, dog cart and brougham, plus his two ponies, Joey and little Tommy. At that age, where such qualities of kindness and human consideration were involved, I gained strong, enduring impressions.

My work-room was at the end of the servants' quarters and had a bench on which stood a hurdy-gurdy contraption for cleaning table knives. A handle was turned to rotate the cleaning vanes and there were slots around its outer perimeter to take six knives. One morning, in an endeavour to ginger myself up a bit, I turned that handle very quickly. At the precise moment when Major Luddington arrived to change his muddied brogues, I found myself with six buckled knife-blades.

'What is the meaning of this?' asked the major, examining his ruined cutlery. Spluttering to reply, I was interrupted and given instructions. 'Put in six more. I will turn the handle!' In seconds, six more knives were distorted and ruined. The major winked. 'This is OUR secret, Cedric Mays. Don't tell Miss Hawes. If you do we'll never hear the last of it.'

Miss Hawes was the cook, who ruled the kitchen staff with a rod of iron. In great secrecy the major helped me bury twelve knives good and deep in the peat floor of the wood shed. Later, he taught me to ride, to groom and, in the field of Woodshot, to shoot with 12-bore guns and a small calibre rifle. 'It will put some interest in your bird-scaring.' On my second day in marksmanship, I fainted. I had started my bird-scaring day in feverish excitement but – because our larder had given out – with an empty belly.

From then on the observant major arranged that I should take my midday meal in the small room adjacent to the butler's pantry. There were conditions! 'He must have the same food as myself. He is not to be embarrassed by eating before the household staff. They might comment!'

Walton's was like that!

Leila Luddington, the charming and lovely lady of the house, could not have been more kind. Her frequent visits to the lowly cottagers helped to relieve their grinding poverty; to mitigate their loneliness and suffering long before the miraculous powers of penicillin and antibiotics were discovered. Nourishing soups and broths, egg-rich custards, thick dairy cream and Place Farm butter the colour of marigolds were prepared in her kitchens for the lonely sick and aged ones of our village. Fresh-picked fruit and vegetables were taken to the homes of the sick and to the wards of Saffron Walden and Cambridge hospitals. Usually Mrs Luddington would accompany her baskets; invariably she would take her purse and her friendly smile.

Unlike most women of her social standing, she was not to be seen on race courses; but one could lay long odds that she would be found each Sunday – with her daughter Elizabeth and her ward Miss Drusilla – in the second pew from the pulpit at Ashdon Church.

According to Walt Nunn, 'That there Miss 'Lisbeth be a fair caution, there's no mistake.' And so she was. Rumour had it that she had been put on a diet and was forbidden sweets. But Miss Elizabeth was not readily deterred. With help from me she spiked the guns of the prohibitionists.

After a very broad wink from Miss Elizabeth, I would find

in a secret place of my dog cart half a crown and a pencilled order for new stocks of confectionery. I would buy these as I went to the village each night to post the mail.

Once there was a bit of a complication. My Miss Elizabeth had mispelled 'nougat' as 'nugget'. Instead of a favourite sweetmeat, and without asking my advice, old Vic Eason the grocer packed with other sweets a large tin of Nugget Boot Polish. If Miss Elizabeth's palate suffered deprivation on this count she gave not a sign. Perhaps the extra polish I put on her footwear did something in the way of compensation for I reserved that tin of Nugget for her walking shoes alone.

During my approach to adolescence, the remotest appearance of Miss Drusilla would play havoc with my emotions. Her glance would induce in me a strange paralysis. Her word would set me flushing and stammering. And her request that I should pick flowers or fruit for her would create in me the proud illusion that I had just been nominated for a knighthood. The music of her name affects me still – after all those years.

Freeman told me that Miss Drusilla came from 'furrin parts ... Darjeelin', somewhere out Africa way!'

Freeman, the butler, was my immediate superior.

He taught me the mysteries of lighting boiler fires and charging them to maintain a constant supply of hot water for the household. He schooled me in making bee-hives and collecting honey, unveiled, from the busy insects to which he was unreciprocally devoted. With roots and herbs and a battered saucepan he would concoct hellish brews as antidotes to bee-stings, none of which gave me much solace or relief.

In the field of antidotal experimentation I surpassed my mentor by sheer accident. Between the kennels and the rookery half an acre of the garden bristled with blackcurrant bushes and Freeman's bee-hives. The grass was lush and inviting, so one day I laid me down on it and fell off to sleep. When I woke it was because a queen bee had decided I would make an excellent swarming ground. Bunches of bees were over my head in settling formation. In desperation, there being no other escape to hand, I thrust my head deep into a currant bush, seized branches with both hands and shook them furiously round my head. The bees flew off, leaving a few stings on my face and currant leaves on my shirt. I rubbed a currant leaf on the hottest sting. The pain stopped. I rubbed it on other stings with the same results and hurried to tell Freeman.

Freeman was one of those persons who could not generate any enthusiasm for discovery unless he made it himself. Since bees were involved he displayed a mild interest. 'Come along a-me, then!' He took a broom stave and stirred up a hive of bees. He got us both well and truly stung and he made careful applications of currant leaves to his own stings, not to mine. To my delight, however, he made a grudging admission. 'Drat it, boy! I bleeve you're on to summat. They suttinly takes away a bit o' the pain.'

There was also an occasion when he did not agree with me. Among my many chores was the provision of firewood and kindling. For this I would take the dog cart to Home Wood to collect dead wood and chips from the tree fellers. On a very wet day when a big shoot was in progress over the estate – and there would be lots of sodden tweeds for me to dry out for the gun-bearing gentry – I made a startling discovery. I had run out of firewood. I remembered seeing odd boxwork in the cellars about a month previously. In fairness it should be known that these labyrinthine cellars had no lighting, apart from my candle-stumps, scrounged from the brass lamps of the brougham. And it was with a candle-stump and a sharpened axe that I explored the dark depths on this occasion and found bottles of wine, Vichy Etat table waters, trusses of hay and straw, and boxwork. I got busy with my axe. In less than two hours I had enough kindling to last me through a brace of Arctic winters.

Next morning, a near-apoplectic Freeman stooped to me in wrath. 'What the hell do you mean by choppin' up my bloody bee-hives?' he thundered. And it was from that precise point in time that there began for me a protracted course, after normal working hours, in bee-hive construction.

Another of my jobs was the plucking of game fowl and the skinning of hares or rabbits. Although inept in personal performance, 'all on account o' me weak stummick, boy', Bill Leonard, the coachman and chauffeur, put a bit of life into the itchy, feathery business by introducing a competitive element – my manipulative dexterity versus the hands of his silver half-hunter watch. 'I'll give ye foive minutes fer a chicken, foive fer skinnin' hares an' conies, but fer geese an' turkey an' duck yew can hev six minutes – on account o' they big owd wing 'n' tail feathers an' all that owd fluff 'n' down.'

Mid-season, when many guests dined at Walton's, I was to be found in my wooden plucking shed by the stables, knee-deep in and half choked by feathers, or alive with chicken fleas. Close of season presented even greater hazards. As there was no refrigeration it was customary to 'well hang' the game fowl, to postpone their eating until the last 'safe' moment.

One morning Miss Hawes, the cook, handed me a brace of pheasant and another of partridge. 'Pluck 'em, boy, quick. Unexpected visitors!'

Both brace had been shot a fortnight earlier, on the last day of the season. My first inkling that all was not well came with an involuntary sniff of disgust. Inspection revealed that three of the birds were on the verge of disintegration. As he had taken the brougham to Cambridge to fetch Lady Bate, Mrs Luddington's mother, my friend Bill Leonard was not available for advice or consultation. A wordy encounter with the frenetic cook was the last thing I wanted, so with game-keeper's ferreting spade I interred the decomposing delicacies in an appropriate grave – a dung heap.

One hour later a dishevelled Miss Hawes appeared.

'What abowt them birds, then? You've had 'em long enough ter cook an' eat 'em!'

With due solemnity I doffed my cap and informed her of the last sad rites and the resting place. She did not mourn, she shrieked.

'You bloody boy, you! You was born to get hung! Go an' dig 'em out. Clean 'em an' pluck 'em!'

'But they are rotten, Miss . . . ' I began.

'They ain't rotten, jest nice an' ripe. Go, do as I say!'

In the interests of self preservation and estate concord, I dug, exhumed, cleaned, plucked and was sick. The least said about the seething details the better. I had two hopes; that not one morsel would be given to my Miss Drusilla . . . and that Miss Hawes should forcibly be fed with both brace.

With Lady Bate came Mr O'Boyle, her Irish butler. Apart from the Canadian soldiers, this was my first encounter with a 'foreigner'. Throughout his long stay Paddy was a constant source of companionship and entertainment, with his personal behaviour and his stories of the eccentricities of fellow Irishmen.

A born philosopher, he found mirth and delight in every human situation and was particularly interested in the inferiority of 'the English', in Miss Bertha Cox, the between maid, and in the conservation of human effort – in that order.

We used to work together once a week in Freeman's pantry. It was sheer delight. There were we, all green-baize aproned, polishing away at Mrs Luddington's silver, with Paddy philosophizing like fury about every aspect of this 'English' estate.

'Let me be tellin' you, m'boy, the hot water systems of Ireland are far superior to the trash you have here. If it's hot water we want in Ireland, 'tis hot water we get, without all this silly ole stokin' an' shovellin'.'

Later in the morning, in Bill Leonard's harness room, he

tried to give a practical demonstration in support of his denunciation. Behind the harness room stove there protruded a vertical brass spindle threaded with weights. 'Here we are, indeed. See these silly ole weights, m'boy, they're for controllin' the water pressure.'

Paddy removed one weight from the spindle to demonstrate, and handed another to me for inspection. With a hiss and a clatter the water pressure took the remaining weights to the harness room ceiling. In less than a minute the harness room and all that therein was – including Paddy and me – were saturated.

Paddy did not know how to stop the torrent. Nor did anyone else, except young Lawrence Bidwell who, with his new-fangled tractor, was ploughing the field of Thruskell's.

Bowler-hatted and bicycle-clipped, Paddy pedalled furiously to Thruskell's. He returned with Lawrence, who quickly turned some hidden tap and the deluge was halted; but it had gushed over the boots of the many onlookers and had brought down a fairish bit of plaster from the ceiling by that time.

'The trouble of it is, m'boy, you never can tell what stupidities these benighted English plumbers will be gettin' up to next. Now in Ireland . . . '

Paddy's aquatic antics did not end there. Every day I would fetch drinking water from George Midson's spring well. I would take for this quarter-mile trip to George's cottage home my dog cart, with little Tommy between the shafts. In the cart would be one bucket, one funnel, one twelve-gallon wicker-encased earthenware jar. On arrival at the well I would leave the big jar in the dog cart. With six dips of my two-gallon bucket I would funnel the water into the jar. Too heavy for me to handle alone, the jar would be lifted from the cart at the big house by Freeman, who always complained about the things this lifting did to his 'poor owd back'.

Paddy was disgusted by this primitive 'English' system, and suggested improvements. 'Leave behind that silly old bucket an' funnel, m'boy. Fetch a bit o' rope, an' it is meself who'll be showin' a bit of intilligence to you.'

We set forth in the dog cart, without bucket or funnel, but with a bit of rope with which Paddy tried to lasso dogs and cats *en route*. At the well he tied the rope to the jar handle. With an overdone display of Irish strength he lifted the jar from the cart and hurled it into the well, keeping a tight grip on the rope's end. He tilted his bowler, sang a snatch of bawdy song, and looked me in the eye. 'Hark now, to the music of the water gushin' into the throat of that silly ole bottle, m'boy, with not a bit of work for us at all, at all.'

At that stage Paddy's system seemed superior, but he had not bargained for the weight of the twelve-gallon jar when filled. With feet astride the well he heaved on the rope and purpled; but the bobbing jar refused to leave the well. He took off his bowler and black jacket and rolled up his shirt sleeves. He gave me a wink and a grin, spat on his hands . . . and then disappeared into the well.

When I pulled him out I was helpless from laughing. Strange curses in Erse rang out. Fearful spells were cast on the English.

Back at the big house he slunk down into the cellar and I tried to do what I could to dry him out. From Constance Ranner, Mrs Luddington's personal maid, I borrowed a flat-iron and an old sheet. I smuggled these to where Paddy was shivering in short shirt and ugly underpants before my cherry-red water-heating system – still talking about the inferiority of English drinking-water systems. I rigged up a laundry table with bricks and scaffold planks and placed the flat-iron on top of my red-hot stove. Paddy was still grousing and grumbling.

I picked up the iron and spat on its bottom to test its temperature. But Paddy snatched it from me. 'There's not one bloody Englishman alive who is fit to press the trousers of an Irish gentleman, there is not!'

He pressed the iron on the sheet. There came a hiss and a stench as he burned through sheet and best pin-stripe trousers. 'Oh, m'boy, m'boy. What a day it has been, to be sure. Every bloody thing in me favour has bin against me, it has!'

Although the wheel rims of Paddy's spit-new bicycle shone like burnished steel, he insisted on polishing them again and again with Goddard's Plate Powder. I asked him why. 'Cleanliness is next to Godliness, it is. And, as sure as God made little apples, it's meself an' me boike that's goin' to Saffron Walden on Sunday for Mass, we are!'

As sure as God made apples of all sizes, Paddy went to Mass. But not upon his pride and joy – his beloved new bicycle. On the Saturday night snow fell until a thick blanket covered each inch of the road to Saffron Walden – five long miles from Walton's Park. Walking beside his gleaming bike, Paddy swore, sweated and pushed it to the church. Having there been absolved for the sins of his cursings on the outward journey, he pushed his bike back to Walton's – to defeat the English snow.

Bertha Cox was 'between maid', whatever that was. In Bertha's case the title was singularly inappropriate. Her 'waist-down' dimensions would preclude her intervention between persons and objects not widely spaced. Gipsy black was her hair. Full and red and ripe were her lips and her dark eyes smouldered and fired as she followed her habit of looking man-wards to the yards and stables, a habit which, unjustly, had earned her the title of 'spy'.

O'Boyle had different opinions about Bertha.

'She's a foine, strong, healthy young colleen she is, m'boy, with the arse of an Argentine steer, she has. An' it's a foine, strong man she's needin' an' is lookin' at this minute,' said Paddy, settling his bowler at a rakish angle as he sought to capture Bertha's attention. Next morning, however, having suffered an overnight repulse, he changed his song.

'There she is, now, m'boy, looking straight into the eye of me from her bedroom window, the harpy! As sure as God made little apples, I'd loike to ...' He hesitated, like the gentleman he was, in consideration of my youth.

'You'd like to what?' I asked, in salacious anticipation.

'I'd loike t'creep up behind her, I would, an' shut down the window on her lush, fat back, an' then ...' he hesitated again.

'And then?' I insisted.

'An' sloide a big, red-hot pertater up her petticoat, an' howd it down hard on her fat owd arse.'

The window slammed shut. Bertha vanished. Paddy was no 'whispering' baritone.

The female domestic staff of Walton's Park was divided between kitchen personnel – under the charge of Miss Hawes – and the housemaids, who were supervised by Constance Ranner. The 'kitcheners', as they called themselves, were at the lowest rung of the domestic ladder and seldom went to other parts of the house except to the servants' sleeping quarters. In some big houses a kitchen or scullery maid might work for years without meeting her employers. Occasionally, perhaps when attending the kitchen to discuss meals with the cook, the 'lady' would deign to ask about their work, if not their welfare. It was not so at Walton's, for Mrs Luddington took a great interest in the personal problems of her staff, called them by their Christian names and always regarded them as human beings.

In places elsewhere cooks and upper servants, or maids, were the real bosses, and some ruled their underlings – particularly the new recruits just from school – with great severity.

Kitchen staffs usually began their apprenticeship in the scullery, where they would spend most of their days in washing up great piles of plates, dishes and cooking utensils. The next best thing to a 'day orf' was to be employed in polishing the brass and copper utensils, of which there were many. Most of the girls took great pleasure in doing their jobs. There were reasons! Their bedrooms were clean and roomy, with ample linen; their meals were regular and substantial – a great improvement on what their family life had been if they happened to be daughters of farm workers, as many of them were.

Housemaids tended almost everything except the kitchen and scullery, to which they seldom went except to eat their meals from the big communal kitchen table. Most of them preferred housework and needlecraft and were experts in both. All lived in, and the wage was seldom more than twenty pounds per year for the seniors. 'Scullery slaves' were lucky to get ten pounds.

But what a pleasant sight it was to see them going a-walking in the sunshine! All spick and span, with white frilly aprons and immaculately starched caps set on masses of feminine well-brushed hair, so shiny that the sun shone from their gleaming heads.

Constance Ranner (Con to most of us), Mrs Luddington's personal maid, was also a sight for sore eyes. Never seeming to walk she would glide from room to room, and sometimes from garden to garden, like some dell-reared fairy. On 'recreational afternoons' she would thistledown-nestle in the depths of her roomy armchair, to produce masterpieces of the daintiest needlework, and crochet-work like frost crystals. Her voice was quiet, musical, compelling. Too honest a person to indulge in estate gossipings or scandalmongerings, she would gracefully glide away if disobliging things were said about her colleagues. There was one exception, but it was a person to person exception. When Bertha Cox, the between maid, admitted to Con that for the past three months she had been 'goin' steady' with Frederick Green, a young painter and Casanova from Saffron Walden, and ended by saying, 'I s'pose that'll be a nine days' wonder, Con!' Constance countered with an enjoinder which ran through the estate like wildfire ... 'You mind it won't be a nine MONTHS' wonder, Bertha dear!'

Miss Hawes, the cook, was an enigma. Reputed to be secretly in love with Freeman the butler, she could be charming and considerate, but only within earshot of Freeman or her 'superiors'. Her vocabulary seemed to be restricted to peremptory words of command. Her gestures were like the lunges of fencing masters and one received the impression that her rearing and education had been based on manuals of military law.

Her face was as flabby and doughy as the contents of her mixing basins but when she smiled it was transformed into that wistful beauty so characteristic of the love-deprived. When that smile came, one fully expected to see flour fall from her mouth wrinkles – and was disappointed when it did not.

Paddy O'Boyle had a theory about Miss Hawes which lacked nothing in biological and psychological significance. 'She's a foine ole cook, indeed she is, m'boy! Give her one tough ole buck rabbit an' two pithy ole radishes an' she'll be turnin' out a banquet, she will. But it's vinegar that's gone to her soul from picklin' ole hens' eggs an' from the want of a foine, strong man.'

Freeman was the only male servant on Walton's domestic

staff. He was a kind but lonely man and had gone prematurely grey and dignified. Apart from his beloved bees he had few interests. I never saw him take up a book, but his handwriting was almost copperplate in its neatness. Not that he was addicted to writing, for the only signs of his penmanship were the lists he gave me to go shopping in the village store and post office. Later he committed suicide in the quietude of the rookery.

The menfolk of Walton's were hard-working, God-fearing individualists, ever resentful of interference in their particular functions. All were highly skilled in their crafts.

George Midson was the head gardener. He was sixty-plus then, and had a stoop which gave the impression that he was loth to be far parted from the rich soil he tended with patience and love. From the cunning of his skilled, calloused fingers, riots of bloom cascaded down mellowed walls, through the hazy heat of the greenhouses, in the tranquil splendour of the green-carpeted library gardens.

George lived for flowers.

Each Sunday morning, as we went to Sunday school, we found him waiting at his garden gate to pin rose or carnation in our buttonholes or on our jerseys. To the girls he would say, 'Here's a nice red rose, m'dear, to go with they pretty cheeks!'

And when I sometimes helped him in the gardens he would teach me a thing or two, not only of flowers. 'When I looks into the heart of a flower, lad, I can see my God. Hoe the soil, lad. Let the air of God breathe into it, an' it'll pay you back a hun'd-fold. Tells you that, lad, in the Big Book.'

George's main fear was that he might become consti-
pated. To ward off some cunning attack of this evil he would
mix great measures, shandies of Epsom and Glauber salts,
in the seclusion of his holy of holies – the potting shed.
Then, scorning the primitive alfresco privy close to hand, he
would shuffle off to his own privy in a hurried ungainly gait
which suggested that all had not been well with his timing.
Yet, one could synchronize watches and clocks, or tell the
train departure time from Bartlow Station, by George's
'movements'.

He loved best the month of May and would spend hours
beyond his working time between flower gardens, fruit gardens and kitchen gardens. Most of the work was concentrated
upon his beloved roses. He would mulch them, disbud them
and, with razor-sharp secateurs, cut out the suckers before
rearranging the briar wood into new positions. In the fruit
gardens he would bark-ring trees of over-vigorous growth,
spray fruit trees with derris, remove suckers from raspberries,
and walk miles with his little camel-hair brush to hand pollin-
ate the fruit blossom. His last job was a black one, with soot,
lightly to dust the new strawberry plants.

In the kitchen garden he would put in the seeds of cucum-
ber, marrow, sweet corn and maize; thin out the seedlings of
onions and carrots; sow runner beans, and put in sticks for
them to climb to fruitfulness; and do all manner of plantings –
celery, indoor and outdoor tomatoes. Nor did he need a calendar to guide him; he got his timing from the sun.

In those splendid gardens George had been assisted over

different periods by Bill Albin, Tom Symonds and my father, John Mays.

Bill Albin hailed from Bartlow and a blacksmith father. His main responsibilities lay in the maintenance of lawns and drives, and work in the vegetable gardens. Bill loathed the donkey work of digging but when each new spring arrived he became inspired. With little Tommy between the shafts of the heavy roller he would draw lines of light and dark green upon the immaculate lawn surfaces as if he had used a straight-edge. At the end of each lawn crossing he would stoop and cast an appraising eye along the last line drawn. If satisfied, his tongue would loll spaniel-like and he would salivate like a pricked water-blister. 'Thasser straight'n, bor. Carn't hev straighter!'

Biologically speaking, Bill was big-headed. It was not until one conversed with him that it became evident that a big casket contained but a meagre treasure. Lacking the capacity for the meanest of abstract thought, believing in only what he could see, he was convinced that 'light and shade' had nothing whatever to do with his immaculate lawn lines.

''Tain't a mite o' good you arguin', boy. Any fool can see they owd lines is made by the weight o' the roll, crushin' the grass blacker-like!'

Tom Symonds, who preceded Bill in those gardens, had the frame of a giant and the soul of a child. With his great strength he could lift three great wheat-sheaves high in the air on his two-tined pitchfork. Without a falter he could carry the slithery weight of two full sacks of linseed – one under each of his massive arms. I once saw him lift my pony, little Tommy, across his broad shoulders, without apparent effort.

But when, years later, I last saw Tom he was rotting to his death in his tiny Church Hill cottage. He had been shut away from the gardens and fields for months. He lifted the top sheet and disclosed a leg swollen to thrice normal size; blacked and purpled; yellowed and greened. From the lightest contact of that flimsy sheet he would flinch in agony. In his night turnings and twistings strips of rotted, smelly skin were peeled.

He looked like a frightened child.

'It's good to see you, Ced, bor, an' thasser fact. S'pose the Lord knows what's best. But what's best for He ain't a-doin' me a power o' good. Carn't recall on doin' nobody no harm deliberate though. Mebbe I'm a-payin' for the sins o' my owd father, Ced. He were the wickedest owd varmint alive!'

Tom died soon afterwards, but his flowers live on.

Bill Leonard was the coachman and chauffeur. He was a tall, boyish-faced man with a charming wife, two bonny children and an urge for practical joking. Bill taught me to drive . . . not one of those new mechanical motors, but a real live horse.

Joey had a mouth like silk. Well schooled for riding and driving, from the pressure of my skinny legs, or a tickle from my whip tassel, he would respond like a cavalry charger. On the occasion of my first driving lesson Bill and I were sartorial contradictions. Resplendent in livery and shiny top hat complete with cockade, he sat beside me in the driving seat of Major Luddington's brougham. I was garbed in cut-down trousers from Grandfather Ford's old corduroys, green stockings, hobnailed boots, grey jersey, white celluloid collar and black butterfly bow tie.

'Ease an' feel them reins, boy. Remember, owd Joey's got a hunk o' steel in his mouth. You wouldn't like one in your'n! Don't holler at him so . . . Unkind words'll hurt a hoss more'n heavy hands, go easy!'

Although the power of twenty horses lurked and throbbed under the bonnet of Major Luddington's Austin – the only motor in our hamlet – Bill's kind eyes shone brighter by far when, by reins and bit, he controlled the power of Joey. On wintry nights I would go in the Austin with Bill to Audley End station to meet Major Luddington from the Liverpool Street train. I would sit close to my liveried chauffeur feeling like a millionaire. Headlamps would stab into the country blackness with twin fingers of revelation, picking out each stone in the road, making frost crystals wink and scintillate from fairy frosted trees and rimed hedgerows like diamonds in the night.

Sometimes those trips would supplement our larders. Startled rabbits would bolt from hedges to fall victims to the Austin's cruel wheels. But that was only seen by me on the outward journey. Homeward bound I would see not a thing. Covered by a warm Royal Stewart rug, I would crouch on the floor of the driving cabin, inhaling petrol fumes and the smell of Major Luddington's cigarettes. And never once did he suspect he had a fellow traveller.

When repairing an inner tube with vulcanizing equipment one day, Bill noticed that George Midson had left his new

Wellingtons in his garage. This was the first-ever pair of Wellington boots in Ashdon and George had brought them in to show off Mrs Luddington's gift to him, perhaps to make us envious. But one week later, when George collected and inspected his now 'united' footwear, he wondered by what miracle of adhesion they had become inseparable. He shuffled off, shaking his head, clicking his tongue and looking to the sun. 'Must be this owd summer time they've jest started up. Makin' birds git up an' sing afore their time. Don't howd with it. An' now, by the look on it, they've gorn an' mucked abowt with the heat o' the sun.'

For some days Bill had been puggling about under the Austin's bonnet, with instruction pamphlet in hand. 'Now,' said Bill. 'I'll show you the power that drives this owd engine.'

He held a steel spanner close to a sparking plug. I was fascinated by the blue streaking between spanner and points. 'That's how it looks . . . Now, cop howd o' my hand an' you'll feel it a-throbbin'.'

I 'copped howd', but felt nothing. Then, inadvertently I put my disengaged hand on the chassis. At once there came the sensation of being pole-axed and the fact of being hurled to the garage floor. First to my feet, I saw a shocked Bill still reclining – hoist, in a manner of speaking, with his own petard.

Later, he tried to get to the bottom of the experience by asking philosopher O'Boyle.

'It is the volt which gives the power to drive the ampere, it is,' said Paddy. 'You must have stood in the path of the volt and the ampere, you must.'

'Well then,' said Bill. 'How the hell am I a-goin' to stop gettin' shocked in future?'

'That is easily done, it is. Blow up the bloody English motor an' buy yourself a fine Irish geldin' instead.'

Chapter 9

The Bonnett

Less than two hundred yards from our home stood the Bonnett Inn, where the squire's employees gathered most evenings for warmth and drink and companionship and once each year to give thanks for harvest home.

Standing high above other cottages in the hamlet's centre, under the proprietorship of Bill Cooper for the brewers Greene, King, the Bonnett pub was our community centre and social club, and a most companionable place. In winter a great fire invariably roared up the chimney. Pokers would stand ready and waiting for the 'beer warmers' to perform their ritual. With their backs shielded from draughts by the tall backs of the settles they would start by ordering up.

'Le's hev a quart an' a pinch, then!'

The performance would then begin with the following procedure:

Stand frothing quart pot by the fire. From nutmeg (pinch) scrape a dusting into the froth. Let it soak until froth disappears. Place poker in fire until cherry-red. Remove poker from fire and plunge into quart of beer. Retrieve and replace poker. Lift quart and down half of it.

Result: Ecstasy, rapture ... Repeat as required.

Walt Stalley, Reuben Ford, my grandfather, and Toe-Rag Smith, the horse-keeper, all had their places. Walt and Reuben had stools and their own pots.

'Git the cards, then!'

Cooper would return with dominoes.

'Come on, Jack' – to my father – 'we'll see 'em twice round the board fer a coupla quarts.'

Sometimes there would be conversations and no dominoes ...

'They were round ag'in yes'day, I sin 'em.'

'Who were that, then?'

'They owd draymen, Greene, King's.'

'What, they owd fat 'uns?'

'That be 'em. Looked like they'd had a tidy few.'

'Not so many as larst summer, bor. Her, her, her!'

'What were that, then?'

'They druv up, the pair on 'em a-sittin' on that high owd seat like a coupla tom-tits on a bull's arse. The big 'un hollers to Bill Cooper to bring 'em out a quart a-piece. They had three a-piece, laps their owd tongues round theer chops, an' owd fatty said it worn't a bad gargle. Arter that they got down an' come in fer a few.'

'Ar, I remember now, come to think on't. But the thin 'un were the wust of the pair. They reckons he put poor owd Wimbish in his grave afore his time.'

'How were that, then?'

'Wimbish were tidy bad, there's no denyin'. He knew he were a-gooin', but worn't ready and towd the drayman he were frit to goo. He just laughed and towd him not to goo worryin' abowt dyin'; there worn't nuthin' to it. Trouble were he'd be bloody stiff nex' day.'

The old tales would be told and re-told.

'Remember that fust harvest in Holden Field?'

'Oh, ah . . . Le's hev it ag'in.'

'There were three on 'em. Wuddy were loadin', Jack an' Walt a-pitchin'. Started harvest to roights. Got outside half a gallon o' dandelion wine afore breakfast. Straight arter breakfast they put paid to a gallon o' best bitter. Wuddy gets in the wagon to load, but couldn't stand hardly. He worn't there long. The very fust sheaf Jack pitches to'm had a swarm o' bees on it. Wuddy got stung bad. He were too bluddy drunk t'run.'

'Worn't it owd Joslin who took 'em the gallon?'

'Thass roight. He were thatchin' at Overhall Farm an' brought 'em a gallon from the Bricks. He were courtin' at the time.'

'Wouldn't say courtin'; she wouldn't hev owd Joslin at any price.'

'Thass where you're wrong. Joslin wouldn't hev Nellie Thompson. He wanted a gal who wus religious, like hisself; an' he ups an' asks Nellie straight:

'"Hev you found the Lord Jesus, Nellie, dear?"

'"No!" Nellie towd him. "Never knew he were lorst!"'

Barney Chapman would walk in.

'Ev'nin' all. Pint o' bitter, missus.' Then, seeing Cribby sitting chewing a straw:

'Sign o' snow, ain't it, when yer see an owd hog chewin' straw?'

'Ev'nin', Barney,' said Cribby, not in the least put out.

'Tell us about owd Harry at the auction, Jack,' and off my father would go:

'Harry'd bin at market all day. Good ten sheets in the wind. Sees a light in the village hall. Staggers outer his owd cart and goes in. They helps him to a chair, an' there he sits, blinkin' like a bloody owl. One of the Women's Institute howds up an owd jug.

'"Who'll bid half a crown?"

'"Foive bob!" says Harry, quick as a flash . . .

'"I'm bid five shillings," she says . . .

'"Make it ten bob!" hollers Harry . . .

'"I am bid ten shi . . . "

'"Make it a pownd, me dear. Make it a pownd."

'"I am bid one pound; who will . . . "

'"Twenty-five bob, m'dear. That's me larst wud!"

'She hands Harry the jug.

'"Oi don't like the look on't. Set it up ag'in. Here's twenty-five bob."

'"Thank you, Mister Hutchings," she says, howdin' it up for the second time. "Who will open the bidding?"'

'"Foive bob!" says Harry. Nobody else bid, an' he bid ag'in hisself another twenty-five. Paid up, never took the jug, but they slung him out. Best auction ever.'

Clay pipes were the order of the day. Some had long churchwardens with stems two feet long. Others smoked the remnants of such pipes. With notches filed into what remained of the stem to get a toothhold, they would suck away at the blackened clay bowls making stenches and gurgling with glee.

'What you got in there, bor? Smells like camel shit!'

'Yew ain't far out. Picked it up in your hoss-stall larst night. It's a ripish owd dottle. You orter give they owd hat-racks o' your'n a bran mash now an' ag'in!'

At threepence a pint for mild and fourpence for bitter, the beer was very good. But the beer was by no means the main attraction. Some would sip slowly away to make a pint pass the whole evening, even though they could afford to buy another.

They were in communion with their fellows, with a warm fire, good company, no children under their feet or wives to nag them. Women came seldom to the pub, and then only to the back door to buy beer to take to the fields. Pubs were almost exclusively the clubs of working men or male adults.

Occasionally a young lad under eighteen years would be asked in. This was considered to be an honour, a token of appreciation of occupational prowess in the fields or a recognition of approaching manhood. The publican would turn a blind eye on these occasions.

To hear them speaking of the fields they loved, mentioning them by name in what was almost a caress, was an inspiring experience – one which underlined what a great part these humble people played in the life of the nation without the recognition they well merited.

Three slender things that best support the world:
the slender stream of milk from the cow's dug into the pail;
the slender blade of green corn upon the ground;
the slender thread over the hand of a skilled woman.
Three sounds of increase:
the lowing of a cow in milk;
the din of a smithy;
the swish of a plough.

Grandad Reuben Ford liked solitude, silence and Yarmouth bloaters. It was a delight to see him cook his bloaters. Sometimes he would grill them at home, sometimes at the Bonnett. From bits of wire fencing he had fashioned his own toasting fork, with a very long handle and five prongs. First, he would cut a thick slice of bread and place it in the fireplace in a good fat-catching position. Next, he would spear the bloater with his fork and toast it before the fire; sometimes moving the bread with the toe of his clodhoppers to catch the mainstream of the dripping fat. He would lick his chops, moisten his beard and salivate in gleeful anticipation; and God help the boy who uttered a word to disturb his ritual.

Grandad loathed company, particularly the company of women and relations. One Sunday we were all invited next door to have dinner with Granny Ford. It was a lovely meal, with lots of meat and all the best vegetables, but there was no Grandad present. He had gone to the Bonnett to dodge the company and the chattering.

Just before closing time Granny Ford sent my sister Poppy to the Bonnett with Grandad's dinner; all protected and covered with top plates to keep it warm, and wrapped for ease of transportation in his big dinner handkerchief. 'tell him,' said Granny, looking more furious than I had ever seen her, 'tell him to eat his vittels where he drinks his dratted owd beer.'

Poppy returned in five minutes – with a message.

'Grandad says where's the pepper and salt?'

In that old taproom, beneath their deceptive straw-chewing exteriors, astute self-reliant farmhands gave to that village vitality. Among these lads and men of Place Farm there existed a recognized hierarchy, based on age, experience and occupational prowess. The horse-keeper was George Smith and, in Farmer Bidwell's absence, he assumed command. George once gashed his foot with a careless scythe-sweep when mowing the headlands of Shorthill. Lacking first aid equipment, he had bound a dock leaf around his all-but-severed toe with the tail of his flannel shirt. Ever afterwards he had been known as 'Toe-Rag'.

He was marvellous with horses. Without any veterinary training he could diagnose thrush, colic, strangles and pregnancy by his sense of smell and equine experience before there were any actual symptoms to be seen. To my knowledge, he was never found wrong.

Toe-Rag had a wart on his lower lip – a horny unsightliness which he tried to hide by his constant chewings on oat straws. Mention of that wart, or a sly peep in its direction, would cause him profound embarrassment. This was underlined one day when Tom Symonds, who it was alleged had inherited psychic powers from gipsy ancestors, offered to charm it away. 'Put a mite o' siller in m'hand, Toe-Rag, an' I'll wish that owd wart o' your'n roight away.'

George looked Tom in the eye and spat in the horse-stall. 'Thankee, Tom, I can do me own wishin'. An' roight now I wish y'd mind yer own bloody business!'

When sheaves were carted, George's tenor rang out across the golden stubbles in exultation. Ships and sailors figured largely in his songs, possibly because he, like Grandfather Ford and Walt Stalley, had never seen the sea. 'The Dark-Eyed Sailor', 'Shenandoah', 'When the Fields are White with Daisies I'll Return', and so on. George sang those songs in fields whose names are music in themselves; Old Lay, New Lay, Sparks's, Thruskell's, Long Mead, Short Mead, Holden, Woodshot; Little Bourne, Great Bourne, Hungerton, Bartlow; and many more, for every field and meadow and path had its name.

George had poetry in his soul, and it was from him that I

learned this old rhyme of Essex country place names:

> Willingale Doe and Willingale Spain,
> Bulvan and Bobbingworth, Colne Engaine;
> Wenden Lofts, Beaumont-com-Mose, Bung Row,
> Gestingthorpe, Ugley and Fingringhoe;
> Helions Bumpstead and Mountnessing,
> Bottle End, Tolleshunt D'Arcy, Messing;
> Islands of Canvey, Foulness, Potton,
> Stondon Massey and Belchamp Otton;
> Ingrave and Inworth and Kedington,
> Shallow Bowels, Ulting and Kelvedon;
> Margaret Roothing and Manningtree—
> The bolder you sound 'em, the better they be.

Next in status to George came Walt Nunn, a long gaunt man whose face seemed almost as long and horsey as his legs. He covered the ground in great strides, as though wearing seven-league boots. His vocabulary was strange and rich in Anglo-Saxon oaths. Perpetually raised, his brows conveyed the impression that he was always surprised and this impression was strengthened by his two pet expressions, descriptive of persons and situations alike: 'There's no mistake', which covered the conventional, and 'A bit of a caution!' which sufficed for all unorthodoxy. Both expressions were used lavishly when Walt 'fust heered that owd wireless'. By this time Chris Ketteridge and I had made a crystal set, the first in the village. Financial stringency precluded the purchase of two sets of headphones, but by splitting the flex leads we used one ear-piece each. For weeks we heard nothing – due to a spurious crystal. We got another and erected a magnificent aerial on the top sail of the old windmill, aiming it at the lowest central portion of Savoy Hill. We twiddled the cat's whisker and to our great delight we heard snatches of music punctuated by the speech of an unknown language.

Breathlessly and jubilantly we searched adjacent fields, hoping to find another human to share our joy. We found Walt Nunn. We hustled him into the mill, sat him on a mill-stone and clapped both earpieces over his big hairy ears. Breathless, we watched his eyes protrude, his brows rise even further in wonderment. We awaited his congratulations.

'Well, thasser bit of a bloody caution, there's no mistake. I don't bloody well believe it.'

Chris winked at me, but looked solemn when he spoke to Walt. 'Best be careful about swearing, Walt. With those head-phones on you, every word you say can be heard in London.'

Walt tore off the headphones. 'Well, bugger me! Thasser bit of a caution, there's no mistake. But if they owd Cockneys start spreadin' tales abowt me an' my owd woman, I'll hev the bloody coppers arter 'em, there's no mistake.'

He hurried from the mill, deep in thought.

Wuddy Smith came third in seniority. He was a strong man in more ways than one. Not addicted to daily ablutions, his presence was ripe, particularly in summer. He had a brother who had actually been church-christened Pudden and distant relatives at Camps End who, sometimes, but only when there was an acute dearth of labour, were recruited as casual har-vesters. There was justifiable doubt about their surnames and total ignorance of their Christian names, but their nicknames were household and taproom words:

> Pipper an' Pie, Nickett an' Ninn,
> They can allus be found
> At the Holly Tree Inn.
> When they bain't full o' beer,
> They be sodden wi' gin.

Pudden Smith, who went to live with Wuddy after his wife died, kept pigs with varying degrees of success. Some he ate, some he sold, but he had one special porker upon which he lavished all his pig-rearing wit and experience, and hoped to cash in on his enterprise at Saffron Walden market. This was a Gloucester Spot, a breed well thought of in East Anglia. After the sale Pudden was approached by a neighbour.

'Did the owd pig fetch a good price, Pudden, bor?'

'Fair t'middlin',' replied Pudden. 'It di'n't make me as much as I thought it would; I di'n't think the bugger would!' and Pudden spat in contempt.

Before his wife died Pudden was sitting with her in the fading light. When he awakened from a short nap he could not see across the room.

'Light the bloody lamp, woman. Anybody gooin' past an' seein' us a-sittin' in the dark'll think we've gone ter bed.'

'I can't find me matches,' came the quavering reply.

'Then strike a bloody light, woman, an' look fer 'em!'

Wuddy Smith had the biggest holdall basket in East Anglia. Made from plaited and woven rushes, he carried it over his shoulders slung by a bit of plough cord, and its ends projected from him like the wings of an aircraft. So capacious was this 'frail' that in addition to the porterage of his daily rations – a quartern loaf and half a pound of cheese – he toted therein his hedging equipment: billhooks, sickles, rubstones, whetstones and bits of plank to put across the ditches so that he could stand on them when trimming hedges. He also carried in the bag a large alarm clock and a blue-enamelled two-pint tea can. There was ample room left for any other oddments he might need. It was fortunate for Wuddy that he lived in an age of little traffic. When he met someone on the narrow roads he had to turn sideways to allow the person to pass. Should he encounter a wheeled vehicle he had to stand in the ditch and lean well back on the bank so that his wings did not obstruct its passage.

One day Wuddy's hand was seen to be bandaged with his red handkerchief, and he was asked why.

'Oi were jest a-gittin' me shop things owter the basket on Saturday night an' cut me hand on me bill.'

'How were that, then?'

'Jest as I were a-puttin' me hand in, a bloody grut rat jumped owter me basket. Oi clarred (clawed) me hand owt sharpish, an' dang me if I di'n't drag it straight across the blade o' me bill.'

'Where d'you reckon that owd rat come from, then, Wuddy?'

153

'Owter me cottage, bor. There's scores on 'em runnin' abowt there o' noights.'

After one of his ear-shattering throat clearings and a big friendly grin, he continued. 'T'other week oi had a rare owd abser (abscess) on me face. It was mighty sore. Afore I went ter bed I made meself a red-hot linseed powtus (poultice) an' slapped it on. I woke up in the middle o' the noight an' felt suffin narrin (gnawing) me; an' there were a bloody grut rat, its tail a-ticklin' me tongue as it chewed away at me powtus.'

Wuddy paused.

'Do y'know,' he continued, 'afore I come proper to me senses that owd rat had et up the powtus an' started on me abser. Good job, too, I were cured on it overnight!'

Twice widowed, Wuddy had lived alone for some time, but in his later years he was joined by Pudden, who had also been twice widowed. His cottage was almost opposite ours and only a short way from the Bonnett. Throughout the years of his lonesome tenancy Wuddy wasted not a shred of energy on cleaning. His meagre furniture was encrusted with dirt. That there had been a floor covering was evident from bristling tufts of coconut matting around the table legs, and there were bristly remnants along the outer edges of the path his clodhoppers had made to the table, the door and the cupboard.

Wuddy's sole relaxations were his pipe – an almost stemless, black atrocity of clay which stank – and his pint of beer which he bought at the Bonnett, less than thirty yards from his rat-infested cottage. It was in the Bonnett that he indulged in his only recreations: cribbage, dominoes and rings. Only once was he prevailed upon to try his hand at darts.

The dartboard hung over the fireplace, its top but an inch from the low ceiling, and there was a thick oaken beam between the board and the throwing point which sometimes baffled the experts.

Wuddy's first dart hit the quarry-tiled fireplace with a shower of sparks. His second hit the jamb of the mantelpiece, a foot above the floor. Undeterred, he puffed away at his foul pipe and threw his last dart – straight into the fire. Joining in the laughter, then pausing to take breath, he made his excuse. 'Oi don't reckon I pitched the buggers high enough!'

Nell, Wuddy's second wife, died suddenly one midnight. Next morning he said quite laconically, 'Oi di'n't loike to bother nobody at that hour, so I got into bed with her. She were good an' dead, anyway, so I jest went off to sleep aside of her. I knew she wouldn't be disturbed.'

Then came Barney Bland. Although misshapen by a badly humped back, he was not physically handicapped. He could whistle like thrushes and blackbirds and could perform the whole of the farmhand's toil with meticulous conscientious-ness and enviable ease. His edged tools were like razors. Not a speck of rust or mud could be found on his fork, spade and shovel. Nightly they would be oiled and wrapped, cared for as puny children would be by anxious parents. Examination of a hedge or ditch which Barney had trimmed would reveal the cleanest of cuts on every severed twig and blade of grass. He should have been a surgeon.

Noise was the characteristic of Frank (Poddy) Coote. At 4 A.M. boot-thumpings in his terraced cottage would resound throughout Collier Row, accompanied by loud curses, as he endeavoured to get the unyielding leather of his hobnailed clodhoppers over his size fifteen feet. In addition, he was forever singing hymns. He had learned by rote every hymn in *Hymns Ancient and Modern* and every psalm in the psalter, together with alternative tunes and chants. Given an opening line or a whistled bar, he would sing the lot word-perfect, in a nerve-shattering bastard tenor, for beer or bets.

One weekend in 1922 he went off on his only holiday in years, and for weeks afterwards wore a strained, pained look. He ceased to sing. We wondered for months what had happened to him. Then, the following spring, dressed in new corduroys with polished straps and wallies (buckles) below his ugly knees, he made a blushing, valedictory confession . . .

'It were on that owd holiday I 'ad! I met a young gel, on the sands. She axed an' offered me. I were willin' an' we did! Now I be a-gooin' to she for good!' Singing 'All Things Bright and Beautiful', Poddy strode manfully to Bartlow Station, to be off to the seaside and romance. Over his shoulder, one shovel, one bricklayer's hod.

These were some of the men of Ashdon; my mentors; the salt of the earth, the frequenters of the Bonnett Inn.

Chapter 10

Horkey

It was in the Bonnett, too, that harvesters would gather for the Horkey, the ceremony of thanksgiving for a successful harvest. The squire would give five pounds for the occasion. The tenant farmer would give two pounds, and the remainder would come from pay-point collections weeks in advance.

Horkey day would see Bartlow Hamlet in turmoil. Apple-cheeked women would scurry from their homes to the Bonnett with baskets laden with cooked meats, hams, pickles, home-baked bread and home-made cheese. Each would vie with the other to produce the best looking and most palatable cakes, pastries, sausage rolls and jams. The old taproom would quickly assume a mantle of colour and perfume. Bowls of fragrant roses, vases of mixed flowers and special sprays of sweet peas and asparagus fern would decorate the snowy table-linen. Upon the walls would hang ponderous pumpkins, majestic marrows and scrubbed potatoes – King Edwards, all pinky of eye, kidneys, all purple and polish. The pods of peas and beans would be pregnant to bursting point. Cabbages and cauliflowers would be as round and solid as Cromwellian cannon balls. There would also be parsnips and pears, carnations and carrots, radishes and roses; and strings of mighty onions, each half the size of a choirboy's head. To set it all off, and to symbolize the whole, Toe-Rag Smith's handicraft would be evident – in the skilfully plaited cottage loaves; in straw of wheat, barley and oat.

All would be ready and awaiting the harvesters by 7 P.M.

On the day of my first Horkey when I was ten or eleven, I was leading the wagon-horses in the field called Woodshot. Most of the harvesters were bragging about the quarts of ale and plates of beef they intended putting away that night, Poddy Coote particularly. There was an air of excitement and expectancy which increased in intensity as the corn shocks dwindled in that last field to be harvested. Climax came when Tom Symonds pitched the last sheaf to the loader. Bronzed and sweating, naked from the waist up, Tom looked like some harvest god.

Toe-Rag, as was his right, gave the ritual orders.

'Unhook Captain!' That was the name of our trace-horse.

'Take the Horkey Bough!'

Tom uncoupled the traces from the chestnut gelding and replaced them with a rope, whose free end he looped over a branch of a nearby oak. He made a running bight and nodded to Toe-Rag.

'Up, Captain!' The massive Clydesdale dug in his hooves and heaved. There came a mighty cracking and swishing as the oak's limb was slivered from its bole. Our cheers rang out. The Horkey Bough had been 'taken'. It was hoisted to the top of the last load of grain. Boys and men, our mugs were filled with Greene, King's strong ale to drink two toasts; one to the last sheaf, one to the Horkey Bough.

Slowly and majestically the steel clad wagon wheels rolled to Place Farm. With wheat ears and oak leaves in their caps – pitchforks and jackets over their shoulders – the labourers followed.

Harvest was over.

After washing and dressing in Sunday best, we gathered in conversational groups outside the Bonnett, waiting to take our appointed places at the table. Traditionally, Toe-Rag was last to his place. As soon as he sat he rose again, and all rose with him.

The old horse-keeper looked a bit awkward in blue serge. His ginger whiskers were out of place against his starched, white wing-collar. But when his golden tenor led us in the singing of the harvest hymn it seemed of no account. Humble men were giving thanks.

> Come, ye thankful people, come,
> Raise the song of Harvest home:
> All is safely gathered in,
> Ere the winter-storms begin;

God, our Maker, doth provide
For our wants to be supplied;
Come to God's own Temple, come;
Raise the song of Harvest home.

Each word of every verse was sung by all present without
reference to books, for there were none. No one would suggest
that the Bonnett was God's own temple but there was not a
man or woman present who was not deeply conscious of the
words and their significance. The annual miracles of sowing
and reaping were part and parcel of their hardworking lives.

'You can say Grace, boy!' said Toe-Rag, looking at me. But
I could not say Grace. My emotional reaction to that honest
singing had temporarily erased those simple words from my
recollection. Slowly and clearly as at each of our meals at
home, my father said the words for me . . .

'For what we are about to receive, may the Lord make us
truly thankful.'

The gruff communal 'Amen' was followed by chair-leg
scrapings on the brick floor. Conversation, good-humoured
badinage and laughter swelled. Aproned women flitted with
meat-laden dishes and foaming frothy jugs.

The feast was on!

After an hour and a bit of eating and drinking, Toe-Rag
started the round of individual singing with a song I had not
heard before, nor have I heard it since; but I shall never forget
the swinging of his watch-chain and charm as he swayed to
the lilt of his pretty song:

> Ring-ting, is 'ow the bell goes;
> Ring-ting, you pretty young thing.
> If you'll be my wife,
> I'll buy the ring;
> We'll have servants to wait
> On our ring ting-ting.

In turn, everyone rose and made some contribution – until it came on Wuddy Smith, who, beer-wobbly and salivating, was silent.

'Come on, Wuddy, bor,' bellowed Poddy Coote. 'Sing, you owd varmint, sing!'

Wuddy was no nightingale but, with his hiccup-punctuated rendering, he brought the good old Bonnett near to hysteria.

> Eggs'n ... hic ... bacon,
> Eggs'n ... hic ... bacon;
> If y'think I'm gonna ... hic ... sing a song,
> Ye're bloody ... hic ... well mistaken.

The clock hands stood at well past midnight when landlord Bill Cooper shouted: 'The owd copper's abowt. He's 'ad a couple o' quarts but 'e's startin' ter git a bit sarky-like. Best be a-gettin' to ower beds!'

Toe-Rag stood up. He banged his pewter ploughing-match prize on the oak table.

'Afore we goes, m'lads, we'll sing the evenin' hymn. Sorftly now, sorftly!'

And softly and reverently it was sung:

> The day Thou gavest, Lord, is ended,
> The darkness falls at Thy behest:
> To Thee our morning hymns ascended,
> Thy praise shall sanctify our rest.

I walked out through that open door with wet eyes. Listening to that hymn stealing softly through the starry night, under the harvest moon and over the dark fertile fields of my East Anglian hamlet, I recalled the words of a Persian, taught to me by William Tuck, my village schoolmaster, who used to loan me his poetry books for my 'silent reading'.

One glimpse of it within the tavern caught,
Better than in the temple, lost outright.

And then I was certain that the Bonnett could lay some claim to being God's own temple after all.

Next day, all food left over was taken to the homes of those who had little, to our war widows and the old ones. For every pair of bloodshot eyes in our community there was a big heart.

Chapter 11

The Village

There were other pubs in Ashdon besides the Bonnett. Pubs outnumbered shops. There were five of them, all cosy, human places where farmhands, tradesmen, shopkeepers, farmers, retired gentlemen and travellers met most evenings in winter and summer.

The Lamb Inn was the tiniest one, standing on the Ashdon–Saffron Walden road about two miles from the village centre; it got most of its trade from travellers, farmhands living at Church End, and from farmers passing to markets who could not resist calling. Some of the latter's horses would never pass a pub and would slow to a halt from whatever speed they were travelling at. To the locals the Lamb was home-from-home. Always with a good fire in winter, and with sometimes hanging on the chimney hooks a smoke-cured ham from which could be cut a generous slice to eat with a handful of spring onions and a half-loaf of bread for fourpence, it was more than a home; it was an hotel – an hotel where one's own seat was never sat in by others, be it chair, stool or settle.

In each pub, too, there was always the communal quart pot from which every new entrant was expected to drink in cordiality. Anyone who declined on grounds of fastidiousness or hygiene was never asked again. The refusal would be regarded as an insult.

The Fox Inn and the Rose and Crown are both in the village centre. Each has several rooms compared with the Lamb's one. The pattern for these two pubs was much the same; seats were reserved for the exclusive use of the regulars, mostly in taprooms where cribbage boards and dominoes were much in evidence. The younger element took to darts, and was constantly reminded by the old ones that this game was not a patch on quoits and horseshoe throwing, at which they had been adept when young. Work and politics were the main conversational topics of both and there was more talking than drinking unless there was something to be celebrated, like the birth of a son, the killing of a fat pig, a wedding or funeral or christening, or even the release from gaol of a popular poacher. There were a few who always could produce a reason or excuse, even though it be the lack of something to celebrate.

The Bricklayers' Arms stands low in the midst of a group of terraced cottages, near the T-road junction of New Road Hill and the Ashdon–Bartlow road, and about forty yards from another village pump, where the womenfolk of Knox End and Roger's End would fill their pails with drinking water and gather to exchange gossip about the women who were filling their pails from the pump at Crown Hill. The pattern was the same for the 'Bricks'.

Cousin Ellen, two years my junior, daughter of my dead Aunt Harriet, was brought up next door by Granny Ford. If anything she was even prettier than her mother had been. Because I saw her almost every day I did not fully appreciate her beauty.

Her cheeks were soft and downy, like George Midson's sun-kissed peaches on Walton's walls. Two great braids of golden hair hung to her waist, with a ribbon bow on each to keep them plaited. Almost every day I would give them a good tug, the moment I caught her. She would yell and whine: 'Granny, that boy Ced's bin pullin' my hair ag'in. Fetch him one!'

If I was within range I would feel the sting of a damp dish-cloth.

Ellen's eyes were soft and kind but full of loneliness. Her speech had become a whining, unhappy thing, a liquid lamentation.

Except when she was with Dorothy Whistler, the daughter of Aunt Polly and Uncle Bert – the uncle who had been killed by German machine guns – she was unhappy and looked it.

Dorothy was Ellen's opposite. Raven black was her hair; her eyes like twin Aphrodites, radiating the fire of life; her voice clear and strong as springtime daylight. I never once pulled her hair; I could not catch this dancing will-o'-the-wisp.

Her reflexes were instantaneous, her agility and energy incredible. Although I tried often to catch her as she raced laughing from me to the Old Mill Cottage where she lived next to my friend Chris Ketteridge, she would be through the door, with a foot against it to keep me out, before I arrived panting, baffled and infuriated.

Ellen and Dorothy had two things in common. Each had lost a parent. Both were regarded as the finest shoppers and errand-runners in the hamlet. Almost every day of their holidays they would go from door to door, from cottage to cottage with baskets and note books.

'Want anything from the village?'

Orders would range from carbolic soap to collar-studs, to be purchased from one of two grocers. Chattering merrily away, comparing orders and making comments upon orders and orderers, they would set off down Ashdon Road on the mile walk to the village.

Vic Eason's shop stood at the village focal point, next door to the Rose and Crown Inn, not far from the village school, but still nearer to the village pump – where the village women would congregate with pail-laden yokes to pump out drinking water and gossip. At that time Eason's shop had a dual function because Eason was also the village postmaster, the sub-postmaster of a post office about three feet square situated at the window end of his Church End-side serving counter.

Bill Allgood, ex-regular soldier of the Suffolks, my father's old soldier comrade in India and other places, kept the smaller grocery near Ashdon Chapel, on the Radwinter road. He also kept Johnny Purkis, the defaulting church organ-blower, twenty-four cats and his wife – who gave piano lessons. With monotonous regularity Cousin Ellen would attend there for musical instruction. After three years she learned to play one melody, 'The Bluebells of Scotland', but to a Scottish ear her rendering would be a reminder of Culloden.

Both shops were the epitome of versatility – Eason's more so than Allgood's, for in Eason's were also to be had postal orders and postage stamps.

I think that I was the best customer on the post office side. Each night at five o'clock Freeman, the squire's butler, would hand to me a locked leathern satchel containing Major Luddington's outgoing mail, together with a blue linen bag with money and a list of items to be purchased, 'Careful, now, there's a tidy bit a money in that bag. Some o' them letters are for furrin parts and I ain't sure of the charge. Get Eason to check it an' write it all down!'

Sometimes I would walk to the post office. But if little Tommy the pony had not been pulling the roller that day and was not tired, I would go to Eason's on horseback, but without a saddle because I preferred to ride bare-back to be closer to my charger. On the way down New Road Hill I would put him into a canter, fancying myself to be one of the dragoons who were portrayed in Eason's shop in a picture I loved to look at. Between the Epsom Salts and the Lifebuoy soap it was – a representation of a cavalry soldier resplendent in scarlet tunic with facings of blue and gold. His eyes gleamed and challenged, his moustache was nearly as good as my father's. His buttons seemed like nuggets of the purest gold. On his proud head was a busby with a scarlet plume, fastened under his manly chin with links of glistening silver. 'Second to None' was written above it, and underneath, 'Smoke Greys'. He was a Dragoon of the Line, a Royal Scots Grey, and, despite my longings, I never thought that one day I would look like him. Nevertheless I continued to play a cavalry pretend-game when I rode little Tommy.

Eason's shop was a confusion of smells – nice smells of bacon, cheese, onions, oil, cinnamon, shag tobacco, soap, paraffin, vinegar – all blending to make an essence of richness but yet remaining separate. Shelves were packed with every-thing the village community usually needed – socks and shirts; girls' and women's dresses; pinafores, aprons, button-up boots, candles, lamps and clothes pegs; big jars of boiled sweets, humbugs, Pontefract cakes, sticks and straps of liquorice and liquorice tubes stuck into sherbet bags; clothes lines, bill-hooks, sickles and axe-heads; slabs of home-made toffee and boulders of coarse chocolate; scrubbing brushes, crockery and tin ware. If Eason had not got what was wanted, he would get it from Haverhill or Saffron Walden, always with a kindly smile and the greatest of courtesy.

Sometimes, on the way back to the hamlet, the girls would stop and check the contents of the shopping baskets against the orders, to put them in the right sequence for delivery. Once there was an accident. A jar of mincemeat fell to the road and the glass was broken, but held together by the viscosity of the contents. It was for Granny Ford. Ellen handed it over, blushing furiously.

'Sorry, Gran, it were an accident!'

'Accident! There's no such things. Accidents are excuses for bad happenin's. It's a happenin', 'cos you're clumsy, drattle yer hide, gel, be more careful!' Then, looking at the jar, 'Thank God! Half of it's whole!'

Albie Bassett had the shop I liked best. It was the saddler's. Standing at the bottom of Rectory Lane, on the main Ashdon–Saffron Walden road, it smelt beautifully of leather things. From hooks high to the ceiling hung spotless light-brown reins with fancy white stitches and gleaming brass buckles to attach them to the bits. There were head-collars, girths, surcingles, stirrup-leathers, stirrup-irons, bits, curb-chains, whole saddles of pliant skin and ornamental riding crops, beautiful to behold. On shelves were tins of saddle soap, dock-sponges, soap sponges, body-brushes, dandy-brushes, hoof-picks and curry combs. On lower shelves were jars, bottles and tins brimming with brown polishes and metal polishes; the browns ran from light tan to ox-blood and stood on bigger tins full of soft soap.

Albie's hands were highly skilled. He could stitch with his beeswaxed threads and needles of bristle as well as any house-maid. Short, slight, bespectacled and apologetic-looking, he was never at ease with humans, but show him a horse and he became inspired. He would take his hands from the pockets of his white apron, rub the heels of them on his backside and from nowhere would produce sugar lumps to feed to little Tommy.

'Ain't he a little beauty, now? ... Here, Tommy, here. Here's yer fives's. Carn't call 'em elevens's this time o' the day!'

One evening he made a mistake and slipped poor Tommy a lump of heel-ball. Ever afterwards Tommy looked at Albie with a shifty eye.

Apart from the butcher, baker, coal-merchant and cobbler, these were the only persons tending shops for these were all we had. There was not a tailor's, nor a proper shoe shop, but if the need was urgent and the sizes were known, Eason or Allgood would get the goods from the town. They would fetch them, and deliver them free of charge, with cheerfulness and courtesy.

Although scattered in area and sparsely populated our hamlet lacked little in the field of communication. Tradesmen called, tallymen, gipsies, tramps, wandering gardeners, itinerant musicians and flock-garnering parsons from distant parishes – not only at our cottage but at those more remote – to create diversions and scandals by their newsmongerings. Tales would be told of abortions, rapings, marryings and christenings, of arson, late drinkings, poachings and of sentences inflicted upon the deserving.

'She were up the gut, all right, so they towd me. But the owd mole-catcher put 'er t'roights with slippy willow, a tidy few gins arter a hot bath. She got rid on it, I were towd, an' young Sid were pretty glad. He knew it would be hissen – if it were born – but towd me he never took no precaution. Jest let hisself go to give 'im peace o' mind.'

170

'Glad they copped howd on him. Bin at it some time 'cos the owd farmer never took him on fer harvest. Set a-fire to two ricks an' the barn. He's safe now, they towd me. Carn't set fire to much in Chelmsford gaol, bor.'

'Deserved what he got. All right enuff to take a pheasant or two, but it don't call fer beatin' an owd gamekeeper senseless. Lucky he only got six months!'

'You will be glad to know, Mrs Mays, that the ladies of Linton are coming to see us next week. Do not tell anyone. It will be in the Parish Magazine.'

Most of this news concerned the activities of village characters, but spice was added by the fact that most of the news dispensers were the greatest 'characters' of all.

Eddie Miller lived in Ashdon with my Uncle Jasper Miller (then the Walton Park gamekeeper) and my Aunt Jane. He had left our hamlet before I arrived but from time to time he would return from his tailoring in London to become re-humanized. On one such return Eddie and my father were invited by Harry Hutchings, the farmer of Overhall Farm, to attend a pre-wedding party at Hadstock. By this time there was a second motor car in our village. It belonged to Harry Hutchings who would drive it to and from market at a great lick, drunk or sober.

After the celebration Harry went merrily to get out his car from where he had parked it – backed into a farmyard gateway with its rear wheels uncomfortably close to a ripe dunghill. But when he tried to move off, with Eddie and my father in the back seat, the wheels churned whirringly in

the stinking mire and that was the only discernible movement.

'Come on, John, bor. How abowt you an' owd Eddie givin'
a mite of a push?'

Conforming to Harry's request they pushed like mad.
Unfortunately, the gear was in reverse. The car chose that
moment to grip, shot backwards and pushed them smack into
the filth, white carnations and all. Harry then changed gear
and the car sped off to Ashdon, eight miles from Hadstock.
Half an hour later it pulled up outside our front gate. My
mother was in bed but wide awake and heard things; first, the
opening and slamming of a car door; then, from Harry
Hutchings . . . 'Goo'-noight, Eddie, bor; goo'-noight, John,
bor. Thanks fer the push!'

My mother then listened to the car going towards Overhall
Farm and was puzzled by the fact that not another sound
could be heard; not a whisper nor a footstep. 'I bet they've followed owd Harry on foot to get another drink,' thought my
mother and got up to investigate. There was no sign of life
anywhere. It was then half past midnight.

Three hours later she heard Eddie and my father walking
up the road. She went downstairs and taxed them about their
'disgustin' behaviour'.

'You've bin drinkin' in that owd market since ten this
mornin'. You stink worse'n a pig-sty an' you hed to go up
Overhall Farm to get more drink from poor owd Harry. Why
didn't you come in when he stopped?'

It took several days to sort things out. Mother could not

and would not believe that they had walked eight miles from Hadstock. They would not believe that Harry had stopped to let them out, reasoning that he could not have, because they were not in, and Harry would not believe that they had not been in his car when he stopped.

Walter Smith was the youngest son of the slightly mentally retarded roadman, Cribby, who was employed by the council and trimmed hedges and ditches bordering on public highways. Walter, like his father, was a bit unorthodox, to say the least. He once came early to our house in the hope of selling to my father his poaching rifle. John Mays took the gun, loaded it and drew a bead on a knot in our front fence. When he squeezed the trigger the slug fell about one foot below the point of aim. Father reloaded and took extra careful aim at the same target, with the same result. He handed back the gun to Walter . . .

'It's no good ter me, Walt, boy. The sights ain't true!'

'Ar!' said Walter. 'I knows all abowt they owd sights, John. That's why I be lettin' the gun goo cheap. I reckon it were my fault, John. I were a-tryin' ter shoot an' owd 'are on Bartlow Field. Now that owd hare were a helluver long way orf. I reckon I sprained they owd sights a-tryin' ter shoot too far!'

Charlie Petitt was one of the best at retailing the local news. Twice a week, on Mondays and Fridays, he could be scented before being seen. Charlie was six feet plus. Clad in frock coat and striped trousers, a greasy, greenish bowler, with a rose in his buttonhole, he purveyed paraffin and reeked of it. Charlie was liberal with his 'haspirates'.

'Hare yew hevin' hany hoil ter-day, Mrs Mays?' That was always his opening remark.

Our hamlet children loved him. He would talk to them all, tell them preposterous stories and – if their parents were not there to stop him – take them for pony-rides in his 'covered wagon' as he called it. This was jam-packed with paraffin, vats of vinegar, soaps (carbolic and Lifebuoy), grate polish, metal polish, blocks of brickdust and whiting, brooms, brushes and all manner of tinny household wares. And if children rode for ten minutes in the 'covered wagon' they would reek for weeks.

Cecil Chapman was renowned for rat-catching. We would go with him when the threshing-tackle was busy at farms. Like ships' rats, stack rats always try to leave a sinking stack as soon as they become aware of what is happening. We would take forked sticks to hold them down for the terriers, or to give them quietus with a steel-tipped heel of our clodhoppers.

Not so Cecil Chapman. With a big red hand he would snatch a rat from the rick, take it to his mouth and, with a quick snap of sharp incisors behind the rat's ears, he would sever the spinal vertebrae. With his killings there was never a squeak or a wriggle. And despite these unorthodox and un-hygienic activities, Cecil was never ill.

Joslin was a professional thatcher, an artist at the job. People would flock from miles to see and inspect his handicraft, on corn stacks and on cottages. Whether he thatched with straw or with reed the result would be the same – perfection! He was also, by impulse and belief, a hot-gospeller. Wherever he went, either to thatch or to preach, he would go by tricycle, wearing tail coat, pin-striped trousers, grey spats, starched wing-collar, cravat, tricycle clips and a mothy top hat. On the nearside handlebar, in a red handkerchief, he would carry his 'levenses; on the offside handlebar, his hot-gospelling handbell. With the latter he would summon the sinful to salvation. He would ride always in the middle of the road.

On the Saffron Walden–Cambridge road he was once hooted at by an irate chauffeur. Still hogging the road centre, Joslin pedalled on. Finally the chauffeur all but rammed him, but stopped instead. A dignified lady then emerged from the shiny limousine.

'I wish to get to Cambridge. Am I on the right road?'

'Hallelujah, sister!' said the irrepressible Joslin. 'God be praised! I'll put ye on two right roads. Cambridge fust! You jest foller me an' you'll be there in no time. That's where I'm a-headin' fer, God willin'!'

Cambridge was twelve miles from that point.

Martin Mash, a corruption of Marsh, hired out pony-traps and wagonettes on Sundays. Families would go off in them to visit relations in neighbouring villages. If in funds, one could hire a driver from him, but it was cheaper to 'self-drive'. Women would turn out in finery and furbelows, all mutton-chopped at sleeves, ruffly at neck and bustly of bottom – wearing be-flowered and be-feathered hats so large as to provide ample shade in sunny days for all the pony-trap's occupants.

Martin's ponies were on the slim side. When mother, father

and several children entrapped the girth would tighten alarmingly under the poor pony's belly, sometimes so tightly as to make him almost airborne between the shafts. Once on the move, however, after a bit of pushing down of the shafts by bystanders, the pony would be able to maintain contact with mother earth.

On such an occasion we were once embarrassed. My father decided upon a pony-trap trip to Great Thurlow, Suffolk, where my paternal grandparents lived.

To see a pony-trap on Sundays was a great event, and, as was the custom in most East Anglian villages, the youths of the parish would congregate at the village centre loudly to comment and criticize persons leaving the morning service. Unfortunately just as Thurlow's home-going congregation reached the critics, we drove past up the incline leading from the village centre. What with the rise in the ground and five of us in the trap, it seemed a bit too much for our poor pony who registered his displeasure by pushing out loud *flatus* blasts – so prolonged and machine-gunny that they lasted all the way up the rise.

My mother crimsoned with shame. My father looked stern and applied the whip. The rest of us thoroughly enjoyed it because laughter is infectious and quite a lot of it was coming from youths and church-leavers alike.

'Stop that silly nonsense,' said Mother. Then, to Father, 'Next time, get the wagonette!'

But it was always a great delight to ride through those pleasant country villages in spring and summer. No one ever tried to overtake. No one ever hooted or tried to drive us off the roads.

Uncle Will Ford, father of my cousin George Dry-bread Ford, had two nicknames: 'Owd Geezer' and 'Snobby Ford'. No one knows the significance of Geezer, but Snob was the local name for cobbler, which he was. He had not always been a cobbler. Gravely wounded in the Kaiser's War, he had narrowly escaped amputation of his legs. With my father's help, as secretary of the Comrades of War (forerunners of the British Legion), he had succeeded in getting vocational training as a cobbler and a very fine cobbler he was. Although he had great difficulty at first in holding his lasts between his crippled legs, and would go ashen-grey with pain at every early attempt, he persevered and triumphed. 'Geezer's Snob Shop' was one of the social meeting points. All the old men of the village and many young ones, too badly wounded to work, would try to pay him a daily visit. Some would help by hammering out the big chunks of leather he had soaking and softening in zinc baths. Others would hinder him by telling stories or by hiding his tools. Children would call at his shop after school, always asking the same question: 'Hello, Fordie, dear, what you got for dinner today?' Always he gave the same reply, making the most awful faces: 'Arf a brick an' no taters, me dear!' Although they heard it every day, they never wearied of it. But he did other things for children. Even when he had insufficient money to go to Saffron Walden to replenish his diminishing stocks of leather and rubber, he would still contrive to repair children's shoes – on the book, a book that was forgotten often by both parties.

Duggie Bateman and Sonny Pearson were the village butchers before Charlie Peploe took over their shop. Their speciality was pork sausage. There have never been before, and never will be again, such succulent sausages. Sonny was the comedian. When children went to his shop asking for a pound of sausages, he would put them on the spot: 'Pownds, m'dear! Pownds! I never sells sausages in pownds! Didn't your old mum says yards or miles?'

If the children appeared concerned at having misunder-stood their mothers, he would take them to the store where hung his masterpieces; chains and chains of them, looped over great steel hooks, all smelling of rich pork, not of soggy breadcrumbs.

'There they are, m'beauty, miles of 'em. We sells 'em by the mile in the towns; in rods, poles an' perches in the villages; but in yards to the hamlets. Come now, you jest weigh yourself a pownd, m'dear. I dunno how!'

Martin & Thompson, Bakers and Coal Merchants; these were the tradesmen who delivered bread and coal to almost every house in Ashdon by pony-cart and wagon. Hail, rain or snow, I never knew them let anyone down if they lacked food or fuel, as many did. The Martins founded the firm. Len Martin, the son, had the broadest Essex accent, a most kindly disposition and a great sense of humour. He was always con-cerned about the illnesses of his customers. He would take them to Dr Brown's Rose and Crown surgery on his bread cart, collect and deliver their medicines and make constant enquiries of the children about their parents' state of health. At one time my mother suffered two ailments, phlebitis and varicose veins. During that period Len met me at the gate.

'Hellow, Ced, bor, 'ow are ye? 'Ow's yer poor owd Mum, bor? She were lookin' suthin' chronic larst week. Takes it owter yer, that owd 'bitis. What with hevin' 'bitis, an' they owd various veins, she's got a tidy owd plateful. Roight, two quarterns an' a bag o' flour. Cheerio, Ced. Give yer owd Mum me best respex!' He married Marjorie Green, a dark-eyed beauty equally kind and considerate of others, and it was always a joy to see them together with so much love and understanding in their eyes.

Harold Thompson had been a railway clerk at Bartlow Station. When he teamed up with the Martins he became the coal-delivery expert, for most of the coal came to them from Bartlow Station. His accent was broader than Len's but it was not of Essex. Harold delivered bread later, baked by Drybread Ford, who also delivered coal. George was a practical joker of no mean consequence and one who put my Aunt Frances in her place before she married Baldy Rodwell, the estate gamekeeper.

Aunt Frances was my mother's eldest sister, and a very frosty one she was. Thin and sanctimonious, she looked as if she had been long pressed between the leaves of her Baptist Prayer Book. Her hair was as iron-grey as her fiercely penetrating eyes. For a time she worked at Walton's Park on some laundry job, at which she excelled. Possibly because no one had ever invited her to go 'bluebelling' in Langley Wood, Frances suffered from semi-submerged biological urges and took it out on tradesmen, her only callers. They were made the targets for her verbal darts of denunciation and abuse.

'Flour! It's stale an' yeller-lookin'. Orter be white. Take it back!'

'Well-baked crust? Cinders I call it. Take it back!'

Dry-bread Ford got his ticking off when he made a coal delivery.

'Call that coal? It's dust. It's allus dust. Take it back! Fetch me lumps, like you takes to they owd farmers!'

Dry-bread went to Bartlow Station coal-yard. With a borrowed pick-axe he whittled down a massive coal lump until it scaled exactly one hundredweight. Choosing a day when he knew Aunt Frances would be at Walton's, he made for her a special coal delivery. He lodged the great lump across the seat of Aunt Frances's little privy with the result that she had to lower her pride and ask permission to raise her skirts elsewhere.

It was about this time that Aunt Frances met Baldy Rodwell.

Henry Rodwell had been married before, was getting on in life and had a grown family of his own. He had not a hair on his face, and only one on his otherwise bald head, which earned him the nickname 'One Hair and a Nit'.

They courted in the leafy glades of Home Wood, but not unobserved. Each Sunday afternoon those children who did not attend Sunday school would visit Home Wood, trailing behind Henry and Frances and giving certain advice. 'Why don't you do somethin', then?' 'Why don't yew get married?'

Eventually, Henry Rodwell made his confession to my father.

'John, I've arsked fer the banns ter be called, nex' Sunday.'

Because Frances had not sampled Holy Matrimony before, and Henry had, my father persuaded old Henry to have a practice wedding in Granny Ford's bakehouse. Bunches of flowers were stuck in rafters, in the keelers (kneading troughs) and even in the twenty-four gallon copper. Two nieces, carrying flower bunches, acted as bridesmaids. My father put on a long white nightie, Mother's black sash, turned his starched collar back to front and went through the marriage service like an expert; so well, in fact, that Frances asked for a repeat performance, which was most merrily given after deep samplings of the seven-year elderberry wine.

Everyone in the village was extremely interested in the affair – a bit too much so for the liking of Frances, who asked permission of Mrs Luddington, whose brougham had been kindly loaned for the wedding, if, instead of driving through one part of the village, they could use the Carsey, the private road leading to Walton's Park from the Bartlow road. Permission was granted but my father had already thought up a counter-plan. He insisted on sitting with the coachman as footman, all togged up in borrowed livery and a top hat, and instead of going by the Carsey as Frances had wanted the coachman drove through part of the village. Not only that, but my father had fixed a spring bell to the back axle and tied to it a cord which he tugged regularly as they approached Holden End, thus bringing out the villagers in force. In the event, Frances was delighted. Never before had so many wished her good luck, waved to her, thrown her flowers and blown her kisses.

With eyes not fierce any more, but good and moist, she gave her opinion.

'It were the best weddin' I ever bin to!'

Bob Matthews was small in stature but his role in the village was big and indispensable, for at some time or another everyone would require his services. He could measure a pair of feet and cut out uppers to fit them first go from a bend of leather unaided by a machine and make a sturdy pair of boots complete with hobnailed soles and cut a pair of leather thong laces to go with them. Long before Uncle Will took on the job of village cobbler Bob was the only cobbler and shoemaker. He made boots by hand and his finished footwear was far from elegant, for it had been fashioned for sons of the soil who often had to stand deep in water. Bob's boots were watertight and lasted for three years. He made the waxed thread himself to stitch the stout uppers to the welts, for he had no machine. His cobbler's shop was the meeting place of the village lads, particularly in winter, and they were forever playing practical jokes on him. He could not afford to quarrel with them for they were potential customers. Sometimes they would lure him from the shop long enough to allow one of the lads to climb to the roof and place a slate over the top of his stove pipe, and poor Bob would be seen to emerge coughing away like a cab horse.

He did not always cobble, for he helped with harvest, with threshing the corn and was a member of the village fire brigade and a rat-catcher. The Rural District Council had launched a rat-killing campaign and paid one penny per tail for each rat caught. Bob took on the job of rat-tail agent in the village and would buy tails in bunches of a dozen. Being very near-sighted he often failed to detect odd bits of cord in the bunches, but he used to store them away in his ramshackle shed. The lads knew the hiding place, and often poor Bob bought back bundles of tails he had already paid for.

As a fireman Bob made an incongruous figure because his uniform and leather helmet were several sizes too large. He had to tilt his helmet well back on his head, otherwise he could not see. The fire engine was maintained by a retired army officer, Captain Reville, and was operated by a crew of four whose prompt attention on several occasions averted serious conflagrations pending the arrival of the Saffron Walden Brigade. Farm fires were frequent around Michaelmas time when rents were due, and there were often lurid glowings in the night sky when hay and corn stacks were fired. It is on record that on one occasion, when the four stalwart firemen of the Ashdon Brigade had already mounted their engine and were about to speed off at a slow trot to fight a fire, there came an anxious shout from old Bob.

'Whoa there!'

As he ran towards his home to repair an omission, he shouted out his reason.

'Howd hard fer a bit, I hain't got me bacca!'

Donald Petitt did not deserve the kick up the backside my father gave him one day. He was a love-child. Wuddy Smith and his Nellie had lived near us for years. Although Donald was not their child, they took him in, but subjected him to anything but kindness and when Nellie died my mother took pity. Rather than that orphan Donald should go to the work-house, she contrived to bring him up. A little mentally retarded, with a pronounced stammer, he was not notorious for wit . . . until the day of father's kick!

Castle Camps Fair was in full throttle, we could hear the roundabouts in the wind, and Donald wanted to go. My father had no money to give him, but to disguise that fact he said to Donald, 'There're better things to do in this world than go to owd fairs an' such. Only fools go to fairs!'

'I 'spect you'll be a-gooin' then!' said Donald, and provoked the uncalled-for kick.

Gipsies were always knocking at the doors of the district, selling clothes pegs, telling fortunes and scrounging clothing. They would tell extraordinary tales about their poverty and misery and would always carry bags to take away the vege-tables my mother would give to them. Other villagers would hand them old clothes which they either sold to rag merchants or to other families in our village. We first rumbled this when one of the boys Stone turned up in school wearing a cast-off from one of the Symondses.

Sometimes the gipsies would ask if they could use the privy, but in time we learned that this was an excuse for them to spy out the land to see if and where chickens were kept; and chickens used to disappear without trace of feathers left by foxes.

It was quite a common sight in those days to see twenty to thirty dirty tramps selling matches, bootlaces and worthless trinkets, dressed in several overcoats and jackets, carrying fire-blackened cocoa-tins in which they made tea. They would knock at doors and pester the daylights out of villagers until they were given morsels of food. 'I'm on me way to Linton Union (the workhouse) and I've had nary a bite o' food fer two days, lady!' And although we could ill afford it, my mother sometimes asked them in, gave them a meal and let them wash their filthy feet in the bakehouse. But she put a stop to it when she found out why more tramps called at our house than at others. It emerged that some of them carried a bit of chalk and would make a sign on our black fence which would indicate to the others that something useful could be got from us. Although the object of their hiking from Union to Union was to ensure for them a night's doss under a roof – in return for about two hours' work – most of them would not work and were nothing but mendicants.

Tallymen came several times a week from Saffron Walden and Haverhill. With wicker baskets full of clothes, they would let anxious mothers have clothing they could not afford on the instalment system, sometimes for as little as threepence a week. Most walked from village to village with great boxes strapped on their backs. Without knocking they would walk into cottages, usually by the back doors, and throw open their boxes to disclose shirt lengths of flannel, corduroy trousers, ribbons and scarves, fancy buttons, stockings and all kinds of dress material for the women. Once they were inside it was difficult to get them out again without making an unwanted purchase. Some sold crockery, dinner and tea services. Others had pudding basins, mixing basins, tin saucepans and kettles and cutlery, which were usually the objects for bargaining: 'How much will you offer fer this nice little lot, then?' and so on.

The Pig's Belly Man was always welcome. He would come round singing in his cart to sell tripe, pigs' trotters, pig's pluck, chitterlings and big basins of lard he had rendered down from pork fat and chitterlings. He wore a blue and white butcher's apron, with long knives and shiny steels stuck in his belt, and would sing out one of two songs. If he had only chitterlings, his song would be:

> Come owt, Nellies,
> See me bellies!

If he had pig's pluck as well, he would sing:

> Livers an' lights
> Are great delights;

Come on, Granna,
All fer a tanner!

In those days one could buy a whole pig's pluck for only six-pence. Liver, lights and crinkly fat to fry them with onions was a favourite dish and sometimes the chitterlings would also be put in the hot fat to make them deliciously golden brown. Most cottagers bought the pork dripping, for it was very tasty. Often it would have thick brown jelly at the bottom and was far cheaper than butter. My mother would buy pigs' trotters and a shin of beef if we were in funds and would make the most delicious brawn, all stiff, jellied and tasty.

Granny Ford was an expert on chitterlings. She used to clean them herself. The worst job was the first cleaning when all the muck had to be squeezed from yards and yards of pigs' intestines and the big 'granny cap'. She would then light the copper fire and boil twelve gallons of water. While it was boiling she would get to work and wash the dirty bellies three times in cold water. After that she would do her 'magic' as she called it. Holding one end of a few yards' length of pig pipe in one hand, she would open up an end and pour in from a jug about a pint of water. Then, quick as a flash, she would lift both hands in rapid succession then leave go one end ... A jet of pig-filth would shoot from it like water from a fireman's hose. She was doing this one day when Grandfather Ford happened to be walking to the back of his cottage unknown to his wife, and he received quite a spraying.

'Now then, Sue, I've growed enuff!' he growled. 'Why don't you squirt it on me taters?'

We had two blacksmiths, Clarky Cooper and Bill Smith. Bill was old, bent and part-crippled by rupture. Always in pain, his groanings and gruntings were frightening to hear, but he could shoe horses far quicker and better than Clarky who had his smithy in Chapel Road. We used often to go to Bill's forge in the school holidays, help him pump his squeaky bellows and watch the iron being transformed from a lifeless bluey-brown into white-hot splendour. Bill would puggle the hot iron about in the fire until he saw it was at just the right heat for hammering. With a quick flick of his tongs he could whip the glowing iron from fire to anvil and thunder away like Thor. Sparks would fly and dance, iron would ring on iron, and in next to no time there would be a great horseshoe, with only the holes to be punched in it for the nails.

'Wanna make friends with hosses, boy?' he asked me one day.

I nodded.

'Watch this, then.'

In the smithy stood a big Suffolk Punch.

Bill went to him and peeled a layer from one of the 'chestnuts' on its fores.

'Smell that, then!' He held it to my nose. 'What's it smell of, then?'

'Horses!' said I.

'Let me tell you summat. If ever you gets a bad hoss to handle, peel a bit orf one of his chestnuts, rub it on yer hands an' then rub it all over his muzzle. Keep a-talkin' to 'im, soft-like, an' you'll soon git round 'im!'

I have tried it often, and it works.

In repayment for our voluntary stints on his bellows, old Bill would make for us boys the most magnificent iron hoops and guiders. We had to make the wooden handles ourselves. Sometimes he would charge us sixpence, more often nothing at all; but he would also iron-runner our sledges for us in winter time although often doubled in pain.

Clarky was held up to us as an example of wickedness. More often in the Rose and Crown or the Fox Inn than in his smithy, he was the best swearer in Ashdon, and children were scared stiff at the sight of him.

Florrie Greygoose lived with and kept house for her uncle Ben Symonds. About three hundred yards from the Bonnett Inn, they lived in a red-brick cottage surrounded by their smallholding and magnificent orchards. Florrie and Ben were both stone deaf. Although they were unable to lip-read, and knew not the deaf and dumb alphabet, they could converse with each other fluently and with ease in low voices almost inaudible to those of normal hearing. But they could not understand anybody else. When talking to strangers they would shout at the top of their voices and gesticulate like fury, seeming exasperated at not being able to 'get through'.

In August and early September they were to be seen in their orchards and gardens throughout the day, pegging down the strawberry runners for layering the new growth; layering the tips of the loganberry canes; and – the best job of all in which we were often invited to help – gathering apples of all kinds. Russets, Golden Nobles, pippins; and later Blenheim Orange and the best pippin of all apples, Cox's Orange. After picking we would wrap them in paper ready for the market, or clean them ready for storing in the straw lofts. Then to the William pears, leaving some to ripen on the top branches – there is not a pear in all this world to beat a William that has ripened on its tree. We would also be there when plums, greengages, damsons black and damsons white, and purply, sultry sloes had to be picked for selling or bottling. In reward, when we helped, we would be given – instead of wages – all the fruit we could carry away. For we did not want silly old money wages; we were delighted with the more useful fruits of the earth. Poor Florrie! She withered to a wisp when old Ben died. She had no one to talk to any more.

George Goodwin had lived near Chapel Farm before coming to the hamlet. He was the classical 'Rural Man'. Outspoken, honest, fearing neither God nor man, he worked on the land and was a kindly, homely person and good neighbour. His vocabulary was strange but entertaining and became even more entertaining when he spoke about his wife Edie . . . particularly when poor Edie became indisposed.

'Hedie's hill. Hi got she some heggs, but Hedie were too hill to heat they heggs!'

Nicknamed 'General', Gordon Goodwin, George's cousin, lived near Place Farm. His wife Hilda was a most magnificent person with valuable human qualities but was a bit on the homely side. After General married her he invited Ron Fisher's attention to his good fortune.

'Ron, I got suthin' ter show yer. This is Hilda, my missus. I'm married now, bor. She ain't much to look at mebbe, but she's all MY!'

General had an excellent ear. On the blackest night, when not a thing could be seen, he could tell who was walking about. He knew everyone in the hamlet and most of Ashdon's villagers, by their footsteps. I have not met a happier and more genuine couple than General and Hilda.

Brother Leslie hit the character headlines while still at school. He read somewhere that Londoners were donating door-knockers, railings and steel for munitions and that others were being advised to follow their example by collecting iron and handing it over. Mother knew not a word about his patriotism until one Saturday morning – the day our shirts and surplices were ironed for the three or four shifts of church attendance. When she went to look for them, there was not a flat-iron, fire-poker, fire-shovel or even a boot-scraper to be found. And in some farmers' fields where had stood on headlands the ploughs and other agricultural implements, it soon emerged that rein-guides, plough-spuds and spare coulters and shears were missing. Leslie had taken them to the blacksmith who, totally unaware of Leslie's intention, was on the point of rendering them down in his furnace when the plot was discovered.

From 1914 to 1924 I gained vivid pictures of village life. Many of the villagers were characters, individualists. Frank, outspoken, fearless, but God fearing, they gave the village its vitality. Hardened by daily exposure to the elements, grinding work and the common poverty prevailing, they were rich in valuable human qualities. Humble but proud, skilled but ill rewarded, they aired their grievances in their only club – the village pubs – where they collected pennies and even half-pennies to buy clothing and coal for the needy; to raise a bit of good wind for the sick and for burials. They provided their own amusements. The social life of the village and its survival depended solely on their self-reliance.

Chapter 12

A Family Addition

The sleeping problem at Brick and Stone Villa had been increased ...

Late in July 1917 I became aware, by the obvious signs, that my mother was going to have another child. Worldly-wise by now I calculated that I should have a new brother or sister before Christmas.

Poddy Coote was not unaware of the circumstance.

'Wanna bet, Ced?'

'What about?' I asked.

'Bet yer a tanner your ole Mum'll drop that lump she's bin a-cuttin' the bread on afore a month is owt.'

I took him on and lost sixpence.

My father was then stationed with the Canadians at Knotty Ash Camp, Liverpool, for this was his final wound, and had applied for leave for the 'delivery'. He had got his inspiration a bit late in the day, for Jack – my new brother – was born on 4 August and my father did not arrive until the 6th. On the afternoon of his arrival the new voice could be heard wailing a protest. My mother's voice was scolding like mad and my father's apologizing. The reason was this . . . He had gone to sit in the bedroom to keep my mother company. Taking a mean advantage of her dozing off, he had decided to have a furtive smoke – a delight denied in her bedroom. But something had gone wrong with his pipe-lighting. A bit of hot tobacco had flown and alighted on the new baby's wrist. Hence the noises.

After silence, there was laughter. My father came downstairs grinning sheepishly.

'Go up an' take a look at your new brother!'

Mother laughed as she showed me.

On the left sleeve of un-christened Jack Aubrey's nightgown Father had sewn, at the appropriate height, one of his wound stripes. After that all was well and the bedroom smoking ban was lifted.

During her confinement my mother was attended by Liz Wright, the village midwife. District nurses had not yet come upon the scene, and this midwife, although not certified as such, had plenty of experience. For a few shillings she would be present at deliveries and would continue to attend mothers and to do odd jobs about the house until the mothers were fit again. These untrained women did marvellous jobs, but were not held in the high regard which was their due. In fact they were known as mole-catchers and body-snatchers, the last title being descriptive of their performances at laying-out the dead.

Our cottage changed overnight with Jack's arrival, turning into a world of small shirts, woollen boots, nighties and nappies by the score. Our shirts were changed but once a week, Jack's several times a day, and I became extremely upset by all the washing and laundering, mainly because I had to do most of it myself.

By now we knew almost everyone in all the Ends as well as those who lived in the village, but certainly not with the same intimacy that others insisted upon knowing us. Intended to be friendly, there would be what I considered undue intrusions upon our privacy. All kinds of people barged in through the back door with never a knock. I would watch their eyes roving over our few possessions. Though not ashamed of what we had, I was sensitive and would have preferred our poverty to be hidden.

I once looked up from a book to see in our living-room a Haverhill tallyman and the village grocer; neither had knocked.

'Why didn't you knock at the door?' I asked the grocer. He merely laughed.

'It's rude of you to ask such a question,' chided my mother.

'Not so rude as coming in without knocking,' I replied, just managing to dodge a clout.

'Children should sometimes be seen an' not heard,' she replied, finding the target on my left ear. And though I disliked answering my mother back, particularly in front of these intruders, I felt that my honour was at stake; that mine was a personal crusade against the evils of ignorance, inquisitiveness and discourtesy. I would not be silenced.

'Grocers should be heard before they are seen in THIS house,' I said angrily. 'He didn't come when we had no money!'

As I walked out to the garden to hide my anger, I heard my mother say: 'Don't take any notice. He's far too sensitive!' And then I thought that she was either on my side, or was putting on a bit of a front in case we got really poor again.

This fear proved right. Shortly afterwards Father's pay suddenly stopped. Someone in pay records thought he was dead. In fact he had been invalided out, and was in Addenbrooke's hospital in Cambridge. When the army at last remembered we got an unexpected windfall of all his back pay.

After the summer holiday of 1918 – during which I had been working at Walton's Park and Ashdon Place Farm – I returned to school, sun-tanned, invigorated and feeling almost a new man. I had also earned some money towards the cost of my new suit – a Norfolk jacket and short trousers. These were of inferior tweed but better far than Grandfather Ford's old cut-downs. Mother bought me a nice new shirt to go with it and I lashed out by spending a whole ninepence, in wild extravagance, upon an oval tin of greenish, smelly brilliantine. It took me a long time to get my hair brushed back from the front with no parting whatsoever because some of 'they owd

Cockneys' said this was the Pompadour, the fashion in London.

Mother did not approve: 'You'll drag it owt by the roots, that's what you'll do. If God intended hair to go back'ards instead of for'ards, He'd hev set it that way. An' you can stop that owd smokin'. You ain't old enough to smoke. I'll tell the policeman. If God intended fer you to smoke you'd hev a chimney-pot on your head, boy!' and so on.

But there was method in my seeming madness. I had begun to notice the girls. All at once they seemed to be pretty – some of them. Although I knew most of them by heart, every frock and ribbon, they all began to look different. I had not noticed before how pretty their hair was when the sun shone on it through the school windows; how delicate were their hands; how red their lips and shiny their eyes. A glimpse of the white flesh above their long black stockings dislocated my capacity for other forms of thought. I was generally discomposed and disturbed but knew that nature intended it because I was growing up.

Previously I had helped tug their pigtails and with the big boys had tormented them at the 'offices'. We had been in the habit of hopping over the black fence at the back of the boys' playground at playtime to pick nettles. Then, bobbing down low so that our heads could not be seen over the fence-top, we would creep to the lavatories, lift up the wooden hatches at the back where the cleaners used to pull out the buckets and tickle up the girls' bottoms with the stinging nettles.

It had seemed great fun to hear them yell. But all at once

I thought this a nasty and disgusting thing to do and I did not want to do it any more – the more so after having gone walking with Cilla.

This was just before the end of the summer holiday. We walked round the rookery, and went into its greenery to throw stones into the pond. We talked about nothing in particular but were both on the fidgety side.

'Come on, Cilla, let's walk to Home Wood,' I said at last.

'Whaffor? It's quiet enough here!'

Anyway, we walked about half a mile to Home Wood, she on the offside of the cart-track between the fields of Old Lay and New Lay, I well on the near-side separated by a good wagon's length. We didn't speak much on that walk but we kicked the seed-puffs off dandelions and decapitated buttercups. The sun was shining into the big glade. We lay on a mattress of pine-needles, a century soft, chewing grass, making small talk. The heat of the earth seemed to penetrate my being, telling me what to do ... no, imploring, commanding, because she was so close. I knew what was required. She was laughing, hot, heavy and greedy-looking. She puffed up bits of red-brown hair by blowing against her protruding bottom lip. I watched the wisp fall over her eyes. I was tortured, tormented, ashamed. All kinds of things came into my mind – bits from the Bible as when they stoned the woman for giving herself; snatches from the Commandments, including 'Honour thy father and thy mother' ... 'Thou shalt not commit adultery' ... 'Thou shalt not covet thy neighbour's wife, nor his ...' And then I thought, Cilla is not anybody's wife, at least not by marriage, for I had heard the tales about her in school.

At this point she took my hand in her hot hand, squeezed it, looked me straight in the eyes . . .

'Well, we're here then!'

I believe I gulped.

'What are you a-lookin' like that for, then? Are ye frit? Doan't you worry, bor. I dunnit afore!'

I was eleven.

Chapter 13

Armistice Day

The communal and social life of our hamlet were characterized by our close connection with the earth. Most of the village and hamlet events, like the Horkey, centred round the produce of the earth, and swarms of villagers would go off together for fruit and vegetable shows, fêtes and galas, to other villages. There were however local events of worth.

'Get your pillow cases, we're goin' nuttin'!'

Langley Wood's nut-hazel leaves had mellowed from green to gold. Husks had grown to a brown brittleness; so loose was their hold upon the ripened fruit that the wind of one whirring wing of a nuthatch would send them falling to the thick undergrowth, to be lost for ever. If our hamlet's nutters were not soon off their marks they would be nutless for Christmas.

Nutting Sunday was the day when all would go off together, but would split into family groups at the wood so that each could pick their own drives; so that there would be equal chances for all. It had to be Sunday, the only day when the menfolk were not working on the land.

With us we took crooked sticks and forked sticks; pillow cases for nuts and baskets for blackberries. Off would come the jackets and on would go the scarves and kerchiefs to protect hair and eyes from falling husks and dead wood. At each shrub one vigorous shake would bring down into waiting open aprons a cascade of nuts, later to be stored on straw for Christmas.

At Easter there would be similar excursions – but without the menfolk – to gather palms, pussy-willows and, later, blue-bells. Children would go in droves for bluebells and would emerge from the woods, their little arms laden with the glorious blue blooms. Sometimes a few pairs of adolescents would accompany them. The age and antics of these would betray themselves the moment they left the wood, for they carried not a bluebell.

Throughout the Saturdays of summer the cricketers would be in action. Park Mede, the meadow opposite Walton's Park, was given to the local club; rollers were loaned when required, together with horse-drawn mowers to keep trim the pitch and outfield. Some of the regulars boasted white flannels but the majority turned out in rubber-soled shoes, ordinary trousers, coloured flannel shirts and braces. Except for haytime and harvest there would be practice, without nets, two or three nights a week. The most attractive feature of the Saturday matches against neighbouring villages was – for me – the scoring; for, including the bowling analysis, the results for each over were carefully notched with shut-knives upon hazel or willow sticks. This was a great day for the old men of the village, who would cluster in senile groups and tell impossible stories of their achievements with the ball and the willow . . . 'when we was young 'n' agile, bor'.

'I remembers owd Starchy's relation . . . Slogger Williams they called him. Larst toime I see he play he knocked three rooks' nests clean owter they owd elms. He could bowl better'n Jimmy Furze . . . Knocked one set o' stumps a-flyin' so far they never did find 'em.'

Football was also played on Saturdays throughout the season with villagers nearby, but these games were sparsely supported compared with the cricket matches – until the evenings. Then all would gather at favourite pubs, to wet the whistle and to praise or console according to the result.

Captain Reville and my father were mainly responsible for the first troop of the Ashdon Boy Scouts. After his discharge from the army my father threw himself into every possible spare-time activity, including signalling and physical training instructor to the Boy Scouts. He also instructed Miss Elizabeth and Miss Drusilla in physical training.

But he did not stop at instruction and he made himself a great deal of extra work. As the troop had no funds, he made and stitched the blue and white signalling flags, cut their poles from the hedges, then, having supplied the flags, set about training boys to use them very well for morse and semaphore signalling.

Very soon there could be seen on the fields and meadows the newly trained signallers, flags always in hand, but sometimes only arms for semaphore, signalling like mad to brothers and school friends on distant fields; transmitting messages of great import, such as: 'When is Father coming home?' ... 'Tell him not to forget choir practice' ... 'Go for Dr Brown, Mother is ill.' 'Meet Bill Chapman tonight Three Hills eight o'clock.'

Although this had advantages in a village lacking in communication, it was not appreciated by some, and was even suspect.

'Oi reckon they've gorn stark, starin' mad, bor. Trampin' abowt the fields an' medders, a-flappin' owd rags abowt loike a lot o' bloody bird-scarers. Tellin' tales, too!' So said Wuddy Smith.

Mabel Eason did her best to start dancing classes at the Conservative Hall. The first night was disastrous – for the polished floor. Most of the lads turned up in hobnails. Leslie and I were not there on the opening night but the second week we turned up in hobnails and corduroys. Having learned her lesson, Mabel would not allow us on the floor.

'You can stay and watch, and learn,' said Mabel, 'but for goodness' sake hide yourselves behind that curtain.'

We did and had a whale of a time tripping up the others as they tripped past us. We were sent home in disgrace and never went again. We could not afford dancing pumps.

Now and again people would invade our village to give magic lantern shows in Ashdon Chapel. Occasionally there would be whist drives, concerts and sing-songs, due in the main to the sterling efforts of the Women's Institute and the Mothers' Union.

From time to time throughout the months of summer our highways and byways would be gay and alive with the mass migration of families flocking off to fêtes, galas and flower shows by pony-carts, wagonettes and broughams. All the womenfolk and children would be in Sunday best – whips beribboned, girls beribboned, horses, donkeys and ponies bristling with rosettes and flowers. There would be tapestries of flowers being taken for the judging. Beautifully arranged in delicate floral baskets, they embellished the wagonettes, flaunted their colours and perfume, and made our world gay indeed. Much work would have been done before the migration. However poor the people they could grow flowers, cut and pack sandwiches and fill useful sized bottles with the good wine they had made from their pickings and gleanings.

Anxious looks would be cast to the skies; prayers would be prayed for fine weather; and titbits would be taken for the horses, to inspire them to great effort, and juicy carrots for the donkeys.

At the fête or gala the pattern would be much the same. But the fête for all time, Ashdon's own, was on the first celebration of the Armistice.

This was a day for real rejoicing. The senseless slaughtering had been stopped. Park Mede had been handed over to the villagers lock, stock and barrel, to do with it what they wished. My father who had been home some time would have liked to have been there, but his wounds were playing him up and he was too ill. But at last he had received his back pay. When he wrote to the paymaster to prove that he was poor but alive, there had been complications. Letters came to say he would have to return to Canada to be demobilized. He had refused; until somebody in London agreed that he could be demobilized in England. Lots of money came then. We had trips to London and to Cambridge and were all rigged out from top to bottom and looked very smart. Some of the villagers did not approve of our new splendour and said unkind things, like 'starve yer belly ter clothe yer back'. But we did not worry much about that. Our Dandy was home with us. The war was over and he would not leave us again.

I would have liked Bert Whistler to have been there, my favourite uncle, but he lay quiet in Flanders, full of German machine-gun bullets. Many of my schoolboy friends were worse off, their fathers having been killed.

But Park Mede was gay that day and dressed overall. Allied flags flew from the tall tops of great marquees. Fat brewers trundled beer barrels into bell tents. Hokey-pokey and hot pie stalls sprang up like mushrooms. Two bands played all day and half the night – at the same time and with different tunes; but 'Land of Hope and Glory' did not get so high in the 1919 top ten as 'Pack Up Your Troubles'.

Yes, Park Mede was gay and it was there we saw a remarkable

transformation. All the old men of the village seemed to have turned young overnight; we had only old men left … men so worried by war and deprivation that until that day they had forgotten much about laughter and happiness.

Every device was used to provoke human laughter. Perhaps the organizers knew there would be many there who would have little to laugh about for years to come. Many sons had been reported missing and in the *Saffron Walden Weekly News* there was about to be published a mammoth casualty list.

But this was a day for celebration. Although the fighting had finished in Flanders the finest fights were just starting when I arrived at Park Mede.

Old men were bashing the living daylights out of each other in a comic boxing ring. Half were dressed in white tights, half in black – white versus black. Although there was not much of that health-giving commodity about at that time, the boxing gloves of the 'whites' – white linen bags – were filled with flour and those of the 'blacks' with soot, presumably from ancient fires, for it had been some time since Ashdon's chimneys belched out coal smoke.

The old boys pummelled away at each other in clouds of black and white until our bellies were sore with laughter. Older men also raced each other, in wheelbarrows, sacks, under tarpaulins, through blazing paper hoops. Some played in comic cricket matches, all in fancy dress; some took part in comic football games; and others tried to lift a heavy rope to take part in a tug-o'-war.

Clowns abounded. Two comic curates came in handy to help little children run short races; suffering from malnutrition and rickets, they were too weak for the 100-yards.

By mid-afternoon almost everybody over twelve was good and sloshed on Greene, King's strong ale. We then tucked into plates of beef and pork; wolfed down mountains of sandwiches; crammed our bellies with cockles and mussels and asked for more. Children danced round maypoles festooned with ribbons and flowers. Village maidens danced till they dropped. Village youths ran races, danced, sang with the bands and made open unashamed love to maidens. This went on until it was dusk, then up shot the fireworks. The resulting oohs and ahs could be heard for miles.

But the highlight of the celebration had yet to come, and perhaps because it had not been subjected to the formalities of organization it turned out to be the best.

Old Thatcher Joslin made the day.

As usual, he wore his frock coat, pin-striped trousers, wing-collar, cravat and spats. He had on his top hat and had ridden to Park Mede on his tricycle, carrying as always his hot-gospelling handbell.

But for the first time in his blameless, abstemious life, Joslin had knocked back a couple of quarts of strong ale . . . 'I'm jest a-takin' wine ter celebrate the arse-end o' this wicked owd war, my brethren!'

Later, under the trees by Park Mede entrance, he tried to sleep it off. After dimmit light, when all the birds had gone to bed and the sun had long gone down, he wakened – to see in the sky a blinding white light. Scared out of his wits, bemused by his drinking, he leapt on his tricycle and pedalled furiously around the neighbouring Ends, ringing his hot-gospelling handbell.

'Come out, dear brothers an' sisters,' he was shouting, 'this is the end of the world; Retribution has copped us; come you on out an' be saved!'

Like most religious fanatics, old Joslin had got himself steamed up unduly. That blinding glare in the night sky was not connected with the fire and brimstone we deserved. Ashdon had got itself lit up deliberately with the aid of a government surplus naval flare; so brightly, indeed, that Chris Ketteridge was able to read his Pelmanism book in our old mill a good mile away from the fire.

Quimm Walls, a farmhand who walked as though permanently poised on stilts, was also scared out of his East Anglian wits. He glared at the sky and trembled . . .

'It's that owd Kaiser, ag'in. The owd sod's started up ag'in. He's a-sendin' they owd Gothy airplanes an' Zeppelins ag'in. Tha's what it is. I can see 'em, comin' over in swarms an' swarms, loike bloody gr't 'ornets. I'm a-gooin' ter grownd, me owd matey, gooin' t'grownd!'

And to ground he did go, in a field of mangold wurzels.

The Peace celebration was our villagers' chief topic for long afterwards. As Toe-Rag described it, 'I reckon Peace celebration were a day an' a half!' But our villagers remembered the tragedy as well as the comedy. In the practical manner of men of the soil, they dug gardens and allotments for war widows and for the blinded and maimed who would never again put tine of fork into the soil they loved.

There would have been far fewer callers at our cottage when the war was over if my father had not become secretary of the Comrades of War. Night after winter night we would all sit in the one room listening to conversation between wounded ex-soldiers and my father. Usually they would come to give him particulars so that he might try to get them pensions.

Bunk Thake came one night. Pasty-faced and flabby through long hospital attendances, he pleaded with my father: 'Do yer best ter help me, John, bor. I'm proper lonely an' bloody miserable inter the bargain.'

'I'll do me best, Bunk, lad. Let's hev your particulars!'

'I'd loike one like your'n, John; not one loike owd Captain Lucas!'

'But Captain Lucas don't get a pension and mine ain't up ter much,' replied my father.

'Ar, I ain't a-talkin' abowt owd pensions, John,' replied Bunk. 'I'm a-talkin' abowt 'taches. Ye see, John bor, I wanna gel or a woman ... Everybody in the village who's got a 'tache has a gel. 'Cos I'm clean-shaved an' carn't grow whiskers, I thought yew might give me an idea on how ter start. I want one like your'n – a big un – not one like owd Lucas!'

My father did have a nice big moustache and he had a lot of humour lurking behind it. Bunk was instructed to 'take a letter' to Captain Lucas, who lived at Tenpots, near Whitten's Mere Farm. No one ever knew what my father wrote to

Captain Lucas. But later in that week Bunk attended several Saffron Walden fishmongers trying to buy cods' heads. It emerged that Lucas had told him that the only way to grow a ''tache' like John Mays' was to go on a special diet – to eat nothing for two weeks but the heads of codfish and raspberry jam.

Chapter 14

A Sting in the Tale

If Wixie Barrett had not got wasp-stung I should know less about wasps and bees.

The tiniest man in Ashdon, Wixie – sometimes called Crixie, but his name was Arthur – had the biggest cap, tightest choker, ballooniest shirt, and braces so wide as to look like horse harness. He also smoked the dirtiest pipe; so short was the stem that the rank smoke of the plug tobacco in the pipe's bowl went up his skinny nose to make him coughy and spluttery. Too tiny to work on the land and also too weak on account of his war wounds – everybody was strong enough and big enough for wars – Wixie worked for the council but only when the weather was fine and dry. Succoured and shielded by Cribby Smith, the parish roadman, he would arrive in late spring or early summer pushing a council hand-cart packed with tools – brooms, shovels, rakes, hoes, edge-trimmers, sickles and bill-hooks.

'Oi've come ter give the owd hamlet its spring-cleanin', m'dearie, a short back 'n' sides!'

They had come in fact to trim verges, ditches and hedges owned by the parish – those bounding the highways and byways – and to collect horse-dung from the roads. There was a lot of it to be seen in those graceful days. If we were not sufficiently alert to nip out swiftly with the fire shovel, to get some good stuff for Father's allotment and Mother's flower beds, Wixie would swipe the lot to swop for hens' eggs.

There was always horse-dung near Sparks's, where the stream ran over the road and horses stopped to drink, the more so as Ashdon Place Farm had now twelve great horses, Clydesdales and Suffolk Punches. After their hard work in the fields they would be put out to grass in the meadow behind our cottage.

What a wonderful sight it was! Like the charge of the heavy brigade they volleyed and thundered from stables to meadow, without guide, leader or drover, for they knew where the sweetest grass was to be found. When they had rested my father would take sister Poppy to open the gate of the meadow for them to charge back to the farm for their more substantial meal of good oats, chaff and linseed cake. They would tear back down the road to their horse-stalls, manes and tails a-flying, filling the air with whinnies, farts and kicks, spraying out dung faster than old Wuddy with his four-tined fork. Poppy loved to watch them. There would be lots of dung.

Anyway, Wixie came one day to our back door.

'Look at me, Mrs Mays. See what they've done!'

Already his eyes were closing.

'Sit you down, Wixie. What were it, bees or wasps?'

'Feels like bloody 'ornets, missus. Two on 'em can kill a hoss!'

My mother bathed his face with her special herb lotion and rubbed out a few stings – wasp stings!

'Glass o' dandelion, Wixie?'

'Sooner hev a quart o' paraffin an' burn the bastards.'

'Wixie! Your language!'

'Sorry; jest a drop, then. Thankee, Liz.'

'Thass all right.'

'See the boys hev took all the droppin's ag'in. Damn good mind not to show 'em the wasps' nest. Put me hook straight in it, an' they fair flew at me.'

'Where is it, then?'

'Opposite the tap, bit low in the bank. You tell 'em.'

I knew about bees but not about wasps.

After I had annoyed butler Freeman by chopping up his bee-hives for kindling he had partly got his revenge by teaching me about their inmates. There are many species, all very confusing at first, but he kept me at it by asking questions.

'How many kinds o' bumbles, boy?'

'Scores.'

'Right! Name three an' describe 'em.'

'Er, bumble white; jet black; yellow collar; yellow belt; white tail. Er, bumble hot-arse, all black except for his behind

213

an' that's red! Er, bumble yellow, all yellow 'cept for his black belt.'

'Right! What colour's a field bee?'

'Field bee? Black belly, two yellow belts near his tail, orange thorax.'

'Right! Wood bee?'

'Wood bee, er, yellow body, two black belts round thorax, red arse!'

'Thasser 'nough o' that. Jest say red "tail" not red "arse".'

'But you towd me . . .'

'It were only to get it in yer mind. No need to keep harpin' on it.'

So it would go on, all very instructive and useful. But Leslie had the edge on me about wasps.

I should explain that among the many callers at our hamlet cottages was the tinker. With a funny cart full of tools and a grindstone – the cart painted in all colours and weird designs like gipsies paint their caravans – he would shatter the hamlet stillness with his cries of 'Kittles ter mend. Kittles ter mend. Knives ter grind an' kittles ter mend!'

There was a treadle low down between the cart handles which turned the wheel attached to the grindstone's spindle with a leather strap. When he pumped away at it with his cunning foot a stream of sparks used to shoot off scissors and knives like fireworks. We were surprised that they did not burn us when we put our hands into the flow of the sparks to try to catch a bit of fire. When we looked at our hands we had caught nothing. Sometimes he would let us have a go at making sparks with odd bits of steel from his trays and we would treadle away like fury to make life sparkier. He had funny hammers which beat out the dints in saucepans and frying pans, but he would always ask to come inside to poke his soldering irons in our fire. When they were hot enough he would rub them in a tin of flux, making lots of splutters, then 'tin' them with long sticks of shiny solder. In next to no time he would mend holes in kettles and saucepans and stick brand new spouts on tin kettles.

Once he cured me of my sore finger. I had a whitlow and from the middle joint of my finger to its tip there was a swollen yellowness of pus.

'What ee got wrong with that owd finger, boy?' he asked.

Because I was the only one in Ashdon with a whitlow, I was only too pleased to show him and took off my fingerstall.

'I'll soon cure ee o' that. Come wi' me, boy!'

He went to our living-room and stuck a small soldering iron in the fire, this time letting it get red-hot. He then grabbed me by the hand and pulled me outside. Next to our iron door-scraper he bored a hole in the ground, about two inches deep, with the hot iron and left it there for a moment. When he pulled it out he put my finger in that hot hole. It hurt me a lot at the time. But next day all the pus had gone and the finger healed in no time.

'Owd Tinkery', as our hamlet knew him, had wasp-indoctrinated Leslie by word and practical demonstration in the course of one day. Leslie had accompanied him round the village, collecting knives and scissors to grind; in return he was taught about wasps.

Later, Leslie passed it on to anyone who would listen.

'Wasps like sweet things more than bees. Bees only take nectar from the flowers to make honey. Wasps eat all sweet things themselves. That's why they pinch our jam even when we're eatin' it.

'Wasps are busier'n bees an' ants. They dig an' build. They can make paper, better'n humans.

'Queen wasps start nests by stealin' owd burrows. They chew it till it's big enough to make a nest in – outer their own paper.

'Wasp workers chew bits of rotten owd wood into pulp ter make paper.

'If you listen, you can hear 'em chewin' the wood. But don't listen close or you'll get stung.

'Tinkery showed me. He made a fire, put sulphur on it and made the smoke all yeller. He blew the smoke in the wasps' nest through a paper. All the wasps got drunk an' couldn't fly. But they still chewed, we could hear 'em.

'Then Tinkery dug the nest-hole. We could see the nest. It was hangin' on a chain thing, all made of paper an' upside down, like a William pear.

'We could see all the baby wasps in their cells, all hangin' upside down waitin' till they growed enough to fly.

'Wasps are miracles. Wasps are better'n owd bees an' ants!'

'I'm fair sick of owd wasps,' interrupted my mother. 'When you're at the table you open your mouth to eat, NOT to talk about owd wasps. Eat your dinner an' keep quiet, boy!'

So it was that Leslie was delighted the day Wixie got stung.

'Where was it, Mummy? Did you say opposite the tap? Come on, Ced, we'll get ready.'

We got ready, with bits of butter muslin over heads, caps on to keep it in place, long stockings pulled up and tied over bottoms of short trouser-legs, old socks on hands, jersey cuffs tucked in old socks. We then collected our wasp-hunting gear – one spade, one forked stick, one sack, Mother's wooden spoon, sheets of newspaper, box of matches and matchbox with sulphur. Armed, we raced to 'opposite the tap, low down'.

But somebody had beaten us to it. A few singed wasps lay dead at the burrow entrance. The burrow bore recent spade marks. Ears close to the burrow we listened. Not a buzz!

'I reckon owd Wixie dug the nest owt an' fired it ter spite us,' said Leslie. 'He were proper riled 'cos we took the horse shit.'

And thus it was.

To save faces and the day, we borrowed a ferret, slipped it into an adjacent burrow and instead of a wasps' nest we took back to Mother a rabbit. She was delighted.

Well loved in the village and the hamlet as a mild-mannered little man, it was often said of Wixie Barrett that he would not hurt a worm, and that was literally true. To compensate for his legacy from the war – chronic arthritis – he was possessed of a pungent, ready wit and a boundless humour which buoyed him up and made him bear his affliction with apparent cheeriness.

Throughout his periods of unemployment he would take

long walks to the village Ends and to our hamlet. Invariably he carried his hazel cane and claimed it had the property of divining beer with greater speed and accuracy than the wand of a dowser could divine water. Once or twice a week he would walk towards the Bonnett. When he approached the bend which led *away* from the pub he pretended he was doing his best to avoid temptation. But before he rounded Reuben's Corner his hazel stick would whip smartly round and point at the Bonnett. It would appear to be quivering and twitching like fury – dragging little Wixie with it against his will. He would put on an act of trying to resist; not to be drawn into the pub; but always the quivery stick drew him up the steep path and smack into the middle of the taproom.

'Now, would you believe it!' he would say in apparent seriousness. 'This owd stick won't let me pass this corner durin' openin' time. Look at it now. Quiet as a little lamb!' Smiling his twisted smile he would put the stick on the old settle and sit down beside it. 'Well, I s'pose I might jest as well hev a pint, now I'm here!'

Wixie's resignation to the power of his stick often won him free beer, but that was not his object. He loved to be in the Bonnett with some of its characters, none of whom ever begrudged a sixpence on Wixie's account, whether he entertained or not.

Toe-Rag Smith was one of the few who continued the old Essex craft of straw plaiting. This had once been a booming industry; started in 1790 and continuing successfully for some years, it eventually declined into a cottage industry. There had been 'plaiting schools', and in some north Essex day-schools children had been taught the craft and had earned a few pennies a week. Most of the old horse-keepers knew something of it, and used to plait odd designs and cottage loaves for sale.

Toe-Rag plaited for love, not for money. Upon the occasions of fêtes and fairs his handicraft was to be seen at its best in the manes and tails of his beloved horses. Combed and brushed until they gleamed like fine silk, manes and tails would have woven and intertwined into them cunning and attractive braids of golden straw, offset by rosettes of red, white and blue ribbons. His horses knew they were 'decorated' and would pick up their great forefeet and billowing fetlocks with more than usual majesty.

Sometimes Toe-Rag would plait the horse-manes in 'fine-plaiting'. This was a most delicate operation which involved the use of a bone knife for splitting the straws – one requiring great skill and patience. George had both. For the harvest-home supper he would take great pains in plaiting loaves of bread as table decoration. These were things of beauty to behold, in the delicate 'split-plait' process. His loaves were always of the cottage variety, for it was considered unlucky to plait bread in other shapes.

Like most north Essex folk, George was highly superstitious, and took great care to avoid breaking rules or laws likely to lead to misfortune. He would never walk under a ladder. If he saw blades of knives, sickles or anything inadvertently crossed, he would flinch and quickly uncross them.

There was no end to the prohibitions we learned as young-sters.

Never open an umbrella indoors. Never take indoors May blossom, lilac or snowdrops. Never cross on the stairs. Never look at the new moon through glass. Never eat with a knife during thunderstorms. Never help anyone to salt:

> Help you to salt, help you to sorrow.

Never should dropped pins be disregarded:

> See a pin and pick it up,
> And all the day you'll have good luck.
>
> See a pin and let it lie,
> Before the evening you will cry.

If salt is spilled, take a pinch with the left hand and throw it over the right shoulder. Do not look where it fell. In this last connexion, Cribby Smith somewhat disconcerted Toe-Rag and my father one night. They were sitting on either side of him at a harvest supper. Intending to be helpful, if not good-mannered, Cribby took a couple of good pinches of salt and began to sprinkle them on his friends' food.

'Where d'yer want it, then? On yer taters?' he asked cheer-fully, heaving the balance over his shoulder on folks behind.

We stuffed our heads with many other superstitions: young brides should never marry in green; there was no specified colour prohibition for old brides. Black cats were always lucky, and chimney sweeps; bent oat straw was not. Mirrors, pictures and photographs should be turned face to the wall during thunderstorms. Never sit beneath an oak during a thunderstorm. Never count between lightning's flash and thunder's peal to determine if the storm is arriving or departing. Never put shoes or boots on the table. Never run to church or chapel; people will think the Devil's chasing. New clothes should be worn first on Sunday, preferably in church; if not, sack-cloth and sorrow were likely to follow.

A dropped table fork indicated an early visitation by a female; a dropped table knife, the visit of a male; a dropped teaspoon the arrival of a letter; a dropped tablespoon, a parcel; bubbles in the tea-cup, the visit of a stranger. Ladies' gloves should never be retrieved by the ladies who dropped them. Crossed lacing of boots or shoes heralded disaster.

If a robin rested on the window sill he was the harbinger of bad tidings. If he flew indoors there would be a hard winter. Rooks' and crows' nests high in trees indicated a hot summer. A profusion of holly berries meant a hard winter. A falling picture heralded the death of a near relative. Two tea-leaves afloat in one cup meant travel. Broken in its flight, or upon contact with the frying pan, a tossed pancake spelt broken romance. Children so misguided as to pick the flower of the dandelion would be bed-wetters throughout adolescence. Family letters with bad tidings should always be read to the bees, preferably those in hives, otherwise misfortune would continue. If one failed to wear oak leaves on Oak Apple Day it was necessary to be prepared for the worst. Children were expected to sting non-wearers of oak leaves with stinging nettles. If one saw a new moon – but certainly not through glass – one should turn over one's money.

Cures, too, were passed from parents to children.

Warts could be wished away if the owner had faith in the wisher. Warts could be purchased away: 'I'll give ye a tanner forrit, then it's MY. Don't think about it till it's gone. Then you gits yer tanner back.'

Wuddy Smith had a panacea for the common cold.

'This is how yer gits rid onnit. Fust, cop howd of an orn'ary house-brick – a new 'un. Take it upstairs. Set it on the floor by the bed on the side you sleep. Fill the frog (the hollow for mortar) with spring water. Go to bed. When you starts coughin' and caggin' (spitting) lean down an' howd yer head still over the top o' the water. Then, when the cowd goos down to drink, bugger orf an' leave it … Haw, haw, haw!'

Warts could also be cured by the application of the white of a duck egg; gout, by gargling with carrot juice; sore throats, by wearing a sweaty sock round the neck; piles, by carrying bits of pile wort in pockets; nettle stings, by applying sorrel and dock leaves; sweaty feet, by dusting with Fuller's Earth.

There were odd odes of ominous warning:

> Three swallows make a spring.
> Two don't.

Rooks flyin' high, sun in the sky;
Rooks flyin' low – fer your coat go.

Red sky at night, shepherd's delight;
Red sky at morning, that be a warnin'.

Marry in haste, repent you at leisure;
Years spent to pay, for one minute's pleasure.

It was a miracle that we survived.

There were old men living in Ashdon – and some who were still talked about although they were dead and buried before I was born.

I knew of Dusty Searle, who always referred to his cottage home as the Wukus (workhouse). Long before he had gone to live there that little cluster of buildings behind All Saints–Ashdon parish church – had been administered by the Guildhall Charities as a kind of Poor Law institution. Dusty thought that his name was good enough for such places.

He was a very old man with a great wit and a most endearing personality, and he had been the parish roadman long before Cribby Smith took the job. As a result of his continual stooping to his work he had become so bent as to resemble a human question mark. When he was fully upright his pointed ginger beard was less than a foot from the ground. Forthright in speech and manner he had invented nicknames for all his neighbours. One near neighbour, a very sickly man, he called the Owd Butterfly, because he only ventured forth when the sun shone. A little dumpy woman across the yard he christened the Train, because of her constant shuntings and trips from cottage to cottage to gossip. He was kindness itself to visitors.

'Sit ye down there!' His command brooked no denying, and he would amble off to his diminutive scullery from where there would soon come a clattering of jugs and the gurgling of liquid from a tap. The bent old form would reappear holding carefully at head height – about three feet from the floor – a jug of home made wine.

'Set ye still!' he would admonish if any help was offered. He would open a low cupboard from which he took a glass of crystal clearness and cleanliness with a hand that shook only slightly as he poured generously from the jug. On handing over the glass he would say, 'Howd ye hard a minute, I'll get ye a giggarette.' Dusty would then produce a biscuit tin, prise off the lid with a horny thumb-nail, and proffer the tin with the assurance, 'Sophie made 'em.'

These giggarettes were marvellous confections made by his daughter who had married a baker. Whether they were tarts, buns, sausage rolls or pies, to Dusty they were giggarettes; so tasty that they would melt in the mouth and were worthy accompaniment to the wine.

'I made it,' he would say, 'from rubub an' scaldin' hot water straight from the well.'

Chris Ketteridge saw him shortly before he died. He was busy in his vegetable plot collecting snails, hoddydods, as he called them. But Dusty had seen Chris first and called, 'Come ye here, Dusty wants you.' He then began to feed the snails to his six hens.

'I'm goin' to kill that one to-morrer an' boil it,' said Dusty, pointing to a faded old hen. 'You gotta die, ain't you, old gal, an' so've I, an' I shan't be long.'

Dusty did not live to eat that old bird.

Ashdon once boasted two fine shepherds. Old Riley (George Law) tended the flocks for Alfred Hagger, my grand-father's farmer employer at Overhall Farm. John Baynes was a gentler shepherd and person by far; one who did not con-fine his love to sheep, although his voice was as gentle as the soft bleatings of newborn lambs – and not at all unlike them in sound with those long-drawn a-a-ah's. His beard flowed below his waist in a cascade of creamy silken strands, so pol-ished with daily brushings that sunlight glistered from them.

'All the animals know an' love owd John, bor. You jest watch, now.' And as John slowly plodded the leafy glades and narrow winding roads all manner of wild and domestic ani-mals would leave their grazing and feeding; old horses and colts, ancient cows and young heifers, and even two smelly old goats. They would come to the hedgerows, to peer over or through them, and say their hellos to old John.

'They doan't jest love him, they trust him, bor!' And this was true.

Levi Archer was harnessmaker and saddler long before Albie Bassett took up the trade. His beard was as long as John Baynes's, but he had had more time to grow it to its snow-white magnificence, for Levi died at the age of ninety. Although a master craftsman who took great pride in his craft, he had his own particular claim to fame which he never ceased to advertise. 'I'm a lucky owd man. I were born on Trafalgar Day!' He died twelve years before I was born but was still remembered.

There were characters less saintly: Toby Woodley the official mole-catcher; Mossy Harris the hay-cutter, who travelled from farm to farm on his penny-farthing bicycle and like his friend Snooky Marsh a notorious poacher. Peter Richardson, once an engine driver on the LNER, had retired to drive and maintain big engines for the threshing tackle. He had not retired in terms of dress, for he always wore his engine driver's cap, of which he was mighty proud.

All poached considerably. Our poachers were experts and knew every tree where roosted pheasants, the burrowings of rabbits and the best fields on which to stalk hares and pick them up by their ears. Most wore gamekeepers' jackets - blessed with hidden, capacious pockets. All knew the weather signs, times of full moon, half moon and no moon, the direction of the prevailing wind and the precise location – day and night – of the estates' gamekeepers. All kept dogs, ferrets, curved spades, nets, snares, and guns. Most had been taught to shoot – much to the concern of the farmers – long before the Kaiser's War, in Ashdon's first rifle club.

Along the Ashdon–Bartlow road there was a disused gravel or chalk pit which served as the shooting butts for trainee poacher marksmen. Practice days were days of revelry, music, drinking and good community cheer – an event of consequence. Most of the menfolk – some with their sons – would report early to the butts. All carried something: rifles, shotguns, barrels of ale, baskets and hampers of food, and one or two horned gramophones to make music if they were too sober to sing themselves.

I was never able to discover whether Ashdon Club challenged other clubs to shooting matches; but my old uncle Jasper Miller who for many years lived three cottages away from Granny Ford's – and was the gamekeeper for Walton's Park – had this to say:

'No bloody Germans will ever set foot in Bartlow Hamlet, bor. It ain't safe fer a snipe nor a woodcock to flap theer wings once when they owd rifle club lot puts theer eyes along they gunsights. The way we're a-gooin' theer 'ont be a bloody partridge or pheasant left. I reckon I'll hev to jack my job in and take up knittin'.'

Chapter 15

Scholarship

Another batch of 'they owd Cockneys' came to our school in 1919 when I was twelve. Nellie came with them. She was different. We both knew the moment our eyes met, yet wished not to meet, yet met again. Some volcanic spark was kindled, without words, without touch, later to develop. Although I saw her daily, and her image burned into me each moment in that school where we sat in the same class room, in that first week I could never have described her.

There still were lessons. I did my best, always thinking of Nellie.

William Tuck began to take a great interest in me during my last year at school – autumn 1920 to summer 1921. He came to our cottage one night and spoke to my father.

'Your son is doing very well, but I am alarmed by his

imagination. Last week he wrote a wildly prophetic essay on Future War.'

Poor Mr Tuck, he knew only good books. Little did he realize that I had been guilty of plagiarism. From books by Jules Verne and H. G. Wells and from science fiction comics I had taken extracts about death rays and such. Switching to the personal pronoun I had forecast all kinds of things which, as it happened, were not far off the mark. Tuck was concerned that in one of his classes and in our humble home there lurked a scientist or madman; one who prophesied that future conflicts would need not a sailor, soldier or airman. Just a handful of egg-heads encased in underground concrete, who had but to depress a switch to eliminate their enemies, however remotely situated they might be.

Mr Tuck had brought a book for me. He called it a prize. It was *Tales from Shakespeare*. It has never left me and was in my haversack at Dunkirk and Arromanches. This 'prize' had not been earned by my scholastic ability, but because I had taken him baskets of blackberries and mushrooms – because he was poor and kind. But my father was led to believe it was an award and it pleased him immensely, not only because there was an ornate label in its fly-leaf in gilt and scarlet lettering, with the three scimitars of the Essex County Council, and 'Prize Awarded To' in front of my name, but because he wanted to read it himself.

But what pleased him most was the headmaster's next statement . . .

'I have entered his name for the scholarship and given him

229

a good recommendation. If he succeeds, he will go to Newport Grammar School.'

How I hoped that some miracle would advance the date of the examination!

How I had longed to go to that fine school but without mentioning a word of my longing to anyone. In deep and silent envy I had compared the boys of Newport Grammar with my school fellows and myself. Their caps and blazers seemed to mark or brand a different breed. Their immaculate flannels disgraced my corduroys and leather buskins. Their leather satchels held spotless books, pencils, fountain pens, drawing instruments and slide-rules. My frail, a labourer's basket of plaited straw bound with ravelling hemp, held raw onion, hunks of dry bread and a bottle of cold, unsweetened tea. Their feet wore polished shoes, sturdy brogues with fancy stitchings and perforations. Mine wore shapeless hide mon-strosities, tipped, riveted, soil clogged, hobnailed. Everywhere I went I had to walk. They rode, in parents' pony-traps, wag-onettes and broughams, or on their own gleaming bicycles.

I prayed that I should have these possessions. Convinced after prayer that these things would come to me – if not by God's benevolence, certainly by that of the Education Committee – I could not wait to be examined. When the letter came telling me the date, I became distracted. Sleep evaded me, partly because I took my few books to bed to read through the night.

From his odd job ploughing in Hungerton Field my father took the morning off to travel with me to Newport – only five stations down the Audley End–Liverpool Street line. We had not the fare – until my father sold his fountain pen to Bidwell. This had been his parting gift from the Canadian soldiers – one that he greatly treasured.

He left me where the gravelled drive led through the lawns to the red-brick school.

'Well now, son! Here's your chance. Do your best!' No face could have glowed with greater encouragement. 'I've said my prayers for you. God bless!'

No face could have been kinder. But as his hand went to his pocket there came a transformation. His expression changed to a great weariness. It was as though some evil had passed from his solitary coin to his fingers, as they groped to find so little.

'Oh, I a'most forgot . . . ' his voice had wearied too. 'Here's a shillin'; get yerself a bit of dinner.'

He turned and was gone. He did not look back, perhaps thinking how out of place I looked against that fine background.

Some of the boys looked to me much the same as I thought I must look to them. The majority of them were dressed in Norfolk jackets, knickerbockers to match, warm-looking stockings with fancy hose-tops turned down to show off the colours. Except for me, every boy wore shoes. But my father had polished my old clodhoppers until I could see my face in their toe-caps. He had even picked out bits of caked mud from lace-holes and clusters of hobnails.

A man with a pimply face came from the school. 'Good

morning, gentlemen!' No one had ever called me that before!
'Please follow me!'

He led us into a class room where the differences hit me like
a bullet.

At William Tuck's school, in the 'tops', there were four long
straight rows of forms and desks, to seat on each about thirty
children. They were of Oregon pine, so badly planed, so
rough that it was dangerous to slide along from one's place for
fear of getting a bottom filled with splinters. I once had a
splinter in my thigh and could hardly walk for weeks. It was
poulticed with linseed and bread, and the splinter came out –
two inches long. Our desks were of matching length, of the
same roughly-planed pine, but with not a place for a single
book – just a long, solid, dirty, ink-stained top, with holes
bored at irregular intervals to take ink-wells. Some of these
silly pots slipped through the bigger borings; others lodged
halfway sloshing ink all over our exercise books; a groove had
been gouged to take pens, but so unevenly that at some places
one had to dig deep down with finger-tips to get the pen from
its desky grave. At others the groove was so shallow that pens
could find no resting place and would roll down to spoil our
books.

Here at Newport each desk was of light, limed oak, all
shiny-brass hingy, with lifting tops and nooks and crannies in
which to hide from masters all manner of things. Best of all
there was a separate seat at each desk for the son of every
solicitor, farmer or tradesman.

Through the tall windows I could see the towering rugby

232

posts and was reminded conversely of Ashdon's concrete slabs of playgrounds where often there were falls, broken and infected skin, blood and grime.

Wearing a black silken gown, looking like a churchwarden with indigestion, a fatter man came in and put paper covers on our desks. He then went to a lectern, swished his gown, looked over his spectacles at us one and all, then blew his nose. He then waited for a bit, looked at his watch, then bit his nails.

'Good morning, gentlemen!' He squeaked it out in a high-pitched voice that was frightening.

'You will see in front of you your foldahs. Inside are your papahs. Do not open the foldahs, but write your names on them, Christian names last, plus the name of your school and your home address. You will not open the foldahs until I ring my bell.'

We scribbled.

'All finished? Good!'

He smiled like a fox with a bellyful of chicken.

'When I ring my bell you may open the foldahs and begin. If I catch a boy looking at another boy's work I shall disqualify both and send them home. Understood?'

He looked at us, one by one, for quite a time, perhaps hoping that some of us would go mad and scream for him to ring the bell.

At last! He rang it. We opened up the folders. There were several papers with a time limit to each. I did not look up again until I had finished the lot. When finally I raised my head lots of the boys were still writing – I knew I would have time to check for mistakes, for although I had not a watch – and there was not a watch in our household – I had heard the train going to Audley End Junction and knew that it was only quarter past twelve.

Eventually the folders were collected and we dispersed. Far too excited to eat, I went back to Hungerton Field and gave back the shilling to my father.

'How did it go, son?'

'Not bad, I knew most of it!'

'Well, we'll just hev to wait an' see.'

The suspense was terrible. A whole fortnight passed before Mr Tuck called me out in front of the classes and waved a letter.

'Cedric did well at the examination. He has been highly commended and will probably be going to Newport next year. Now, I think he deserves a jolly good clap!' He started the clapping himself and the classroom reeled.

For once William Tuck was wrong. I did not go to Newport.

I have passed it often by train on my way to Cambridge. On each occasion a lump comes into my throat without my even thinking of Newport.

We could not afford the little cap, let alone the blazers and flannels.

All my mental comparisons of Newport's playing fields with Ashdon's concrete slabs had been in vain.

Most of all it hurt my father.

'You should be startin' out on a new life, my boy. Ter lift you outer the rut. Instead, you'll hev to go to work to help me put food in the bellies of your brothers and sister.'

He looked broken as he said it. I patted his shoulder, hoping my pat would reach his heart.

'I've found a job for you; you've done it afore. It ain't much, but not so hard as the farm. You'll be in the pantry with old Freeman, cleanin' knives an' forks for them who can eat . . . '

I went back to Walton's Park and am glad of it. From the kindly Luddingtons I learned far more of life than I could have learned at Newport.

Chapter 16

Stolen Fruit

During my last year at school, instead of wearing my ugly, comfortable old cap, I wore for a time swaddlings of bandages. Like a Guru of the Sikhs at Amritsar. Eczema was the reason for it. I had it in my scalp and was full of head itchings and urges, and for a short time it was so bad that Dr Brown forbade me to go either to school or to work.

Time was a torture and hung heavily, the more so because I was unable to see Nellie in school. I would have liked to have popped occasionally to the village when the children emerged from school, but I felt a bit leprous and was sensitive about my bandages. Worse still, I had by this time been swept into a net of erotic mystery – the condition of doubt, confusion, anxiety and guilt produced by the onset of the unfamiliar urges that signal the approach or attainment of puberty.

My mind was a-fevered. I kept harking back to Cilla's challenge to my manhood in Home Wood and to what Barney had said about her. He was my senior by six months and one day. But Barney was 'experienced'.

'So you've bin up Home Wood with Cilla, then? Towd me you was scared!'

'I worn't scared.'

'What happened, then?'

'Nuthin', not owd enough!'

'Owd enough! It's size what counts, bor, not age. When they're big enough they're owd enough – if they're willin'. Cilla's big enough, dunnit plenty toimes. She larned me!'

I had felt relieved that Barney had misunderstood. For it was I who had been neither big enough nor old enough – not Cilla. Things were different now, with all this inactivity and time for thought. I entertained hopes that Cilla might give me another chance – if I asked her nicely. But what big, 'experienced' girl would take a second glance at an inexperienced, leprous coward? If I did not pull up my infecund socks, get cured of eczema, ignorance and cowardice before the end of the summer holidays, life might pass me by. So ran my thoughts. I had already been in the world from 5 August 1907 to late July 1920. More than a year had passed since my manhood had been challenged. Prospects seemed unpleasant. Omitting purposely to tell him of the onset of the seven years' itch, I spoke in general terms to my father.

'No need fer you to start worryin', Ced. You're growin' up, an' need somethin' to occupy your mind. Read your books!'

'I've read all I've got. I'm sick of the *Magnet*, the *Gem*, the *Children's Newspaper*, and the bloody *Christian Herald*.'

'Moderate your language, boy,' said my father, landing me a clout on my ear. 'I'll get you summat to read.'

At Walton's Park, Tilbrook's Farm and Hagger's Farm he tried and failed. On the Saturday evening, after I had been subjected to the indignity of having to bath in a bakehouse keeler in front of the living-room fire, in front, too, of my mother, my sister and the discerning Mrs Smith – who commented at full throttle about certain development areas – I changed my eczematic turban and washed out the keeler.

'Put your boots on,' said my father. 'We're goin' fer a stroll.'

Twenty minutes later we were both sitting in butler Freeman's pantry at Walton's Park.

'Mrs Luddington has got out some books for you,' said Freeman. 'There's a tidy owd pile on 'em. Reckon you'll need the dog cart.'

Unfortunately, none of this socially-esteemed literature did much towards the banishment of my biological urges. The *Tatler & Bystander* tittle-tattled interminably about theatricals and sporty socialites who were portrayed in pictures, groups, coveys and droves, mostly clutching either women and champagne, or horses and dogs. The *Field* featured every aspect of country life – except the one that mattered to me – farming, homes, gardens, natural history, women's and children's interests. The *Illustrated London News* dealt with science, art, archaeology, ethnology, travel and exploration. Not a word of advice, solace or guidance in one of them. My mother was delighted with the magazines, however, for she found pictures of many wicked-looking scoundrels for whom she had cooked and served when she was young.

At fourteen years of age she had been banished to Kensington to become first a housemaid and then to graduate by dead girls' shoes and live girls' wedding rings to the envied position of cook. The pattern had remained unchanged for decades. Girls of thirteen and over were encumbrances; their cottage beds were required for new babies, and, like their elder sisters, they would soon be packed off to service, first to live in as kitchen or scullery maids on the big estates, or in the employment of local farmers and professional people. Girls who served such apprenticeships locally were supplied with excellent food, good quarters and sometimes with caps and aprons also. Mostly they were not content to be local 'skivvies' and keenly anticipated that day when an elder sister would write to say there was a vacancy. Then, lock, stock and barrel – in a big black tin trunk or in plaited baskets – their worldly possessions would be sent off, to be followed immediately by the owner, to London or a country town where services were in demand and wages were better. As a result, there were few girls of teen age left in the villages. Boys, on the other hand, were encouraged to remain at home to work on local farms. Their wages would supplement the meagre incomes of their fathers.

Having become anchored to the village through securing employment with local farmers, the school-leaving lads would continue their associations with schoolgirls or with those who had found local positions as maids. But because so many girls migrated, there were too few left, even in local employment. Peacock parades were therefore the order of the day. On Sunday afternoons lads would venture forth in Sunday best – brilliantined, buttonholed and show-offy – hoping to meet a maid in one of the neighbouring villages. There were drawbacks to this 'swainin''. Young maids would be released from their employers' clutches only on Sunday afternoons, usually until tea-time – and for only one night a week or a fortnight – and never after 10 P.M. Thus a minority of the lads stuck to schoolday sweethearts through thick and thin, war and peace and protracted absences. My brother Leslie was one of them, for he married his childhood sweetheart.

Apart from annual fêtes, flower shows and galas, there were no social gatherings for young people – not even a dance hall – and the only cinemas where they could scrape up a casual acquaintance were five and twelve miles distant, at Saffron Walden and Cambridge. There were no buses, no late trains, few bicycles, and a ten or twenty-four mile walking trip on the off-chance was not all that encouraging.

From time to time in the last year of the war the village swains were succoured by the arrival from London of the schoolgirls who had been sent to our village to dodge the Zeppelins and Gotha aeroplanes. These had not the wit – or it may have been inclination – to dodge the young Casanovas of our village school. Soon the 'experienced' schoolboys had winnowed out the 'sures' from possibles and probables.

Convinced it was their bounden duty, in times of dearth, they passed on the information to the hitherto unenlightened.

'Take the bandage off. Put on this ointment, and let the air get at it,' said Dr Brown.

The minute I took it off and felt less leprous I thought of Cilla but deemed it inadvisable to seek her out until I had learned a trick or two. But how? Then it came to me like a flash. Here was I, eager, almost scabless, certainly bandageless, with two female cousins already showing signs of curves and warmth – Dorothy and Ellen – both within striking distance, Dorothy but half a mile distant at Mill Cottage and Ellen next door.

'Ellen! Comin' down to Walt's?'

'Whaffor?'

'You'll see.'

'I ain't a-comin'. You're allus pullin' my hair!' I scarcely noticed her whine.

'Shan't pull it today. Walt's apples are nearly ripe. Get a prop!'

'Promise, then. No hair-pullin'.'

'Finger wet, finger dry, cut out me heart if I tell a lie!'

'Right, then. I'll get a prop.'

We walked the crooked, sloping path at the end of Walt's cottage, Ellen ahead of me carrying one of Granny Ford's clothes props, sporting two long, golden plaits, each with a bright blue bow; her hair blazing in the sun; a yellow fluffiness at her neck; legs firm and rounded.

'He'll know. He looks at 'em every day.'

'He won't miss a couple. Not if we take 'em from the far side!'

'Right, then. Just one apiece!'

We were in Walt's garden. The tulips' flames had died, leaving pokers stiff and blackened with seed. Pinks hit my nostrils, lavender, those old-world roses, Maiden's Blush, the Blood Rose. We could smell and see his picture garden. Enclosed by close-cropped yellow yew less than two feet high, the flower beds rioted with sweet-scented flowers. Gooseberry, red and blackcurrant shrubs nudged the yew hedges. Uncropped grass lushed a carpet greenery under the tall fruit trees. Walt's cottage hid us from Brick and Stone Villa, the shrubs from passers-by on the Ashdon road. A little stream gurgled with glee through Walt's dipping hole behind the density of the green hawthorn and the tree of the Blenheim Orange rose above our heads from the grass carpet. Only the top apples had reddened – those nearest the sun. They had hardly blushed from their green. We knew they were not ripe. Blenheims are not at their best until the blush has been transformed to russet and deep gold; when pips are loosened and rattle like castanets.

We were like those apples.

'I'll prop, you catch,' said Ellen.

She put the 'Y' of the prop under a stem and pushed. An apple fell to my hands. Then another.

'Jest one apiece,' said Ellen.

We sat on the grass under the tree. Apart from the bird-song it was still as sin until Ellen bit into the Blenheim. She shook back her plaits. Her lips were redder far than the apple and juice spurted from the assault of her teeth. She looked very pretty.

'Give us a kiss, then?' I stroked her arm. It was so soft, warm and disturbing.

'Whaffor?'

'I want to.'

'All right, then. But on'y a cousin's kiss.'

I bent over and kissed her. It was not a cousin's kiss, whatever that might be.

I felt a hot, burning sensation. There was a reason for it. Cousin Ellen had landed me a first-class clout on the ear.

Up she jumped and tore towards Brick and Stone Villa.

'Gra-anny! Gra-anny! That boy, Ced, he jest give me a dutty owd kiss!'

Granny Ford shot from her back door, all flour and fury.

'Drattle yer hide, boy. Liz! Lizzie!' She screamed for my mother, 'Git 'is father to 'im. Bin a-tryin' tricks with Ellen. I 'on't hev this owd cousin-wuk. There's more'n enough of it in the village!'

Mother shot from our back door. Bedlam was loose. I ran down the back yard, dashed into the privy and bolted the door. Mother followed but could not get at me and had to demand explanations through the closed door. I explained that it had been a joint enterprise in every respect; that Ellen had agreed to be cousin-kissed; that she had bitten her apple, whereas mine was still intact.

'Filthy, disgustin'. Your own cousin! Wait till your father comes home. Open the door!'

'No, I'm stoppin' in here!'

'Open it at once, I want to use it!'

Oh, the duplicity of women!

Two more clouts the minute I was fool enough to open up ... Three stinging clouts for one little kiss! And maybe more to come.

Because Granny Ford was less swift on her pins than my mother, I escaped by running up her path to the back of the cottage, clearing Grandfather's high chopping block by a good two feet and shooting over the road like a buck rabbit to the safety of the meadow opposite – hearing the while shrieked threats about fathers, grandfathers, policemen, schoolmasters and other disinterested parties. My ears were hot, my emotions tempestuous and I felt physically sicker than when scalp-scabby and turbanned. I needed a confessor but had little to confess. Besides there were no confessors; I would have to work it out myself. As always when disturbed, I perambulated, unthinking of direction, towards the old mill. Chris would not be there. He would be building somewhere. Thank God, I would be alone.

I entered the door and climbed the mill-rope to the first storey. Sitting on the lower stone I chewed at my sorrel leaves; their bitterness was sweet compared with my thoughts about cousins.

'Coo-ee! Yoo-hoo! You there, Ced?'

There she was, the other female cousin. Dark Dorothy ...

244

tomboyish Dorothy! I could not dodge her. She could climb trees and ropes better by far than me. She had seen me; there was no escape except by hiding and keeping quiet. I hid.

'Coo-ee! Are you up the top, then?'

Not a word.

I heard the trip of her feet, saw the rope swing then tauten. Two firm, brown hands shot up through the trapdoor to gain a higher grip. Up came the dark head, bright eyes peering round my storey in vain.

Kicks of the bronzed firm legs and up she shot to the top storey. I crept from my hiding place and seized the rope to slide down. She felt the touch of my hands on it, ten feet above me. I looked up as she looked down.

'You dutty devil. You were lookin' up my knickers!'

'I worn't. Don't wanna look at you!'

'Hev a look, then. No holes. No charge!'

I looked; they were pale blue and full of twin plumpness. No holes!

'Watch out, I'm comin' down.' She was beside me like a sun-burned flash, eyes afire as always, dimpling like a Norfolk dumpling.

'You've got that owd bandage off. What you doin' up the mill, then?'

'Keepin' outer the way; hidin'.'

'What've you done, then?'

'Kissed Ellen, got clouted. It were only a cousin's kiss!'

'Cousin's kisses ain't no good!'

'How do you know, then?'

'Huh! Why ask me? You orter know b'now. Le's go down, it's warmer outside. Did Ellen tell Aunt Liz or Gran?'

'Both!'

'Huh! She would. Where'd you kiss her, then?'

'Walt's garden.'

'No! I don't mean what place ... Where'd you kiss HER?'

'Mouth. She said it were a dutty owd kiss.'

'Was it a hot 'un, then?'

'Fair t'middlin'!'

'Le's go to Mill Pond.'

We went to Mill Pond.

Mill Pond was kidney-shaped and almost entirely surrounded by trees, shrubs and reeds; a little grassy mole of land projected into its centre from the water's edge.

I knew we should be alone because a moorhen kur-r-rucked harshly to proclaim that no other humans were present where dragonflies darted and reed warblers wassailed. The pond's surface wore its vivid green cloak, all water-buttercupped and duckweeded. There was a great stillness, except in me, as we dropped to the grass, Dorothy's dimpled knees but millimetres from mine.

I thrust my fingers into the warm earth, felt the soil fill my nails as I dug out a dandelion, root and all. Its tap-root had snapped to spill its white sap. I pushed the milky-bleedy root on her bare brown legs. Her stockings had been fashioned by sunshine, not by silkworms. In no time at all, where I had smeared that milk there was not a sign. The white became transformed to brown – lost in the dark of her skin. I felt and heard the breath of her – that rise and fall of animality; of life, vitality. Clear as morning daylight she spoke.

'What did owd Gran say, then? Was she riled?'

'Proper riled. Said there was far too much owd cousin-wuk.'

'What did Aunt Liz say?'

'Hollered, clipped me ear, an' she's goin' to tell Father. I'll cop it!'

'Bet he won't say nuthin'!'

'What d'yer bet, then?'

'A cousin's kiss.'

'Oh no! Not ag'in.'

'All right then, a different one.'

'What sort?'

'A hot 'un – if you want.'

'When?'

'Now, if you want.'

Exempt from experience, devoid of any desire, between bouts of adolescent pinchings, pantings and hair-pullings, we shamelessly embarked upon our maiden voyage of natural curiosity and discovery. With teeth and talons, wandering lips and tentative tongues, reconnoitring finger-tips, perspiring palms, inquisitive eyes and mutual inspection, we stroked, pawed and caressed.

We were young. Our sun still shone upon us. Our dragon-flies flitted for us, and our reed warblers ceased not to sing for us. It was all as natural as nature, as natural as the soil in my nails. Not for me one shred of remorse but a revelation.

For my dark Dorothy I made a silver chain – a diadem of daisies with two gems of buttercup gold. I placed it gently on her dark hair and looked at her. We shared a secret. The silence was profound, until there came a call from Mill Cottage.

'Dorthee! Dorthee!'

My war-widowed aunt was calling her young.

'Don't you tell nobody, then. You go down Sparks' hedge. See you tomorrow. Nellie sent me a letter for you. It's in my satchel. She likes you. I shan't say nothing.'

Red lips pouted. Dark eyes danced. 'Last one, then? Not a cousin's!'

Her lips were like warm velvet ... and then she was gone.

I folded my jacket to form a pillow, pulled down the peak of my ugly cap, lay flat on my back on earth's mattress – and thought of a hymn ...

> All things bright and beautiful,
> All creatures great and small,
> All things wise and wonderful,
> The Lord God made them all.

My unsung snatch of hymn was but a mental appreciation of revelation and beauty. I still had to face the music about Ellen. No longer caring, I was prepared for the worst. The tip of the sun sinking over the roof of Newnham Hall Farm told me it was time to go home but I did not skulk in the density of Sparks' thick hedges as Dorothy had suggested. I strutted and skipped down the wide headlands from Mill Meadow, whistling full-throat the latest popular song, 'Butterflies in the Rain'. Slithering down the bank by the pollard elm I thought of Milly who, a year ago, had climbed up there as I had slithered down, her face ashen, her eyes wild, and how she had said to me: 'Stop that owd whistlin', Ced. It's serious. Owd Ben Nunn has hung himself, Chris hev jest cut him down!'

Yes, Ben Nunn had hanged himself from a beam in the barn.

But today I was alive, had never been more alive. I could face anything.

There they sat, around our table with the lion's claws base. My father, mother, Leslie and Poppy, pork and pickles on their plates, were just starting. My chair, the one with its back to the window, was pushed close to the table. There was not a plate set at my place; no knife and fork, no cup and saucer. Frowns were being worn all round. I felt unwanted.

'Where've you been, then?' asked my father.

'Up the mill.'

'Brush that owd grass off your back. Come an' have tea.'

I brushed, washed in rain-water and sat. Mother put out a pork-filled plate and put on the fiercest of faces. I said my Grace and began to eat.

'Want to speak to you when you've done,' said my father. 'Don't you go out ag'in till I've seen you.'

Sweet was the pork and spicy the pickles but the meal was miserable with silence and forebodings.

'Out the garden, then,' said my father, beginning to fill his pipe. We leaned against the bole of our harvest apple tree, now yellow with ripeness.

'This is for you, I reckon. Your aunt found it in Dorothy's schoolbag.'

A crumpled letter. From Nellie. A quick, heart-thumping glance . . .

'Back to Ashdon next week. See you in school. Love, Nellie.'

Simultaneously delighted and distressed, I sensed there was more to follow.

'What's all this about you and Ellen?' He tried hard to look stern.

'Nuthin' much. Jest a kiss, thassall.'

'What's this letter, then? How many gals hev you got, boy?'

'It's only a note. She's in my class. Gone to London for the holiday.'

' 'Cordin' to the note she loves you. Why?'

'Dunno. She's all right. I like her.'

'You jest listen to me, boy. Stop foolin' with cousins an' gals until you get a bit owder. It upsets your mother, an' you ain't got the cradle-marks off your backside yet. When you're owder hev all the gals you can get. If you find one you carn't tackle fetch her back fer me!'

He gave me a friendly prod in the belly and winked.

'Go. Tell your mother you're sorry – an' that I've jest ticked you off.'

I apologized to my mother. She still looked fierce. But somebody loved me. It was in writing. I tore to my little bedroom to read my first love letter – a thousand times.

Chapter 17

Place Farm

For almost two years after school at nights, on most weekdays during school holidays and on what bits could be spared from church and Sunday school at weekends, I had worked at Walton's, delighted always to be with my friends. Between fourteen and fifteen I worked full time as house boy but as soon as I was fifteen I qualified in age – if not stature and strength – to become a farm labourer, to earn an extra two and sixpence per week.

The farm to which I was going was less than one hundred yards from my old workshop in the servants' quarters. There was no need for me to say farewell to my friends, with a bit of luck I would be seeing most of them several times a day. But to me the distance seemed many millions of miles, and I knew that I was going to miss them, to be lonely.

'You're the right age, bor, to get ten bob a week, an' I s'pose we're bound to pay ye ten bob. But you're on'y a little 'un, an' I don't reckon you'll be able t'stand up t'the work.'

That was my introduction to Place Farm, when I started work on the land.

For some years social anthropologists, Oxford dons and others of that ilk have been in the habit of venerating the farm labourer. Physically he has been depicted as having great strength, possessing ruggedness and the capacity for long hours of unhurried work. Mentally he has been regarded as a narrow-minded individualist, opposed to change, resentful of interference in his work but far more self-reliant than the townsman.

It was mostly so of the farmhands I joined at Place Farm. It was one of several owned by Major Luddington and was the assembly point where all the farmhands met each morning to receive their instructions for the day's work from Mr Bidwell, the tenant farmer. 'Old' Bidwell, who had come to Ashdon from Littleport, was not all that old, but he was as bald as a coot and had neither lash nor brow to protect his piercing eyes. Nevertheless, those eyes were kindly and all-discerning. He had a great knowledge of farming heavy land, a devilish smile and a wry sense of humour. That was evident the day Poddy Coote tore his trousers on barbed wire and exposed himself. Poddy went to the back door of the farm to borrow needle and thread from Mrs Bidwell. Bidwell sat in the kitchen, eating his breakfast. 'Well now, Poddy, bor, I expects you to work like a stallion but there ain't no call for you to go about lookin' like one.'

Mrs Bidwell had a strident, jarring voice not in keeping with her character, for she was a most sympathetic and kindly lady with an insatiable craving for work. Not once did I see her in other than her working clothes. Her pride was the dairy; a palace of cleanliness which featured fresh and stimulating smells from her vats of cream and delicious butter – patted and enscrolled with patterns of thistle, shamrock and rose – which she sold at one shilling a pound.

Lawrence was their only son, a sprightly fair-haired young man with an aptitude for new contrivances – motors and tractors – and with an eye for the Ashdon belles. Quite soon after his arrival from Littleport, he fell for the undoubted charms of May Bland, Barney's sister, who ended his predatory prowlings in nearby villages and bore him three strong sons in wedlock.

Lawrence had three sisters, Elsie, Hilda and Freda. Like their mother they were unbelievably industrious and regarded 'work' as recreation and the only reason for their existence. Paddy O'Boyle postulated that the whole family of Bidwell had been mentally conditioned to that state of affairs by their singing of 'chapel' hymns.

'In particular, m'boy, that disgustin' Victorian ole hymn: "Work for the night is coming, when man works no more."'

O'Boyle was not being unkind to the Bidwells, but he firmly believed that only bowler-hatted Irish butlers of the Catholic faith had the divine right to sing at their labours. It was no secret on the farm.

His assessment of toil was simple. 'If it's any ole English job

253

with English tools an' animals belongin' to the heathenish English,' he would say, 'there should be not a note of singin' at all. It's on their knees they should be, prayin' for guidance.'

Standing on the highest point of the farmlands, the farm building was old, three-storeyed, spacious and beautiful. Its mellow yellow plaster and black beams were great attractions as it stood surrounded by stacks of wheat, oat, barley and rye; lofty walnut trees and the towering beeches and elms of the rookery; and in the gardens, all gravel pathed and edged with yellow privet, every fruit tree imaginable. The whole was enclosed by a brick and flint wall and overlooked the stables, the stockyards and the great black barn, reckoned by some to be the biggest tithe barn in Essex.

At the end of each day's work there would be fed and bedded down on oat straw five Suffolk Punches and one Clydesdale, great muscled horses with flowing manes, tails and hairy fetlocks. Punch was the old man, a black gelding, with a white blaze and fetlocks, of nearly eighteen hands. Jockey and Rover, light bays, and Captain, a fiery chestnut, were a good seventeen hands, but were less docile. Both mares, Blossom and Mary, were dark bays. Between them they did most of the hard work on the land, and it was a pleasure to see them, three ploughing teams, all together on some hilly field. The ploughmen would draw their opening furrows on the stubbles at appropriate points, guiding their teams with rein and ropes and words of command. 'Gee, now, gee!' was the order for the team to move slightly to the right. 'Walk-a-meller, walker-meller, now!' was the command for a move to the left. Throughout the day they would paint the golden backcloth of stubbles with long dark stripes of turned earth which got wider and wider until the ploughmen were almost within reach of each other and until all the gold had been turned into rich dark brown. Birds would follow the ploughs, pecking out grubs from the newly turned earth, fighting and wheeling in the air, shrieking and singing for the joy of new-found food. Rooks and blackbirds – the greedy ones – would stay in the furrows, walking and eating behind the ploughs until so gorged they were too heavy and fat to fly.

And in this beginning the earth lay open to receive the seed.

Heavy horse-drawn rollers followed the harrows to break the clods which would be big if ploughing had been done in wet weather, then would follow a second harrowing to break the clods still smaller and to comb out twitch and vetch grass and all manner of weeds and herbs. After each field crossing the finer-combed harrows would be hand-cleaned. Weed piles would be set along the headlands, awaiting burning. They always burned so slowly. Faint blue smoke would be seen rising lazily for days and at night there would be seen faint glowings across the fields, if the breezes fanned the fires, and one would smell the burning herbs throughout the village. Once savoured, that aromatic fragrance would be captured for all time.

Then would appear coffin-like boxes on high wheels and the seeding would be about to start.

Small plough-shares were connected to each coffin's under-side by tubes which could be adjusted to regulate the seeding, thick or thin, according to the crop and the soil. These cut their way through the now 'tilthy' soil, about three inches apart throughout the drill's length, burying the seed out of reach of greedy birds as the drill proceeded. Seed drills, like the plough furrows, had to be straight as a die. This was positive indication of craftsmanship and horsemanship, and was necessary to avoid ridicule in the pubs. Furrows could be seen the moment they were ploughed. Seed drills would not be seen until the first green blades came through.

'Who ploughed Holden, then? I were a-lookin' this mornin'. They owd seed drillin's ain't bad in Thruskell's, but there's a tidy few dog's legs in Hungerton. Reckon owd George had bin to market fust an' took a few jars!'

Many more jobs were to be done before harvest but the big job was over.

Seed now lay in nature's womb awaiting the quickening.

Fessor Smith lived in a caravan. Originally he was called 'Professor', but that was too much of a mouthful for Ashdon. When he was not in his caravan he would be in one of two other places – the Bricklayers' Arms, at the bottom of New Road Hill, or on a traction engine. At Newnham Hall Farm there lived a farmer who hired out traction engines for ploughing, for mechanization was beginning to rear its ugly head in the quiet fields. Every late autumn we would hear a pair of these great engines puffing their way along the roads at about three miles an hour. The object of their appearance was to plough the fields, six furrows at a time. Belching out black smoke they would churn into the fields and take up their positions at opposite ends. Beneath each great black belly was a huge drum around which was coiled a massive steel cable. By that cable the engines would draw Fessor's plough across the fields and Fessor would sit on the plough-seat in sheer delight, steering merrily away with a great red wheel. Although he lived in the village he seldom left his caravan while ploughing was in progress. He fancied himself a cut above the horse-ploughmen but, like the rest of the villagers – who loathed mechanization – the horse-ploughmen held him in pretty low regard. Sometimes he would be completely ostracized, so much so that he was seldom offered a drink from the communal quart pot in the pubs and that was the gravest of accusations – the supreme insult.

Mechanization also began to creep into the finals of harvest, for the same farmer hired out threshing-tackle. Driven by belt from a traction engine's fly-wheel, the threshing machine would beat out the corn, separate the chaff from the grain and push the straw into a huge fork-pronged elevator, conveying it to the stacker who would make the straw stacks. Wheat poured from two delivery holes at the back and chaff from holes at the sides, so quickly that four men would be employed full time to cart it away.

Although it was a vast improvement upon the old system of hand-threshing with flails – the two ash-wood sticks connected by leathern thongs – farmhands and villagers of both sexes resented the arrival, speed and noisy smoky presence of mechanical threshing machines.

Then, to replace the good old mower, his sharp scythe, emery sharpening rub and honing whetstone – and his mate who followed him to gather his mowings to fashion hand-made sheaves and to hand-tie them with bands of corn – there were now to be seen a-reaping the Canadian Massey-Harris harvesters or binders. They cut the cornstalks close to the soil, produced more straw and less stubble; they bound the sheaves in regular sizes with binder string and forked them out at regular intervals and precise rows ready for the 'shockers'. There was less objection to these 'new-fangled owd articles' than to the threshing machine because the binders were horse-drawn; and it was a pretty sight to see three great horses drawing the binder, nodding their heads, making the flimsy sails turn and dip into the corn; guiding and bending it to the sharp, shuttling triangular blades – to put three former corn gatherers out of their jobs.

The mower and the sheaf-maker were not displeased for theirs were sweaty, arduous, back-breaking jobs. But the farmhands' wives were most put out because they were deprived of their ancient perks, the gleanings and leazings. On the other hand there was a compensating factor because they got more meat. As the mechanical reaper circled the field in ever-decreasing circles the rabbits, hares, partridge and pheasant withdrew deeper into the centre of the diminishing standing corn. In the last twenty minutes of reaping the standing corn remnant would bristle with game, and men and women armed with sticks, dogs, pitchforks and guns would converge upon it. In their excitement and anticipation of getting cheap meat for their larders they would sometimes hit dogs and friends with their sticks and cudgels, but usually they managed to direct a couple of good swipes at hares or rabbits and would go off home rejoicing.

Between seed time and harvest there was much to do to ensure a good crop. Hoeing was an essential. Sometimes there would be half a dozen men in one field, or sometimes women; weeding, stone-picking, singling turnips, swedes and mangold wurzels. Usually the men were kept separate from the women, who had different hours to enable them to attend to their household duties. Ten until four were the most appreciated attendances. This allowed the women to attend to their homes before leaving for work on the land. After an hour for dinner, which they usually ate in the hedgerows with their menfolk, they would resume work until four, when they would go off and cook the main meal of the day for their families. Sometimes they got as much as ten shillings a week, never more.

Midday meals consisted of bread, bacon and raw onions. There was an art in eating these. They would be held in the left hand. In the right hand would be the large shut-knife. A hunk of bread would be cut to hold the meat and onion; then the knife would be brought dexterously into play, slicing bread, meat and onion in one slice; these would finally be conveyed between knife-blade and thumb to the mouth. The staple drink was sugarless, milkless cold tea, from old beer bottles or flap-cans. Sometimes there would be a singing of bawdy songs, or a bit of sexual horse-play in nearby woods, but there was not a bit of vice intended and in the main they were happy, contented people.

Soon after my hiring at Place Farm I began to take a hand in all this sowing and reaping, together with a bit of ploughing, hedging, ditching and thatching.

Poddy Coote, who had preceded me at Walton's Park in the houseboy's job, had also preceded me at the farm. Now almost a farmhand graduate, he was my instructor.

My initiation began in the big tithe barn in the preparation of food for the cattle. Poddy and I would spend the morning hours in the barn, singing hymns at the tops of our voices and working like blazes as we measured and mixed the food. The drill was this:

First, on the floor of the barn put a thickish sprinkling of oat chaff; grind mangolds in the slicing machine; grind cattle cake in another machine; keep piles of mangold-shreds and corn and cattle cake in separate piles; go to bin and take out shovels of bean and oatmeal; keep in separate piles.

Then, like bricky's labourers mixing mortar, we would put layers of our various grindings, slicings and crushings on to the chaff and start the mixing. Poddy would always be on the near-side because he was left-handed and I would be on the offside – whether left-handed or not – because I was 'junior'.

After mixing, we would take our mixture in big tubs and tip it into the various eating troughs, taking care not to offend the bull, one which was vicious and had already gored Poddy twice when he turned his back on him.

Off then we would go to the haystacks in a great wooden tumbril with wooden eaves fore and aft to take a good load. At the stack Poddy would slice away into its depths with a large cutting knife, making a wonderful smell of hay so sweet that we could almost have eaten some ourselves. Having cut down fairly deeply, Poddy would load me up in my tumbril. I would have to pack the hay carefully for the road back from the rookery was deeply rutted, making the tumbril lurch from side to side. Sometimes we would put a rope over the load, sometimes not. I always preferred it to be roped and tied because I was still scared of heights and got dizzy going down the rutted road, quite fearful that I would soon be hurled off and crippled for life, but I never was.

Sometimes I would be on my own, the loneliest man in the world, even if not yet a man. When the oats and wheat started to spring through in nice tender green shoots, the rooks and crows would be at them, and old starlings, ruining all the good work we had done before. Bidwell would then send me off to Woodshot, or some other distant field, for bird-scaring. Armed only with a rattle like those used by football fans, and my voice, I would see nothing all day – sometimes for weeks on end – except rooks, crows and starlings. I would be able to see for miles but there would be not a human being in sight save only in the train running from Bartlow Station to Haverhill and that was at least three miles distant – so far away that I would not be able to make out the carriage windows, let alone the occupants.

If the wind was blowing from Woodshot to Place Farm, into the ears of old Bidwell, I would rattle away quite considerably whenever the rooks landed. If it blew in the other direction, and it usually did, I would rattle far less without fear of not being heard rattling.

Then I would move off to the spinneys and copses and do a bit of useful exploring.

In my favourite spinney there were spotted woodpeckers, green woodpeckers, nuthatches, tree creepers, jays, magpies and the tiny warblers – far better than greedy old rooks and crows!

'Yah-yah-yah-yah.' That would be the woodpecker. The first 'yah' would be fairly high and the next three would get lower and lower until they almost faded away. I could pick him out best when he was on the wing; first by his flight which is not unlike a woodcock's, wobbling all over the sky; then by his big head, long bill and stubby tail. If he had a green patch on his lower end he would be a 'yaffle', as we called him, a green woodpecker. I knew that the two other woodpeckers, the greater and lesser spotties, were smaller, with different notes, but that they all make the same noise when they are pecking out grubs and insects from trees.

The nuthatch I knew too, and would watch it run round branches in all directions, even upside down. It was always great fun to observe him eating grubs in springtime. In winter he would change his diet and live on nuts and acorns. He would fix them in a little hollow and hammer at them like a woodpecker until the shell was smashed. I learned a lot about birds when I should have been bird-scaring.

There was another reason for my explorations. Poaching.

Despite the fact that Baldy Rodwell, who became my uncle by marrying Aunt Frances, had threatened to shoot poachers on sight, many a pheasant came to a swift and silent end in Home Wood.

Quite a number of the boy school-leavers were expert poachers by that age, fully equipped with snares, guns and dogs. Leslie and I had no gun. We could not even afford to buy bits of nice square stretchy rubber to make a catapult, but we were better off than the boys of the Ends, for in Bartlow Hamlet Leslie and I had a bobby's lantern, the only one in the village. It was an old 'peeler's lamp', with wick, trimmer and shutter, and bulbous magnifying glass which produced a very strong beam if we remembered to polish the reflector.

To cut down the lateral dispersion of light, we modified the shutter to give a five-inch beam at about three paces – a good pheasant-blinding distance. From a coil of wire left by the Post Office engineers when they rewired the telegraph line, we made good copper-wire snares. These we attached to a stout ash pole. With this equipment we practised until we could whip off ten clothes-pegs from Mother's wash line in ten swift flicks of our wrists. All we needed then was a sack.

On moonless nights we crept off to Home Wood where

unsuspecting pheasants roosted in the lower branches of pine and larch trees. We knew every inch of the countryside and darkness was our friend.

Into the pine-needled woodland drives we crept like ghosts, our bobby's lantern lit but shielded, its unpleasant smoke mingling with our cloudy exhalations in the frost-cold of the night.

'Psst! There's one in this tree,' Leslie would whisper. He could *smell* pheasants.

First, the lantern. We would open the shutter and shine the strong beam into the blinking eyes of a startled pheasant, and before it could blink thrice we would drag it from its perch with our snare. Then would follow one or two convulsive twitches – after I had lengthened its neck across my knee – and Mr Cock Pheasant would be as good as eaten.

Sometimes we took two but never more. We would eat one, sell the other and give the three shillings to Mother, who was terrified by the whole thing ... so she would make us burn every feather and would not be satisfied until she had picked our clothes of bits of feathers and down.

On Saturdays the poachings were legal. From miles around came fine gentlemen in broughams, shooting brakes and Harris tweeds to shoot pheasants, partridge and hares by the hundred-brace. Among them came Mr R. A. Butler, who later succeeded Foot Mitchell to represent other young poachers for the Saffron Walden constituency as a Tory in the House of Commons.

We had other means of raising the wind. Twenty rats' tails produced a shilling and moleskins could be sold at ninepence apiece, provided the skin had not been punctured and had been properly cured by pinning on boards with blackthorn spikes with the inside facing the sun.

Soon after these illegal enterprises had got into a profitable stride my father joined me to work at Place Farm. For him it was the last resort. He had not properly recovered from his war wounds but night after night he wrote letters, answering advertisements in national and local newspapers. Day after day he attended interviews, locally, in London, Cambridge and elsewhere. Each time he would return looking dispirited, disillusioned . . .

'Only officers are getting indoor jobs,' he told my mother, 'and lots of them are being turned away although they are proficient and qualified. There's nothing left except the land. I hope to God I'm strong enough!'

He came to Place Farm where he was interviewed by old Bidwell.

'Can ye take me on? I'll do anything, anything!'

'Can ye plough?' asked Bidwell.

'No, but I can learn.'

'How owd are ye, John?'

'Forty-two. What's age got to do with it, then?'

'Never make a ploughman at forty, bor!'

'Give me a chance to prove you're wrong then.'

Old Bidwell was a sport. He took my father on at twenty-seven shillings a week, two shillings less than those who could plough. There were comments from others.

'Yew carn't larn at that age!' 'Hev to be born to it.' 'Takes a lifetime!'

John Mays confounded the critics before a year was out. He could draw a furrow with the best of them, with prizes to prove it. He became absorbed, entranced with his new work. His health improved and he became an expert in the many skills of the farm. Bidwell, bless him, put me to work with my father whenever it was possible. He taught me to sharpen scythes, axes, sickles, bill-hooks and other edged tools used for lifting and trimming root-crops – skills he had learned long before in the farm at Glemsford. He added to my knowledge of birds, trees and plants. He showed me how best to find partridge and pheasant eggs and nests; to trim hedges in such a fashion that they would thicken the following year; to mow, thatch with straw and reed; and, from a calendar he had fashioned with dates and colour schemes, to memorize the months for sowing and tending flowers and vegetables. He could not teach me about horses for at first he was a bit scared of them; and I could already ride, drive and groom.

One day, Jockey, the trace horse, bolted with me on his back. He went thundering down past the rookery, dragging a great wagon-load of wheat. I had no reins, no stirrups, no saddle; but I hung on until Jockey tired. My father caught me up at the farm when I had just dismounted. He was ashen and trembling. 'You're a good enough rider t'be a cavalry gallopin' major,' he said, with great relief.

After our night meal I got out the chess board. 'I'm not

playin' tonight,' he said. 'Put on your hat an' coat, we're goin' out.'

'Where to?' I asked.

'Come on, you'll soon find out.'

He took me to the Bonnett Inn.

Mrs Cooper emerged from the cellar. 'What'll it be, John? Pint o' bitter an' a ginger beer?'

'Not tonight, Mrs Cooper; two pints o' best bitter ... one fer me, one fer my son!'

The following January saw a strange planting in the field behind George Midson's cottage. It was heralded by the appearance of Jockey between the tumbril shafts and of other tumbrils drawn by Captain and Punch, arriving every fifteen minutes. All were stinking and steaming with ripe dung from the yards. Tom Symonds and my father were at the farm end of the journey, cutting deep into stockyard dung with hay knives, hurling great forkfuls into the tumbrils as they returned empty from the fields. Wuddy Smith and I were at the field with long rakes in our hands. The tumbrils were set at half-tip to make it easier for us to rake out. Our job was to put the dung into even piles in straight lines at fifteen feet apart throughout the length of the field.

The horses were marvellous. 'Up, Jockey!' The bay gelding would heave and take a few steps. 'Whoa, there!' With no one to lead him, Jockey would march straight as a Grenadier and stay stiffly to attention as old Wuddy and I raked out another steamer.

'Good owd drop o' stuff from the pig-yard!' said Wuddy,

taking appreciative sniffs. 'They owd blackcurrants'll fair shoot owter the ground!'

We were 'furtilizin'', preparing and enriching the soil for the first field of blackcurrants in Ashdon's agricultural history. Fed to the teeth with plum and apple in Flanders' fields, our soldiers were about to get a change of diet from the jam manufacturers at Histon, Cambridge.

Afterwards came the muck spreading, with long, light, four-tined forks.

'Flick yer wrist more, boy,' said Wuddy. 'A tidy owd twist an' yer don't hev ter tramp abowt spreadin' it more even-like.' He croaked out his Chinese song:

> Sling-shit-hi,
> Sling-shit-lo;
> The quicker yer flicks
> The fu'ther it go.

Currant shrubs had to be in before January was out. With Lawrence Bidwell and Ted Allen I helped to plant thousands of them. What a back-breaker it was and the talk of the village, for here was something new. 'Fancy that, now. Growin' currants on good farmland!'

They had been placed in even-spread rows, in long lines where the furrows had been drawn and were still to be seen after the harrowing. They were close to hand so that we could 'cop howd on 'em quick' and thus eliminate any superfluous movements. Pushing in our forks or spades 'full spit' we would push forward the handle to leave behind the tines or blade a hole. Into the hole we would quickly but carefully place the roots, ensuring they were not distorted from their natural formation. We would then lift out the fork, tread back soil, and a currant shrub was planted.

Later, Ted Allen the expert would be bent double for weeks, pruning every shrub with his razor-sharp secateurs. After that – apart from running a horse-shim between the rows to let in air and chop out weeds – the currants were left to their own devices. That crop did remarkably well, I remember; just as old Wuddy had forecast when we spread the 'furtilizer'. 'Luvly an' ripe, boy. Black as a sweep's arse,' was how he put it.

Most farmhands could buy a load or two of manure at ten shillings a load for the allotments in which they took such pride. Each would vie with the other to produce the biggest and best fruit and vegetables to enter for the flower and vegetable shows. Strangely enough, after a hard day's work on the fields, they would find relaxation in tending their own plots at places remote from their cottage gardens. They could be heard singing and whistling merrily away, exchanging gossip and banter with their allotment-digging colleagues as though they had only just started work for the day.

Their conversation would always turn to potatoes, the staple food. Sufficient of these were grown and stored to last a whole year by the process of clamping.

First, a spit of earth would be taken out in a circle of about two or three yards' diameter and placed on one side. A thick-ish bed of straw would be laid within the dug circle and on this would be placed the potato crop, great care being taken not to bruise any or to put in a potato which had been even slightly penetrated by a fork-tine. Straw would then be placed over the crop, sometimes a pile of ten to fifteen hundredweight, and the whole would be covered with a three-inch layer of soil. Provided their womenfolk restored the soil and straw after taking potatoes for meals, the rest would be safe from the keenest air or ground frosts throughout the winter.

Sometimes the men would send off for new varieties of seed potatoes but they usually stuck to the old faithfuls: 'King Teddies', Arran Chiefs, Kidney Blacks and Early Rose.

Great pride and care was also taken to grow other vegetables. Peas, beans, marrows, celery, lettuce, onions, shallots, parsnips, swedes, turnips, artichokes, plus various kinds of cabbage, spring broccoli and greens were produced. Even before the shoots appeared there would be trips to the woods and hedges with sharp bill-hooks to cut pea and beansticks. These were carefully cut to the right length and made into faggots bound with nut-hazel withes. These were brought back on shoulders, two or three faggots at a time.

Flowers were usually the responsibility of the womenfolk, for the gardens and plots would be around the cottages close to hand. Particular attention was always given to the front garden if it overlooked a public highway. It was necessary to put up a good show, to surpass the results of other green-fingered Joneses. The women seldom bought seeds or plants from nurseries but harvested their own to exchange with others. I cannot remember a house without a flower garden and I shall always remember the smell and sight of them: wallflowers, night-scented stocks, pinks, cornflowers, larkspur. All the old-fashioned and trusties were there and, in their season, daffodils, crocuses, hyacinths, tulips, Michaelmas daisies, anemones, catmint, alyssum, arabis and, last but not least, profusions of roses: bush, standard, rambler and climber. There would also be small bushes, all with riots of flame in their leaves or in their flowers, together with every shade of lilac and golden cascades of laburnum.

My mother could grow anything at any time. Her favourites were violets from the hedgerows, but in the garden, Sweet William, wallflowers, night-scented stocks and old-world roses whose names I have forgotten.

'You know that Mrs Thingammybob who came from Tottenham to get away from the air raids? Well, at the Mothers' Union last night she made us laugh fit to bust. She went to Walden market on Tuesday and bought three pounds of shallots; brought 'em home; rubbed the skins off with a dishcloth; an' bottled 'em in water, vinegar an' chillies. Joke was they worn't shallots at all. They were tulip bulbs. They'll larn. They'll larn!' My mother was delighted, as most women are at another's incompetence or misfortune.

I went to Langley Wood with my father and old Pipper Free from Camps End. We were there a long time, hewing great trees, rooting out small shrubs and making a clearance of all wood-growth between the two south glades. Our sharp axes and bill-hooks were put to good use and I had not been there two hours before I was put on to axe swinging. This was great fun, not only because I had read about timber-men, lumberjacks and log-rollers; but because my father had been a lumberjack in Canada and had told me marvellous stories of felling competitions between Irishmen and French Canadians. Each time I swung my axe and made sweet-scented chips and bits of bark from the tree boles I fancied myself to be a French Canadian lumberman, the champion of them all.

We would look first at the tree to find out which side was more heavily weighted with branches and which way it was likely to fall. Then we would start with our axes, two of us at a time, making a notch in the tree, opposite the direction of fall. We would try to cut bigger chips than anybody else, but because my father and Pipper had seven-pound axes and I only a four-pound one, they would always win. Later we would collect the chips in sacks and take them home. These were the feller's perks, to make good fires at home.

'TIMBER!' We would shout this like mad just after we had put the wedge into the cut of the cross-cut saw and driven it home with a beetle. Then down would come a great tree, crackling and swishing its branches into standing trees and making jackdaws and jays shriek and croak their protests. One felled tree would keep us busy for weeks, for we had to trim off all branches to prepare the trunk for Saffron Walden's tim-bermen who would crash into the glades with six horses and a log-carrier to take it off to the saw-mill for plank making. Then we would cut the small-growth branches and from them make faggots, which we would prop on their ends in great numbers. Later, these would be sold for fire-kindling to the cottagers, at about sixpence per faggot. With the swishy bits we made besoms, cutting ash or nut-hazel to make handles for them and binding the brush part with withes made from smaller and slimmer sticks of nut-hazels. Even then we were not finished with the great tree. We would cut the bigger branches into four-foot logs and when we had made some good piles of these, would split them into four with beetle and wedges.

This 'beetle-swinging' was excellent practice for Castle Camps Fair, where they had a strength-tester, an attraction for young men who wished to show off to their sweethearts and other men's sweethearts. With one great swipe on to a kind of spring-loaded anvil with a heavy mallet the strong ones would make a steel weight go shooting up a groove in a vertical cylinder about twenty feet high, hoping to clang a cracked bell at the top. There were prizes for the bell-ringers – sometimes a pair of ugly china dogs or cats, but always a girl.

Thatching! Unlike old hot-gospelling Joslin, Father and I did not thatch the roofs of country cottages; but we did thatch corn stacks with reed. It was a job which required patience, skill and many tools including rakes, mallets, knives, bill-hooks, straw of wheat and oat, bucket upon bucket of water and bunch upon bunch of nut-hazel sticks. We would dress for the part in aprons made from sacks and knee-pads made from sacks or leather, these latter tied above and below our sore knees with binder string.

Our stacks would not be thatched too soon after harvest.

Time was required for them to heat, to let the heat seep through the top before we put on the protective thatch.

We would shake up the straw with two-tined forks and damp it thoroughly before drawing out handfuls, keeping it in tight, straight lengths. My father would climb the ladder, beat down straggly bits of sheaves on the slopes of the stack and then we would begin. Usually he would start at the bottom right-hand corner, putting on armfuls of straightened wet straw, one layer upon the other, working his way up from the eaves to the top, where he would leave sticking up a great tuft about a foot above the top ridges. To secure each layer he would drive in with a mallet the wooden staples I had made from hazel sticks by splitting them down the middle and sharpening them to points with my bill-hook. This process would be repeated until both sides of the stack's sloping roof were covered with a good thatch. There would then be put those important final touches; combings down with the rake we had made with long wire nails driven into wood, and a final trim with shears along the tufty top and the eaves, making sure they were as straight as dies for the benefit of the critics, and that stack could stand for ten to twenty years without a spot of rain getting through to moisten one wheat-ear.

Bill-hooks, sickles and a special blade on a long ash stale were brought into play for 'hedging'. It was essential that the fields should be protected from straying cattle and some of them from the prevailing wind.

Alongside most hedges were draining ditches which had to be kept trimmed and clean and it was customary to combine the operations of hedging and ditching. First, the hedge. We would pull out all the dead wood and then get busy with bill-hooks and sickles. Keeping sides and tops even, we would cut back and bend back new growth so that the hedge would thicken the following year. If we cleaned the ditches first we would have to come back to them again after trimming the hedge, an unnecessary repetition which would involve hacking at twigs we had already dealt with. There would be no problem in trimming the ditchless side of the hedge but so that we were tall enough on the ditch side we would walk on three pieces of wood, straddling them across the ditch and bringing the hindermost to the fore on each fresh pace forward.

Those hedgerows were eye-openers. They were full of interest apart from the many small creatures sheltering and feeding in them. They were made up of a great variety of plants with their own characters and habits. These included great yellow tassellings of the hazel, the male flowers and, on the same shrub, those tiny flower-tips of the female – waiting for the hedger, birds, bees or beasts, to shake down the pollen from the drooping yellownesses, to fertilize them and bring forth the hazel nuts. They also included the angular twigs of the elder, the first shrub to put forth its tooth-edged leaves, with nice straight growths of new wood between the nodal joints, all full of frothy pith, just waiting for young lads to make pop-guns from them. Then there were dogwood, privet, hawthorn, blackthorn, sloe and crab-apple. The first was useful for making long-lasting walking sticks; the sloe and crab-apple for wine or delicious jelly. Hips and haws were there, scarlet-clad lifeguardsmen of the hedgerows. Hip wine from these was like a fine liqueur when made by Granny Ford! Also present were blackberry, honeysuckle and black bryony, with its great heart-shaped leaves. In the autumn those green hearts would turn to bronze, setting off the berry strings, first green, then flaming orange and fiery red. Wild clematis (Travellers' Joy or Old Man's Beard) climbed the highest hedges and tentacled into the trees, its beardy feather so profuse as to cover great hedge lengths, making them appear snow-capped or frost-crystalled. Also to be seen were wild peas, or tufted vetch, all kinds of ivy – some flowering in autumn and winter and fruiting in spring – plus that soft red moss growing on the briars of wild roses – old Robin's pincushion.

Through each month of the year there were fruits and flowers, waiting to be discovered by novices; always there to be seen and understood by the countryman.

From Ashdon, alas, those great hedges are gone, leaving a naked bleakness round the fields. There is a dearth, too, of the little creatures who lived there, for now their habits and homes have changed through unnatural migration to the woods.

But in those days, as soon as we had finished our hedging and ditching we would stack the cuttings of sweet briar, weeds and herbs ready for the burning; the burning pyres of Ashdon Place Farm! And oh, the scent of burning briars and roasting herbs! That aroma dwelt and persisted in the rags and tatters of us all, for days.

There were less pleasant days. I still recall with unintentional shiverings row upon row of ice-encrusted leaves, the glacial leaves of the sugar-beet. I recall the iron-shod wheels of a great tumbril standing between those long, perishing rows, where behind that tumbril – each with a curved and sharpened blade in his right hand – were two persons, two persons wrapped in sacks. Sacks slit down one side to fashion clodhoppers' duffel coats. Holding those blades, and in those improvised coats, old Poddy Coote and me.

With our left hands we would tug out the beet. With the back of the knife we would clean off most of the soil. With flicks of wrists we would cut off small roots and slice off the glacial leaves near the beet's crown and hurl the tap-root into the tumbril.

Hymns would ring out as a rule when Poddy and I worked together in the fields – hymns, psalms and sometimes the chanting of responses, for we were in the village choir. But there was silence in our sugar-beet 'lifting'. Ungainly clogged balls of mud, those were our feet. Sack-bound shanks, those were our legs, numbed and lifeless from the knees down. The marrow of our bones seemed congealed, coagulated by the niveous bite of that piercing wind.

I remember how glad we both were when it was all over; when the last sugar-beet was tucked away with tons of its fellows in sweet, warm oat straw under three inches of good top soil, a double defence against the frost and the wintry wet. Sometimes we wished we could be tucked away with them. But convoys had been sunk in the Atlantic Ocean by Kaiser

Bill's unmentionable U-boats. Sugar was rationed. Sugar-beet was thought, rightly, to be the answer. We did our best.

'Well, Ced, bor,' sniffed Poddy, buffeting his frozen hands against his sackcloth, eyes a-rheumy, nose a-dripping. 'Yew can bet a shillin' to a pinch o' shit our nex' job's bownd ter be better'n this bugger. There ain't a wusser job in the bloody world than this'n!'

But spring would follow, and summer, to compensate us in our fields.

Hay had to be mown and carted. I found it sheer delight to sit on the seat of the great iron hay-rake, Punch in the shafts, stealing an occasional mouthful of the sweet hay he had helped to rake into billowing rollers across the ocean of Hungerton Field. And after the hay had been harvested, and the green of the growing grain was changing to gold, there would be knowing and appreciative looks at that welcome changing.

'Best hev a word with Toe-Rag. They've already met at Overhall Farm, an' settled. Reckon we oughter find owt how much we're likely ter git fer harvest!'

Each Friday night, after we had finished our day's work, we would go to the back door of Place Farm. In the kitchen sat old Bidwell, confused by paper and arithmetic as he doled out our pittance. But there was always a kind word, sometimes a rabbit or a few eggs and, in midsummer, a bag of windfalls from his orchard.

In the early weeks of August there would come an important meeting. All would gather in the cart-shed. Squatting on cartshafts, in wagons and in the metal driving seats of binders and hay-rakes, the farmhands would be waiting for Bidwell to 'Settle for Harvest'.

'Well, hev ye made up yer minds, then? What d'yer fancy, Walt?'

'It ain't up t'me. Toe-Rag's the talker.'

'Well, then!' Bidwell would look to George, who looked embarrassed.

'Fifteen pound. Piece-work! If the weather howds, we'll hev it in in three weeks.'

'Bit high, ain't it?'

'Newnham Hall hev settled fer fifteen. Take it or leave it!'

'Are ye all of a mind, then?' Bidwell's eyes would pierce us one at a time. Just nods from each, not a word.

'Right then, George. Fifteen it is. Shake on it!'

They would spit on palms, shake hands. We had 'Settled for Harvest'.

There would be comments as we moved off to our jobs.

'Bit o' luck an' we'll hev it in by a fortnight!'

'Hope the weather howds!'

And the words of my father . . . 'If the weather howds, we'll get you a new jacket, boy. Mebbe boots as well.'

We had settled for harvest.

Chapter 18

Nellie

For almost a year – until August 1921 when I was fourteen and left school – I had fluctuated between peaks of exhilaration and troughs of despair. I was blithesome as a bird when Nellie smiled ... damp and dismal as ditchwater when she seemed not to notice me. We hardly spoke but knew we had something to share, sometime.

When first our eyes met to play havoc with my mind I had become acutely aware of inferiority, of mental and physical shortcomings. I felt I needed gayer plumes. A new suit might do the trick. A general rejuvenation of my outward appearance; a reinvigoration of my wit; and the aptitude swiftly and accurately to answer schoolmaster Tuck's trickiest questions when he orally tested our classes in the 'big room' might also help.

Whether or not I knew the answer, my hand had to be the

first one raised. When Tuck was sufficiently misguided to pick someone else I prayed the answer would be wrong; that he would come to me for the right one.

She was never out of my mind. Because of her I lived in a realm of constant day-dreaming, hallucination and fantasy. I was her hero, her professor, her Sir Galahad and St George. Every one of Tuck's questions was a dragon, ogre, or wicked knight to be slain with the sharp sword of my wit for my Ladye. Nevertheless, I knew the extraordinary scenes I conjured up were not and never would be 'experience'. Although they were more vivid than life itself I knew full well I was merely hoping and wishing; that this state of lovelorn lunacy was but a device generated by my longing to impress her.

I was in love. Nellie knew. Her face betrayed her.

I did not dare tell her. For months we were equally evasive and elusive. We led each other a pretty dance – until that letter of hers came to me via dark Dorothy and my father. After that, each night my restlessness became more unendurable. Before that letter I had got into the habit of staying up very late, sometimes getting up again after going to my bed – just to walk sorrowfully and soulfully past the cottage where she lived; walking always on the grass verges so that none should hear me. She was 'up there', in 'that' room. Yet she was not. She had slipped into my heart, my life.

'I'll hev to hev a word with Chris,' said my father one morning, noting the fatigue on my face, 'he oughter know better'n keepin' you up all hours.'

I would go to the old mill almost every night and Chris and I would delve for hours into the mysteries of his books on Pelmanism and Monsieur Coué's diatribes; or we would read to each other chapter on chapter from Rider Haggard's novels. But little did my father realize I was not always with Chris and that that was not the cause of my fatigue. No sooner had I eaten my 'fry-up' supper, which Chris always prepared after our reading sessions, than I would be off like the wind to the village. Usually I would race across the fields in darkness, hoping, not to see Nellie – who would be long in bed – but just to be near where she lay, unaware of spineless, woebegone me.

After being locked out twice I hit up a scheme to baffle parents who locked out the lovelorn. By driving into the front wall some nine-inch nails I made finger and toe-holds so that I could mountaineer to my bedroom. Sometimes I got away with it, sometimes not.

My world certainly changed with my first love letter. Although she was fifty miles away in distant London when she wrote it, Nellie was close in this world of my own.

Harvest was over. I had attended my last Horkey supper in the Bonnett Inn, after leading horses in the harvest fields. It was a good year. The sun shone hot and kind for weeks and the great sheaves of corn were gathered in record time, leaving golden stubbles shining for miles. Young birds were trying out their wings. The martins who built their nest under the eaves of our cottage for years had returned, laid their eggs and reared the young. These had now been tipped from the neat clay nest and soon with short forked tails and sickle-like wings they would be streaking and scything the sky like dark darting arrows. Great golden corn stacks towered from the yards. The mallets of thatchers could be heard driving home sharp-pointed nut-hazel staples to secure the thatch, to protect grain from rain. And good old Joslin, the best thatcher of them all, would sometimes be seen standing on his head and hands on the height of a stack's ridge – bellowing out Baptist hymns full throttle whilst upside down.

Yes, harvest was over. We had given thanks in our village church and in the Bonnett. At Evensong on Harvest Thanksgiving Sunday we had sung the songs of praise, the anthem and the harvest hymns as the sun shone through the stained glass to transform snow-white surplices and choirboys into living rainbows. The final hymn was the Recessional. We had turned at the end of the penultimate verse to the altar. Then, gliding slowly from altar to vestry down the central aisle behind ruddy-faced Sid Williams carrying the great brass cross, we had sung the last verse . . .

> Now thank we all our God,
> With heart, and hands, and voices,
> Who wondrous things hath done,
> In Whom His world rejoices;
> Who from our mother's arms
> Hath blessed us on our way
> With countless gifts of love,
> And still is ours today.

Although our church had brimmed with flowers and fruit and good things of the earth – and with my village friends who had helped to produce them – my mind was not on harvest at all that time. Six more paces, my thoughts ran, and I would be taking off my surplice and cassock; fourteen hours more and I would be back in school; fourteen hours more and Nellie would be in that school with me.

I was awake before sun and birds on the Monday morning, trying to visualize how Nellie would look when we met at nine o'clock for morning prayers. I was the first to dip our chipped enamel bowl into the water-butt; the first to wash in clear cold rain-water; the one who looked longest into Father's shaving mirror. It was a puny mirror and I could see only my face. I wanted to see the whole of myself on this important morning.

Green gobbets of solidified brilliantine glistened on my hairbrush ready to smarm back my rebellious hair, Cockney style; and polish had transformed my first pair of shoes, bought with my harvest money; my new shirt with faint blue stripes was ready; my very first new bow-tie, all peacocky with blues, greens and yellows, complete with its own push-stud and butterfly stiffeners to tuck under the stiff white points of my new celluloid collar, was to hand. Soon I was out in Mother's front garden carefully selecting the best rosebud for my buttonhole.

Who cared for breakfast on such a day! Quick gulps of scalding tea, then I was out in Ashdon Road. I would not go to school by the fields this morning, although the sun was

giving its best. Dew had not yet dried and I wished not to mar
the shine on my spit-new shoes.

It was ten to nine by the clock as I skipped the steps. I
glanced round the girls' playground. Groups of noisy girls
were carrying flowers for teacher. Clusterings of skippers, with
new white skipping ropes and little bells on the scarlet handles,
were enjoying themselves. A circle of hop-scotchers were hopping like mad. But there was not a sign of Nellie.

I had heart thumpings, misgivings, butterflies in the belly
and sweaty palms. Quickly into the boys' playground I went.
In just five minutes more Mabel Eason would play 'The
Donkey Cocked his Tail Up', to the melody of 'Weel May the
Keel Row'. So I made a dash into the lavatory quickly to read
the well-remembered words of Nellie's letter for the
umpteenth time.

Fred Symonds sniffed at my hair.

'Coo! Thasser tidy owd pong. New suit for school? How
much did yer git fer harvest, then?'

'Mind yer business. Had this suit nearly a year!'

William Tuck then shrilled on his whistle and boys formed
in two ranks. One more whistle chirp and Mabel was at the
tinny piano. Then the boys filed into the classrooms by the
west door and the girls by the east.

She was the palest as well as the prettiest, the others having
been burned by our harvest sun. She smiled shyly and quickly
looked away.

Hornets were in my belly; in my heart rapture, jubilation!

'OwerFatherwichartin'eaven, 'allowedbeThyname . . .'

My final year at school had begun with love in the air at last.

I could and should have spoken to her when we broke class for the midday meal but she was not alone and I was shy. At half past four I watched her watching me as she walked down Ashdon Road. I followed – a good cricket pitch length behind – but not on the road. I skulked along the allotment-patch path, screened from the road by dense hawthorn. She looked back, loitered, then halted smack in the middle of the road opposite the only hedge gap. I stepped through that gap and stood like an oaf.

She came to me.

She came so close that the light wind tickled her hair into my face like an angel's kiss. For a moment we stood face to face, only an inch apart, and looked at each other not saying a word. I could see by her eyes that our minds had been adjusted to love. I knew our bodies would also adjust, some-time.

Something snapped in my mind at that moment. There was excitement in my loins as well as in my heart. I pulled her gently to me. We kissed. Her lips slackened and fired. Her eye-lids fell. Conscious that we were in public view, I released my hold on her.

'I got your letter, Nellie. Did you mean it?'

'Yes, I mean it. You write to me, then.'

'All right. When you want and when I can. But I want to go with you, not write!'

'All right. When I can.'

'Tonight, then?'

'No, tomorrow night. Tell you where after school.'

A look of kindness in her eyes, a squeezing of hands, and she was off like the wind.

One restless, agitated night passed and three parts of one tempestuous, tumultuous day, before we kept our tryst. What an eternity it seemed. I overtook her as she walked slowly up Radwinter Road on the Tuesday evening, took her soft hand in mine and led her into the smithy's shop of Hill Farm, a suitable place for our love to be forged; the smithy ... where lingered the smell of charred hooves and clean-cut frogs of horses shod that day; where loitered the heat of the furnace long after old Clarky had sparked and fireworked his hot iron with Thor-like hammerings, quiet compared with the pounding of my heart.

We were shrouded in semi-dark. So feeble was the light that I could scarcely make out the great rows of horseshoes on their wall battenings. At first we hardly spoke and then in whispers. She took me into her confidence, telling me of her flirtations with London boys ... hinting of her experiences and leaving me to guess, with barbs in my heart. But tonight, at least, she was sweetly mine. I felt rather than saw her mood of love and tenderness. There was a taste to her kiss, feeling in the warmth of her light embrace. The taste and feel of her told me beyond all questioning that we were in more than mere physical harmony, we were like springtime and harvest rolled into one.

'I like you best. You're not so fast as them,' she whispered.

What a two-edged compliment that was to be sure. I wished to excel, to be better and faster than the best and fastest. Here in this smelly forge I was out of my realm.

'Nellie. Let me take you to the woods. Come with me to the woods; it's nicer there.'

'If you want. But not in the evening. Sunday afternoon.'

We met most evenings. We walked together endless measures of footpathed fields, hipped and hawed hedgerows and emerald meadows; clutching, as forever, their old beauty to our new young hearts. There were halts for kissing, for long looks into each other's eyes; intervals for inspection of faces and souls; troths and promises by the score; carvings of hearts and Cupid's arrows in the olive green of the soft willow; initials etched into sturdy stunted oak and towering elm to outlive us. My arm would encompass her willowy waist, her hair tendrils zephyring to my cheek with electric shocks. There would be a sinking to the green of the meadow to fashion for my lady's dark tresses a golden pagle chain as the sun sank in fire of scarlet and orange to herald the next fine day. Then, butterfly kisses would be exchanged, like withered leaves or thistledown meeting in the wind ... more promises, more majesty.

There are not words, nor is there music, to tell how our hearts sang when we were so young and in love.

Sunday afternoons, always to Home Wood, our wood – the remotest, prettiest and most serene of Ashdon's many treelands. There on our wide bed, ten acres in area, palliassed with pine needles centuries soft, we would lie for endless hours. Serenaded by birdsong, caressed by the sun, we were free to move our limbs and bodies, to gambol and frolic like spring lambs. We kissed often and often, with long deep kisses, until our emotions ran amok. I would glide my finger-tip along her thigh, watch her tauten and feel the bliss of teeth that were not mine bite my lips. Then one of us would call a halt, out of mutual respect.

'I'd like to. You know I would. When you kiss me like that I want to. One day, not now. One day!'

We had in all two years and a bit of delight, walking the same footpaths, invariably wending towards our wood to prostrate ourselves on nature's bed, where the magic remained sweet and innocent as the first Sunday. We experimented as time went on, finding mild amative substitutes for sexual fulfilment, only the more to whet our appetites. I watched her with great tenderness as she occasionally slept and escaped child-like from my solitary world of wakefulness, in which time and seasons had no part. Then with tentative, trembling fingers and soft kissings on her closed lids I would wake her to me to make my joy boundless, immeasurable.

In the stark of autumn and winter, when our wood was wetted and our meadows morassed, we met less frequently. It was the final autumn and winter that began to take her from me.

I was working on the farm. Days were so hard and exhausting that I would sometimes fall asleep at my evening meal. In those great, wide, bleak and naked fields there was little shelter from rain, sleet, snow and biting, perishing wind . . . only my old bits of sack, and the kindly, sheltering hedgerows.

Indoors jobs were insufficient to last the winter. Some of them produced hazards worse than the weather. Barley chaff was the bane of my wintry existence for I had to stand in it in the great storehouse ... up to my loins in it. Great sharp whiskers of barley and rye would pierce and penetrate my clothing, remaining for weeks on end, to transform me into an itchy, human hedgehog.

It was degrading as well as distressing. The climax came one morning when, soaked to the skin overnight, tortured with spikes of rye, I took my body to work and Bidwell the farmer quickly took me to task for being late – at half-past six.

'You're late, boy. Them heifers want their feed, an' new beddin'.'

'They're only beasts. I'm human!' said I in righteous indignation. 'They've got food, thick coats. They're under shelter and dry. I'm soaked since yesterday and I've had no breakfast. Bugger your heifers, I'm off home!'

I went home. Father was too ill to work but not too ill to be furious.

'You oughter hev more sense, boy. You know there ain't much work and you're lucky to hev been took on. Go straight back to Bidwell and apologize. Tell him you're sorry.'

Because my fifteen bob and Leslie's ten shillings were our only revenue, I swallowed my pride but not my indignation.

Bidwell was in dry clothes under the sheltering roof of the cow byre, squatting on a stool, squirting quick jets of milk into a pail from Bella's bulging udder. I rested my chin on the top of the bottom half of the byre door.

'I've come back, Mr Bidwell. I never meant to be rude to you but I meant what I said. The heifers are dry and I ain't.'

He withdrew his head from under Bella's belly, turned up one of her teats and squirted her milk right in my eye, all smiley and kind-looking.

'Thass all roight, lad. Fergit it. It's hard fer you. You ain't cut owt fer this owd farm-wuk. God gave you a bit of a brain. Find another job. Go you off home now an' change yer clothes. Stop home in the dry a bit. You'll hev your wages. I know how it is.'

There was no other work. Brother Leslie, too, was ill content. He had started labouring at Engelmann's nurseries, walking five miles there and five miles back, to and from Saffron Walden, every day in all weathers. With his camel-hair paint brush he would tickle some pollen from one carnation, then run like mad to deposit it on carnations elsewhere, hoping by the process of artificial, horticultural insemination to produce for Engelmann his life-long dream – a black carnation. In Leslie's week he walked sixty miles, to work a six-day week of eight hours a day and to glean as a reward one whole sixpence for pocket-money from his total of ten shillings.

It was Bill Symonds, the elder brother of my school-friend Fred, who found the solution.

Bill had enlisted in the Royal Garrison Artillery and had returned to his village on his first leave. He was shining and polished, with yellow-ochred riding-grips on his well-tailored Bedford-cord riding breeches; yellow-ochred puttee-tapes;

burnished buttons and badges; face-reflecting boot shinings; ox-blood bandolier; jingling spurs; and a walking-out whip better than any riding crop in old Albie Bassett's harness shop. Bill told us stories of how he did no other work but drilling on a barrack square at Woolwich – a town where there were cinemas, music-halls, dance-halls, willing girls and long leaves with full pay and ration allowance. We noticed there was not a bit of mud on Bill, not a barley spike!

'It's all laid on fer yer; even wake you up in the morning with trumpets an' puts the lights owt arter you've gone ter bed. It's a good livin'. Plenty sports, plus three an' nine a day, all found. All fer yerself.'

Leslie and I conferred. Father had often told us of his soldiering days in the Suffolks; of lands he had visited, sights he had seen and songs he had sung.

> Hurrah for the scarlet and the blue,
> For helmets glistening in the sun,
> And the bayonets flash like lightning
> To the beating of the old militia drum.
> And the flag of dear old England,
> Waving proudly in the sky;
> I'll tell you the watch of a soldier's life,
> I'll conquer, or I'll die . . .

Nowadays he only sang it when he had more than his usual couple of pints at the Bonnett Inn. Soil-stained and ragged, he no longer looked much like a soldier but we could see by the nostalgic look in his eyes that his heart had been long with soldiers, even though the war had shattered him.

We might well have left it at that had it not been for Professor Martin. Arriving to live in a cottage behind Ashdon Church, he became our scoutmaster and took an interest in our welfare. He was not really a professor. We nicknamed him that because he was horn-rim spectacled and studious looking. He loved the nickname because he had failed to go to Cambridge. Now he tried to help others who had never been given a chance.

In February 1924 he went to see someone of consequence in the Grenadier Guards. Within twenty-four hours of his visit there arrived at our house a magnificent envelope which frightened the living daylights out of Mother because it had printed on it in bold letters 'On His Majesty's Service'. Inside was an attestation form which my parents were requested to sign to give permission for Leslie to become a drummer in 1st Battalion, Grenadier Guards.

'Let him go,' said Father. 'Let him see a bit of life. He'll only get a bob a day as a drummer but he works the whole bloody week here for sixpence.'

I went with Father and Leslie to Warley Barracks, watched him collect the King's Shilling and sadly saw him separated from us.

We missed him. We missed the nine and sixpence for which he had walked sixty miles each week. But letters came from Barosa Barracks, Aldershot – after he had been to the Guards' Depot at Pirbright – to say he was riotously happy, full of food and was learning to play drums and fifes for the Grenadiers. For my mother he sent a brooch in the shape of a grenade, stiff with seventeen points, each point a letter spelling out 'FIRST OF FOOT GUARDS'.

She was so pleased, so sad!

On St David's Day 1924, less than a month after Leslie had become No. 2609406 Drummer L. G. Mays, I was on Hungerton Field leading Jockey and Captain, as my father walked behind the drill with a spud in his hand to clear the drill coulters, to let the seed of wheat run free. Frank Moss, our village postman, with peaked cap awry, whistling away as usual, his great feet protruding from bicycle pedals like the scythes of Boadicea's chariot, spotted us on his way to our hamlet cottage.

'Hi there, Jack. Gotter telegram. Shall I take it up, or will you hev it here?'

My father beckoned him to the headland where we were about to have breakfast. Frank handed over the yellow envelope. 'It ain't fer me,' said my father. 'Here, take it, read it; it's fer you.' He gave it to me.

It was from Colonel W. T. Hodgson, DSO, MC, the Royal Dragoons.

'Royal Dragoons accept you. Form follows.'

Professor Martin had been up to his tricks again. I had been accepted as a band boy in Britain's oldest cavalry regiment of the Line.

Hungerton Field rocked as my eyes swam.

'Let me go. Please let me go!'

'You'll go if you want, son, if you want.'

'What's the form, then?'

'That'll be the attestation we have to sign, me an' your mother, if you're under eighteen.'

I was sixteen and a half.

'Can you manage? You're not gettin' Les's money now.'

'We'll manage, somehow. It's a good regiment – the finest. You can ride hosses, boy, an' like 'em.'

I could not wait to get into old Eason's shop to examine in detail the picture – between the Epsom Salts and the Lifebuoy soap – of that cavalry soldier of the Royal Scots Greys. I had not been in his shop since I was a house boy at Walton's Park. But there he was, as splendid as ever, even though the flies of two years had spotted him here and there. It was he who made up my mind. I *would* be a dashing dragoon, come what may.

Would I be doing the right thing? What would I be leaving behind? I answered my own questions . . . my home, parents, sister Poppy, young brother Jack who had just started school and my new baby brother Frank. Also my friends with whom I had worked and lived and sung in the fields. But most of all my Nellie! Should I shout the news aloud or wait until that form came, I wondered. I decided to tell Nellie first.

By this time I had begun to meet her more often again. March winds were cold but spring was in the air and I helped my father sow lettuce and radish, plant out the hardened cauliflowers and the seedlings of onions and, in our flower garden, to propagate lupins and delphiniums with the shoot cuttings. The green spears of our daffodils were a good foot high and there was that smell of growing in the air plus buds on briars and hawthorns, a change in the song and the flight of the birds and a lengthening of the hours of clear daylight.

I knew where to find her that day of the telegram. She had left school eighteen months but was still in the village. I did not know how to tell her. I remember how and where I tried. We were leaning over a five-barred gate, halfway up New Road Hill, just as the sun was going down.

'Shan't be here much longer.'

'Why? It ain't late.'

'No. I mean I'm going from Ashdon.'

'Where?'

'I don't know, my Nellie. I'm waiting for a form. When it comes I shall know. I'm joinin' up, goin' into the band of a cavalry regiment.'

'Oh, no! No! When?' Her question was like a sabre-wound.

'Don't know when nor where. Les is in the Grenadiers and he's in Aldershot. I might go there but I don't know till that paper comes.'

'Don't go, Ced. I can't bear it!'

'I've got to go, Nellie. But I don't want to leave you. Come Sunday, it might be our last time.'

'I'll come. I'll come!'

We came nearer to full communion than ever before. What a wrench it was to leave her, to go, tasting the salt of her tears.

Sunday came, with wind and rain. Our wood wept for our absence for it was too muddy for us to negotiate the paths and byways. Instead we walked slowly and soulfully to Overhall Farm, under a corrugated roof, to a nest of sweet-scented hay. Our spirits sank as our fevers fired. We sensed somehow that this was our last meeting; that we had not much more to give each other but had more by far to lose.

She was as warm and buoyant as our couch of hay. Too eager for preliminary caressings, she unfastened her frock for me, took me into the depths of her love. The wind whistled and the sleet slashed on the tinny roof. But our summers and springs, our wood and paths, our fields, flowers and sunshine shone in our minds as we floated on clouds of bliss.

I brushed the hay from her. The wind no longer blew, nor did it rain any more. I gave her a brand new horseshoe nail and she gave me an old conker as we parted by the water pump at the bottom of New Road Hill.

'You know now. Don't you? Let me know before you go and write if I don't see you.'

I knew. I would always know. I have always known.

The form came next day. With it was a railway warrant to pay my fare to Canterbury, the depot of Dragoons, Lancers and Hussars. I did not see Nellie before I left, although I tried.

I shook hands with Grandad, who grunted out, 'God bless ye, boy. Write ter yer mother regular!'

I did not kiss the family. There were firm handshakes all round and I could see the tears welling in Mother's eyes as she came to our old front gate to wave me off.

I took one quick last look at the old hamlet and trotted from Reuben's Corner down Ashdon Road, with a new half-crown in my pocket and a little bag with toilet articles and sausage rolls. Out into the world I went – away down past Ashdon Place Farm, to a wave from old Wuddy.

'Careful, now, boy. They owd war-horses are fiercer'n farm hosses. God bless an' good luck!'

Down I went past Walton's Park but there was no one to see me. I thought of old Freeman. Never again would I chop up his bee-hives for firewood.

Past the five-barred gate I went – the gate where I had told Nellie I was leaving . . . past my school, my Sunday school, my church . . . down the little lane to Ashdon Halt Station where the train was whistling like fury as it rounded the bend. Into the train. Away!

Away to Canterbury, the army, and a life that would never again be the same.